NEW ENGLAND
MEN OF LETTERS

WITH A FOREWORD BY HYATT H. WAGGONER
DRAWINGS BY THOMAS EVANS HINTON

WILSON SULLIVAN

NEW ENGLAND
MEN OF LETTERS

THE MACMILLAN COMPANY, NEW YORK, NEW YORK
COLLIER-MACMILLAN LIMITED, LONDON

Library of Congress catalog card number: 75-165574

The Macmillan Company, 866 Third Avenue,
New York, New York 10022
Collier-Macmillan Canada Ltd., Toronto, Ontario

Printed in the United States of America

10 9 8 7 6 5 4 3 2 1

Drawings by Thomas Evans Hinton

FOR PEARL

FOREWORD

The ten nineteenth-century New England writers presented in this volume may at first thought seem very remote from our own problems and interests, hardly "relevant" to people living in this age of world-wide instant communication and space travel, a time of cultural and technological revolution proceeding so rapidly that the phrase "generation gap" has to be coined to point to one of its by-products, along with other new expressions like "pot" and "grass" and "counter-culture." The writers Mr. Sullivan treats knew none of these terms.

Worse yet, it might seem, they were ignorant of some of the realities to which the new expressions refer. "Ecology" was neither on their minds nor in their writing because they had no reason to fear that a combination of technological development and population explosion might one day make the planet uninhabitable. How then can they seem "relevant" if they were unaware of all these and other problems that, quite rightly, seem so important to us?

The answer, it seems to me, must be given in two parts. First, they were not really so unaware of the problems as it may seem, even though they did not use our words for them and the problems themselves did not so urgently seem to demand attention in their time. Emerson warned of the dangers of conformity to outworn customs and ways of thought and tried to wean his generation from what he saw as its growing materialism. "Things are in the saddle and ride mankind," he cautioned an age which knew nothing of television but which gloried in the new inventions of the railroad and the telegraph. Thoreau worried about the human and social costs of the new "factory system," and was horrified by the indiscriminate slaughter of moose in the Maine woods by hunters who, unlike the Indians before them, made no use of the meat or hide but simply left the animals where they fell, satisfied that the pleasure of the "sport" needed no further justification. And it is possible to see Thoreau's retreat to his Walden Pond hut as a kind of "copping out," as his contemporary Lowell saw it, though we ought to recall that he "withdrew" in order to "find himself" and "returned" to society when he felt that he had done so. Hawthorne cautioned his age as strongly as he could against supposing that technological advances, or even political ones, would solve people's basic problems, which he saw as psychological, moral, and religious. Man's really important problems, he thought, were problems of "the heart" and its relation to "the head," or as we should say, of feeling and thought or emotion and knowledge.

Melville, Longfellow, Lowell, and Holmes all tended to be less concerned with technological and social change than with the philosophic impact of the new natural sciences on traditional systems of belief, particularly religious belief. That this problem is still with us is clear from the ferment and inner questioning so evident in many of the churches today. Parkman and Prescott wrote history as their own sensibilities and predilections and the social realities of their times dictated, much as Beard and the younger Schlesinger would do in our century, but they are not worse or more "dated" historians for that reason. History considered as both man's memory and an attempt to understand that memory needs constantly to be rewritten, as the revisionist, "committed" young historians are proving once again today.

The second part of the answer to the question of how these writers are relevant to us can be given more briefly. If it is true that "history never repeats itself"—as it certainly in some senses is, for the conditions are never exactly the same—another "old saw" also has its element of truth: "The more everything changes, the more it is the same." A good many wise men have come to the conclusion that really "There is nothing new under the sun." Of course there are new "things," new conditions, but what these old aphorisms mean is that the central concerns and the deeper feelings, motivations, and reactions of men through the ages tend to be much the same. We can still read or witness a Greek tragedy or a Shakespearean play and respond emotionally in a way probably very much like the way the original readers or spectators responded, though they lived in cultures different from ours in almost every respect.

Of course, the greater the writer the less quickly he "dates," but none of the writers Mr. Sullivan has treated seems to me so time-bound by his own period, so little able to rise above its inevitable fashions of language and thought, as to deserve to be considered by us "not relevant." Mr. Sullivan has helped us to see just how relevant they all are—some more than others, of course; each reader will make his own choice—by showing us how their lives resulted in their works. He has brought them alive as men facing problems not totally unlike our own, while at the same time he has, by a judicious mixture of paraphrase and quotation, offered us generous tastes of the works themselves.

Best of all, he has made us want to go back and read, or reread, the works they wrote.

HYATT H. WAGGONER
Chairman of American Civilization,
Department of English, Brown University

ACKNOWLEDGMENTS

The sources of one's inspiration in creating a work of this volume's scope resist definition. Certainly, my sources include admired teachers who quickened and deepened my interest in the great men whose lives and works I have tried to distill in these chapters—most especially the late Dr. Gwynne Harris Daggett of the University of New Hampshire. My debt to biographers, notably Walter Harding, Randall Stewart and Martin Duberman, is simply too great to assess.

More immediately, I acknowledge with pride the expert guidance and patient emendations of the distinguished critic of American letters, Dr. Hyatt H. Waggoner of Brown University; if errors remain in my text they are incontestably mine, not his. I acknowledge, too, the counsel of Joseph Elder and Joseph L. Gardner under whose unerring but clement editorial eyes this work took final shape.

And finally, I record my debt to my wife, Pearl Steinhaus Sullivan, without whose editorial presence, empathy and love this book would not be.

WILSON SULLIVAN

Hackensack, New Jersey
28 July 1971

CONTENTS

NEW ENGLAND
MEN OF LETTERS

RALPH
WALDO
EMERSON

HE BUILT HIS OWN WORLD

He is, for most of us, a stern and ancient face, with long, gray hair, a Yankee nose, a faint, sad smile. In high, starched collar he looks out at us, lonely and remote, from the pages of a dusty book in some dry attic. He seems never to have been a boy, never to have loved, never to have known the joy and pain that make man's life.

And, in fact, Ralph Waldo Emerson of Concord, Massachusetts, philosopher and poet—greatest of all New England men of letters—often seemed austere and cold, even to his friends. He found it hard to laugh. He was most comfortable alone, with his books and pen, or walking in his silent forest. If some admirers could rank him with Plato and anoint him as no less than "the mirror of the American soul," others, like the novelist Nathaniel Hawthorne, found him preachy, self-satisfied, childishly idealistic in a world governed by evil men in search of power. Still others ridiculed his philosophy as shallow or illogical and his life as pompous or meanly aristocratic.

Perhaps Emerson was something of all of these things, good and bad. No man is all of a piece. But few could see that he came from a people who thought it simply bad taste to show one's feelings. Almost no one saw that behind Emerson's tight, forbidding face was the memory of more than one man's share of sickness and death of loved ones; the memory of poverty and of the loneliness and self-doubt that besiege youth; and, later, the strident hatred of society when he tried to tell it the truth as he saw it. If in his life and portraits he could seem stoically indifferent to human need and pain, he did so, perhaps, because he had learned well the lesson the Eastern prophets had taught him: to greet both joy and sorrow with the same face, to expect from life neither too little nor too much. He never fully cried or fully laughed. He learned to take what came.

Emerson, in a sense, *is* America. He is America not just in a Fourth-of-July kind of way—although he was the poet who told the nation: "Here once the embattled farmers stood / And fired the shot heard round the world." Emerson was America in a deeper sense. He embodied its optimism, its delight in new things, its continuing capacity for self-renewal. If he could look back on America's Revolutionary idealism with unalloyed pride, he could see its errors, too, and scold it solemnly when he found it on the wrong path. He set himself no less a task than keeping America true to itself, true, supremely, to the mission of individual liberty that had freed her from Europe's crippling institutions and offered hope to all those still enslaved.

Looking out from his nineteenth-century study, Emerson saw an America that had strayed far from the path it had set for itself, an America that had substituted Mammon for God, and he rebuked it. He saw an America rushing unthinkingly into a boiling social stew of profit and loss, a heartless factory system where dignified men became mere appendages of their machines, and he begged it to stop. "This invasion of Nature by Trade with its Money, its Credit, its Steam, its Railroad," he warned, "threatens to upset the balance of man, and establish a new, universal Monarchy more tyrannical than Babylon or Rome." Commerce, he feared, would crush the last remnant of the human spirit, of literature, of true religion. Emerson's only hope, as he saw it, was to awaken Americans to the power, the divinity within them, to free them from fear, superstition, greed, and blind imitation of the Old World and enable them at last to build a New. To do this, he set out, as he put it, "to affront and reprimand the smooth mediocrity and squalid contentment of the times." What Emerson did and what he said remain as valid and inspiring in our day as in his.

A less likely candidate for the task of getting America back on course would be difficult to imagine. Ralph Waldo Emerson was born under most respectable circumstances in Boston, Massachusetts, on May 25, 1803, the son of William and Ruth (Haskins) Emerson. His father was pastor of the First Church of Boston (Unitarian) and traced his proud ancestry back through seven generations of Puritan clergymen. Young Ralph, however, was unimpressed by this pedigree. "The dead sleep in their moonless night," he wrote in his *Journals* at twenty-one, "my business is with the living."

Ralph was a quiet boy, shy and serious, more at ease with books and trees than with people. His father's death in 1811 not only saddened the five Emerson boys and their sister, it left them victim to great poverty, which was no less painful because "genteel." Ralph and his brother Edward shared one coat in winter and rose at dawn to milk the cow and lead her to pasture on Boston Common.

Emerson graduated from Boston's famed Latin School and entered Harvard College in 1817. As a Harvard junior in 1820, he began his lifelong *Journals*, which are packed with gems of philosophy and penetrating insights into his own character. He would later call his *Journals* his "savings bank," a collection of ideas and phrases upon which he drew to write essays and speeches. In the early *Journals* the young Emerson despairs, almost pathetically, of his inability to be friendly, to reach people's hearts, and reveals a self-doubt all the more astonishing in the light of Emerson's mature philosophy and achievement. "I find myself often idle, vagrant, stupid and hollow . . ." he writes as a student. "All around me are industrious and will be great, I am indolent and shall be insignificant. . . ." "In twelve days," he writes further on, "I shall be nineteen years old; which I count a miserable thing. Has any other educated person lived so many years and lost so many days? . . . Look next from the history of my intellect to the history of my heart. A blank, my lord. I have not the kind affections of a pigeon. Ungenerous and selfish, cautious and cold, I yet wish to be romantic. . . . There is not in the whole wide Universe of God . . . one being to whom I am attached with warm and entire devotion,—not a being to whom I have joined fate for weal or wo [sic], not one whose interests I have nearly and dearly at heart;—and this I say at the most susceptible age of man." Still later, he laments his "cardinal vice" of aimlessly "strolling from book to book." He felt lonely, unloving, unloved.

After graduating from Harvard as class poet in 1821, Emerson tried his hand at teaching in his brother William's finishing school for young Boston gentlewomen. He appears to have won the respect of his pupils. In any event, by the time the school was closed in 1825 he had gained valuable experience as its new master and a substantial sum of money. But Emerson doubted his effectiveness as a teacher and despaired of personal success. Perhaps as a minister, he thought, he might realize his intellectual and spiritual powers, by preaching and living "the laws of morals, the Revelations which sanction, and the blood of martyrs and triumphant suffering of the saints which seal them."

So inspired, Ralph followed after all in the footsteps

of his clerical ancestors, entering Harvard divinity school. Ill health, including tuberculosis, limited Emerson's academic efforts; in fact, he does not appear to have completed the divinity school's normal course of studies. He was, nevertheless, "approbated to preach" by the Middlesex Association of Ministers in 1826.

From 1829 to 1832, Emerson served first as assistant, later as pastor of the Second Church of Boston (Unitarian). On the surface, at least, the young clergyman projected a radiant self-confidence and subtlety. One parishioner found him "the most gracious of mortals with a face all benignity," his voice more harmonious than the choir's, his sermon punctuated by "occasional illustrations from Nature, which were about the most delicate and dainty things of the kind I had ever heard." But institutional religion, its dogmas and its rituals proved at last too confining for Emerson. It was not truly open, he concluded, to new insights and ideas. It was hostile to scientific discovery. "The Religion that is afraid of science," he wrote early in 1831, "dishonours God and commits suicide." "In the Bible," he noted a few months later, "you are not directed to be a Unitarian, or a Calvinist or an Episcopalian. . . ." He added, "A sect or party is an elegant incognito devised to save a man from the vexation of thinking. . . . Religion is the relation of the soul to God, and therefore the progress of Sectarianism marks the decline of religion. For, looking at God instantly reduces our disposition to dissent from our brother. A man may die from a fever as well as by consumption, and religion is as effectually destroyed by bigotry as by indifference." True religion, Emerson believed, is beyond mere credulity and ritual form. "It is to do right. It is to love, it is to serve, it is to

think, it is to be humble." Even the central teaching of
Christianity—the concept of nonviolence and returning
good for evil—struck Emerson as admirable but impractical.
"An angel stands a poor chance among wild beasts," he
declared, adding that "I admit of this system that it is,
like the Free Trade, fit for one nation only on condition
that all adopt it. . . ."

Emerson's final break with his church centered on the
issue of the nature of the Communion service. He
did not believe, he informed his congregation, that Jesus
had established "an institution for perpetual observance
when he ate the Passover with his disciples," that is to say
a sacrament. In any event, Emerson confessed, he could
not accept the Communion service as such. By early June,
1832 he confided to his *Journals:* "I have sometimes thought
that, in order to be a good minister, it was necessary to
leave the ministry. The profession is antiquated. In an
altered age, we worship in the dead forms of our fore-
fathers." While in the White Mountains of New Hampshire awaiting the decision of his congregation as to
whether he should be retained, he reflected further: "Religion in the mind is not credulity, and in the practice is not
form. It is a life. It is the order and soundness of a man.
It is not something else *to be got*, to be *added*, but is a
new life of those faculties you have." By September, he had
resolved all doubts and resigned his pastorate. "It is my
desire," he explained, "in the office of a Christian minister, to do nothing which I cannot do with my whole
heart."

Emerson's departure from the Second Church was painful enough. It was made more painful by the memory of
the death of his wife, Ellen Louisa Tucker, one year before,

the death of two brothers not long thereafter, and the loss
of another brother to insanity. To relieve this pain Emerson sailed in December, 1832, for Europe, where he hoped
to meet the famed Scottish philosopher and essayist
Thomas Carlyle. The idealistic Scot shared Emerson's progressive philosophy of self-reliance and defiance of old
thought forms and had rediscovered the romantic idealism
of the Germans Goethe and Schiller. From this meeting
with Carlyle emerged a productive correspondence of some
forty years. To Carlyle the shy former clergyman became
"the one of all the sons of Adam [who] completely understood what I was saying and answered with a truly human
voice."

Abroad, Emerson also found pleasure in meeting the
English poet William Wordsworth, whose deeply spiritual
and symbolic "nature" poetry had influenced him greatly.
He met Samuel Coleridge in London. And while he found
travel in one sense futile—didn't the universe exist just as
much in one's heart and mind as across the sea?—this son
of Puritan New England found solace in Europe's old
churches and shrines of the continent: "Welcome these
new joys," he wrote in Malta. "Let my American eye be a
child's again to these glorious picture-books. The chaunt-
ing friars, the carved ceilings, the madonnas and
saints. . . ." In Valletta, Malta's capital, he found a special peace: "How beautiful," he told his *Journals*, "to have
the church always open, so that every tired wayfaring man
may come in and be soothed by all that art can suggest
of a better world when he is weary with this." In his tour
of the classic world he delighted in its preservation of
"pagan and Christian antiquity" side by side. But they
were antiquities, Emerson concluded, "little, positive,

verbal formal versions" of the infinite laws of Nature and man. Emerson, returning home aboard the ship *New York,* was more than ever convinced: "A man contains all that is needful to his government within himself. He is made a law unto himself. All real good or evil that can befall him must be from himself. . . . The real purpose of life seems to be to acquaint a man with himself. . . . The highest revelation is that God is in every man."

If philosophically serene as his ship sailed homeward, Emerson was emotionally troubled. What lay ahead of him? "I . . . wish," he wrote, "I knew where and how I ought to live. God will show me. I am glad to be on my way home, yet not so glad as others, and my way to the bottom I could find, perchance, with less regret, for I think it would not hurt me,—that is, the ducking or drowning."

Returning to the United States on October 9, 1833, Emerson lived with his mother in Newton, Massachusetts, accepting preaching assignments in various New England communities and lecturing periodically. In November, 1834, he moved to Concord, Massachusetts, where he lived with his step-grandfather, Dr. Ezra Ripley, his mother, and his brother Charles in that historic old house of authors, the "Old Manse," a former parsonage located near the Concord Revolutionary battlefield. Years later this quaint old home, now a national shrine, would be occupied by the novelist Nathaniel Hawthorne. In August, 1835, however, Emerson bought a new house in Concord, in which he would dwell for the rest of his days, this wooden frame house located, and still standing, on the Cambridge Road. For Emerson needed a home of his own. He had met the gracious and cultivated Lydia Jackson during a preaching engagement in Plymouth, Massachusetts, and they had become engaged in June. They were married in Plymouth on September 14.

Emerson would find new joy in four children given to him by Lydia; one of them, Waldo, is immortalized in one of Emerson's finer poems. But he found no less joy in the companionship of Lydia, who moved with ease in the most polite literary and social circles. To Emerson, Lydia was "mine Asia," the embodiment of his continuing fascination with the philosophy and religions of the Far East, especially Hinduism and its central concept of God as a force dwelling in all forms of life, from the highest to the lowest. Lydia, in one biographer's words, was "a woman of warm, opulent nature, endowed with humor and patience," qualities notably lacking in the earlier, unhappy years of Emerson's life. Their mutual devotion is unquestioned. Five years after their marriage, Emerson tried to put it in words: "I finish this morning transcribing my old essay on Love, but I see well its inadequateness. I, cold because I am hot, —cold at the surface only as a sort of guard and compensation for the blind tenderness of the core,—have much more experience than I have written there, more than I will, more than I can write. In silence we must wrap much of our life, because it is too fine for speech."

Emerson, one contemporary recalled, was "an iconoclast who took down our idols so gently that it seemed like an act of worship." Not everyone, least of all the Harvard theologians, agreed. But in no single work is Emerson's curious synthesis of radicalism and almost pastoral tact more in evidence than in *Nature*, his first book, published in 1836. With it, writes Professor Sherman Paul, Emerson began no less than "a revolution in thought." In it, Emerson assailed traditional religion, on the one hand, and scientific determinism on the other—the belief that man was the hapless pawn of an impersonal materialistic realm governed by a mindless and ruthless law of cause and effect. "The foregoing generations," Emerson declared, "beheld God and nature face to face; we through their eyes. Why should not we also enjoy an original relation to the universe? . . . [W]hy should we grope among the dry bones of the past? . . . Let us demand our own works and laws and worship." "The essential and liberating idea of *Nature* . . ." Professor Paul adds, "was that by his own constitution and by the corresponding constitution of the universe, man was not the victim of his environment. Mind, not matter, was supreme. Ideas were sovereign, and with them as his instruments man could shape the universe to his needs." At man's rational best, God works through his hands and mind, in an essentially moral cosmos. "Nature," Emerson adds, "is not fixed but fluid. Spirit alters, moulds, makes it. . . . Know then that the world exists for you," wherever you are—in the scholar's study or behind a plow or in a cobbler's shop—no less than it existed for Caesar or Adam himself. "Build therefore your own world." It was Emerson's boldest statement of a credo arrived at after years of pain and self-doubt. At Harvard a young student named Henry David Thoreau read that statement and reveled in its bold vision and challenge.

Emerson's call was heard, too, by a group of like-minded people he had helped bring together. This group, which met at Emerson's home from 1836 to 1843, called themselves the Transcendentalists. Reality, they believed, "transcended" the world of the physical senses. Science could not replace philosophy and religion, as the prophets of the eighteenth-century Enlightenment had insisted. Man's growth and salvation lay not in the gross material world of riches and strife but in harmony with what Emerson called "that great nature in which we rest," the cosmic unity "within which every man's particular being is contained and made one with all other . . . ," a great "Oversoul" to "which every part and particle" of the natural world "is equally related, the eternal ONE." In this universe, the seer and the seen are one. There is no natural and supernatural. All life is equally divine.

The Transcendentalists saw God not as a distant Ruler, but as a vast Mind dwelling everywhere, "in each ray of the star, in each wavelet of the pool," but supremely in the heart and mind of man. Reality was One and indivisible. "Mind," Emerson taught, "is the only reality, of which man and all other natures are better or worse reflectors." Politically, the Transcendentalists opposed human institutions that crushed the individual under the weight of tradition and conformity. They delighted in Utopian experiments in communal living, like Brook Farm in West Roxbury, Massachusetts. There they hoped to purify their lives, eating at a common table, immersed in honest labor, far removed from the influences of a corrupt society caught in a mindless pursuit of financial gain with little thought given to the quality and sanctity of human life.

The Concord group was an eccentric lot: the unpredictable, skittish Henry David Thoreau who found even Brook Farm too social for his part; bright Elizabeth Peabody of Salem; the "Christian Transcendentalist" Unitarian minister Theodore Parker, sworn enemy of orthodox religion, foe of slavery, filled with what the novelist Henry James would call "the sacred rage" in the presence of hypocrisy and injustice; the novelist Nathaniel Hawthorne, brooding and dark, riding well, as Emerson put it, his "horse of the night"; and, unforgettably, Emerson's preachy, pontifical neighbor, Amos Bronson Alcott, educational experimenter and father of the famed Louisa May. Impractical dreamer, diet faddist, and champion of the Utopian commune, Bronson Alcott, in the words of Emerson's friend Carlyle, was "a venerable Don Quixote, whom nobody can laugh at without loving." In one experiment, Alcott founded a school conducted on the disciplinary principle that when a pupil misbehaved the teacher should thrash himself. Alcott's theory, Hawthorne's son Julian writes, was that "the heart of the child would be touched and reformed by the spectacle of his schoolmaster's suffering for another's misdeeds." The result was predictable. The students, of course, "multiplied their iniquities for the fun of seeing the master thrash himself."

Associated with the Concord group, too, was the brilliant Margaret Fuller of Boston, unexcelled *saloniste*, bursting with progressive—and romantic—ideas, a scholar in her own right. She wrote *Woman in the Nineteenth Century*, described by one critic as "the first mature, complete treatment of the subject of feminism by an American writer." Margaret Fuller also edited the *Dial*, journal of the Transcendentalists, from 1840 to 1842, when she was succeeded by Emerson.

Emerson himself had little to do with the Concord group's wilder experiments. He was essentially a contemplative man, more comfortable in his study, really, than among the chattering mandarins of the Boston-Concord set. Literary society, he declared, "must be tasted sparingly to keep its gusto. . . . The dog that was fed on sugar died. . . ." For all his determination not to squander his energies in precious cant, however, the Sage of Concord, as Emerson came at last to be called, was without question the high priest and fountainhead of the Transcendentalist cause.

Beyond Transcendentalism, however, Emerson had much to do in performing the task of "building his own world." And August 31, 1837, marked a historic high point in its construction. For on that day Emerson delivered at Harvard his famous Phi Beta Kappa address, "The American Scholar," which, by itself, could hold him fast in the national memory and still exerts a seminal influence on American thought. At the old meeting house of the First Parish of Cambridge, writes Van Wyck Brooks, Emerson "rose and faced the assembly. All Harvard was there, the old Unitarian war gods . . . and the young men (two named Holmes and Lowell among them) for whom his speech was to seem the Declaration of America's Intellectual Independence. The hall was packed with listeners. He stood there, slender, motionless, serene, with the air of one who heard nothing but the voice within him, indifferent to the movement of the crowd. . . . The older faces grew grimmer with every word, while the younger lighted up with eager approval. . . ."

With eloquence and power, Emerson called now for a truly independent United States. He demanded an end to America's cultural apprenticeship to Europe, which he scorned as "timid, imitative, and tame." Let us not mourn the loss of Old World certainties and aristocratic status, he cried. Let us welcome the opportunity to begin the world again, the opportunity for mental revolution. Each

age, he said, must write its own books. The universe was
not a blind alley, its limits fixed forever before America
was born. The universe is infinite, new every day, its potential for growth, for invention, for progress unlimited.
"Give me insight into today," he declared, "and you may
have the antique and future worlds." The American
scholar, Emerson continued, must think his own thoughts,
not parrot others' or serve as the mouthpiece of social
prejudices. "The office of the scholar," he explained, "is to
cheer, to raise, and to guide men by showing them facts
amidst appearances." Then he reaffirmed his supreme faith
in the autonomy and power of the individual: "The whole
world is nothing, the man is all. . . . In yourself slumbers
the whole of Reason; it is for you to know all, it is for you
to dare all." The "chief disgrace in the world," he concluded, is "not to yield that peculiar fruit which each man
was created to bear."

The very next year Emerson again delivered an address
with comparable repercussion, again at Harvard, this time
to six young seminarians at the Harvard Divinity School.
While this address prompted Harvard's outraged authorities to ostracize Emerson for almost thirty years, it is, read
carefully, entirely within the revolutionary teaching of the
Judeo-Christian prophetic tradition. Hadn't the Hebrew
fathers declared God to be one and eternally new and
claimed to speak in His name? Didn't Jesus teach that
"the kingdom of God is within you" and urge his followers
to emulate not the formal religionists of the temple but
the laws of God and Nature as revealed in Scripture? A
close student of the Bible, Emerson had learned these lessons well. He now assured the seminarians about to embark
on their ministries that God lived in them and spoke

through their lips as much as through those of any prophet of old. "Obey thyself," he told the young clergymen. Who could presume, as the reigning clergy presumed, to claim a monopoly on truth, or dare to imprison infinite truth in mere words and doctrines?

As for Holy Scripture, he said, "Men have come to speak of the revelation as somewhat long ago given and done, as if God were dead." But the Bible, Emerson said, is not a closed book; it will never be fully written, for God and revelation are forever new, forever advancing, open to all men to seek and to preach. "It is the office of a true teacher to show us that God is, not was; that He speaketh, not spake." And Emerson urged the young ministers to "go alone . . . and dare to love God without mediator or veil." Honor great prophets, of course, Emerson declared, "but say 'I am also a man,'" and be unafraid to share the revelations of your own experience. And do not be afraid of science. Truth cannot conflict with truth. He himself, Emerson said, looked for a "new Teacher" who would reconcile the truths of science and religion and so make the church, once again, a creative and relevant force among men.

If the Harvard authorities cared little for Emerson's ideas, the more progressive elements of nineteenth-century America welcomed them and sought to hear more. Emerson obliged—and helped support himself by a series of public lectures and courses in philosophy, religion, history, and the social sciences, his subjects ranging from English literature and theology to Napoleon and John Brown. Emerson's lecture tours took him not only to Boston, but across the Mississippi and, later, across the Atlantic. In Ohio, Kentucky, Missouri, and Illinois, biographer Bliss

Perry writes, "The visits of Mr. Emerson were the bright days of the whole year." London received him with no less interest. Slender, erect, blue-eyed, Emerson was a "spellbinder," a speaker of "radiant presence . . . serene voice, [and] quiet manner," even as he set forth revolutionary ideas. And if some in Emerson's audiences found the Sage's delivery rambling and disconnected, the poet James Russell Lowell replied in his defense: "So were the stars, and were *they* not knit together by a higher logic than our mere sense could master?"

Emerson himself looked at the lecture tours with mixed emotions. Although a legacy from his first wife provided him with a yearly income of $1,200—then no mean sum— he needed the money. Lecture fees ranged between $10 and $50, netting him an additional $800 to $1,000 per year. The income from his books, however, was not significant until after the Civil War. But with a measure of thrift, making do with simple clothing and food, the Emersons lived in comparative comfort, able to afford considerable charity. Still, as he made the lecture circuit, he missed his "Lidian" (he had changed her name so that it would blend more euphoniously into "Emerson"), his children, and his home. And he feared that his public appearances took on, perhaps, the character of vulgar puppet shows and felt, at times, as if he lived "in a balcony or on the street."

On January 27, 1842, the joy of the Emerson home was shattered when five-year-old Waldo, his father's pride, died. His birth had made the universe "look friendly" to the philosopher, and he became "this sweet symbol of love and wisdom." Proudly, the father had recorded little Waldo's first steps. Now the boy who, for Emerson, "decorated for me the morning star, the evening cloud," had given up

"his little innocent breath like a bird." In a tenderly moving elegy, "Threnody," Emerson sought to give voice to
his sorrow:

> . . . Looking over the hills I mourn
> The darling who shall not return. . . .
> And whither now, my truant wise and sweet,
> O whither tend thy feet . . . ?

He recalls Waldo's painted sled, now abandoned; observes
the sticks he had gathered to shore up the wall of his snow
tower; recalls mornings, when Waldo, "chieftain" among
his school chums, rode off to classes in his willow wagon.
"O richest fortune sourly crossed!/Born for the future, to
the future lost!"

But at last he seems reconciled. In eternity, he concludes
there is no death. One's final journey is but the passing of
the infinite from one form into another, or at worst the
"finite into the infinite."

> . . . What is excellent,
> As God lives, is permanent;
> Hearts are dust, hearts' loves remain;
> Heart's love will meet thee again.

Emerson found continued solace in daily walks through
the woods, breathing its sweet, crisp air, exulting in its
beauty and sounds: the "burly, dozing humble-bee," the
rhodora, "rival of the rose"; or Walden Pond where he
owned land, read the classics, and swam well into his
seventies, naked as a jaybird. In one of his best essays,
"Nature," he shares the joy of these hours: "At the gates
of the forest, the surprised man of the world is forced to
leave his city estimates of great and small, wise and foolish.

. . . We have crept out of our close and crowded houses into the night and morning, and we see what majestic beauties daily wrap us in their bosom." We are ennobled by sunset, freed from "the ugliness of our towns and palaces," given new energy by the "foaming brook," learn the wisdom of nature's balance of motion and rest, and gain a new sense of oneness with all forms of life. In his poems Emerson celebrates the sea, the snow, the great mountains and lakes of the northeast. "In the wood," he told his *Journals,* "God was manifest, as he was not in the sermon. In the cathedralled larches the ground-pine crept him, the thrush sung him, the robin complained him . . . the wild apple bloomed him. . . ."

But if Emerson reveled in his woodland walks, he still seems to have been more comfortable in his study, at the lectern, or in the society of his intellectual peers. One cannot imagine him, at any age, building a hut to live in as Thoreau would do, or going to sea to rough it as his friend Richard Henry Dana, Jr., the novelist, would do. Always frail, and afflicted, like Lidian, with tuberculosis for most of his life, the Sage of Concord lived a measured and sedate existence, more in his own imagination than in the world.

Emerson is perhaps best remembered in our age for his essays, at their best gems of concision and epigrammatic thrust. Among them, "Self-Reliance" remains, perhaps, the most famous. It has inspired generations of Americans to trust their own thoughts and follow their own stars. The poet Walt Whitman credited Emerson with giving him faith in himself as an artist. "Insist on yourself," Emerson wrote in "Self-Reliance," "never imitate." For no man knows what he can do until he tries. Society will try to make you conform and stifle your creativity, but don't worry about what others think, for "the sour faces of the multitude, like their sweet faces, have no deep cause, but are put on and off as the wind blows and a newspaper directs." And never be afraid to admit that you've been wrong. Change your mind as often as new information makes it necessary, for "a foolish consistency is the hobgoblin of little minds." Never underestimate your power as a person, for "an institution is the lengthened shadow of one man . . . and all history resolves itself easily into the biography of a few stout and earnest persons." Live neither sadly in the past nor hopefully in the future, but live the present moment fully and richly; it's all you really have. Above all, don't look beyond or outside yourself for strength or truth. "Nothing can bring you peace but yourself."

Emerson was a master of the epigram. His journals and other writings shimmer with witty thrusts at man's hypocrisy and humbug:

> "The Sabbath is painfully consecrated because the other days are not."
>
> "Age gives good advice when it is no longer able to set a bad example."
>
> "Make love a crime and we shall have lust."
>
> "Culture is one thing, and varnish another."
>
> "Politeness ruins conversation."
>
> "Imitation cannot go above its model."
>
> "We must either get rid of slavery or get rid of freedom."
>
> "Do not say things. What you are stands over you the while and thunders so that I can't hear what you say to the contrary."

Emerson's poetry has suffered at the hands of critics. To his contemporary James Russell Lowell, his verse was "not even prose." In the opinion of another, the English poet Matthew Arnold, it was not "legitimate." In our day it has become fashionable to dismiss Emerson's poetry as pallidly intellectual, maudlin, naively idealistic, undisciplined, absurdly unaware of the evil that rages in the human heart. But as the critic Hyatt Waggoner points out, Emerson was in conscious rebellion against both the content and form of poetry as it had been understood. In "Merlin: I," which ranks among Emerson's finest poems, he rejects the "jingling serenader's art." In a poetic line equal to the most cosmic themes, he declares: "The kingly bard / Must smite the chords rudely and hard, / As with hammer or with mace; / That they may render back / Artful thunder." Poetry, he wrote in his masterful essay "The Poet" should not be merely decorative, bound by archaic patterns, "for it is not metres, but a metre-making argument that makes a poem,—a thought so passionate and alive, that, like the spirit of a plant or an animal, it has an architecture of its own, and adorns nature with a new thing." Emerson, in short, was applying to the poetic art the same concepts of self-reliance, self-trust, and individualism that informed his entire philosophy. Poetry was no longer to be concerned with a commonly shared definition of reality, static and unchallengeable, but with the poet's individual experience of life, unique in each man. "The poet has a new thought," Emerson wrote in the same essay, "he has a whole new experience to unfold; he will tell us how it was with him, and all men will be the richer in his fortune. For, the experience of each new age requires a new confession. . . ." Emerson was saying, as Dr. Waggoner explains it, that the poet approaches life and art as if "*nothing* is known, nothing is given, everything is discovered or created, or else remains in doubt." The new poet, Emerson declared in "Merlin: I," ". . . shall not his brain encumber / With the coil of rhythm and number; / But, leaving rule and pale forethought, / He shall aye climb / For his rhyme. / 'Pass in, pass in,' the angels say, / 'In to the upper doors, / Nor count compartments of the floors, / But mount to paradise / By the stairway of surprise.' "

Emerson's influence on future poets, including those overtly hostile to his style and message, was decisive. "Without knowing Emerson . . ." Dr. Waggoner concludes, "we cannot understand our poetic history." In Emerson the central concerns of American poetry were defined: its concern with nature rather than with society, "with the eternal [rather than] with the temporal," and, again, with the *individual* experience reported in free, innovative poetic forms.

It must be conceded that in his own verse Emerson does not always measure up to his own bold standards, to the hope he expressed in his poem "Monadnoc" that "the thoughts that he [should] think / Shall not be forms of stars, but stars, / Nor pictures pale, but Jove and Mars. . . ." Much of his poetry is repetitive, turgid, and anemically abstract. Among his better poems are "The Titmouse," a charmingly metaphysical work; "Hamatreya," "Brahma," "Uriel," "Days" (he is said to have thought this his best poem), "The Snow-Storm," "Compensation," "Each and All," "Limits," "The Bohemian Hymn," "Fable," "Music," "Water," "Bacchus," and, of course, the highly revealing "Merlin: I and II."

It is argued that in the statement of his philosophy in

prose and poetry, Emerson is inconsistent, even contradictory. Indeed, in many of his most eloquent bursts of
social criticism, as Daniel Aaron astutely points out, Emerson was simply attacking "the social consequences of his
own philosophy." His philosophy of aggressive individualism might well free men from self-doubt and conformity.
But it also provided a neat rationalization to the greedy
industrialists rampant in Emerson's century, men who confused individualism with selfishness and exploitation of
men who worked for them, men who considered their
employees as so much property rather than a divine part
of Emerson's cosmic Mind. And surprisingly, Emerson,
while he condemned the meanness of petty traders and
shopkeepers, appears to have reserved a special admiration
for the nineteenth-century captain of industry. He praised
these "men of the right Caesarian pattern," who, in their
daring transformation of the world to their ends, fulfilled
the Divine plan. And he admired Napoleon, despite a few
reservations: "We cannot, in the universal imbecility, indecision and indolence of men," democracy's prophet said
of the dictator, "sufficiently congratulate ourselves on this
strong and ready actor, who took occasion by the beard,
and showed us how much may be accomplished by the
mere force of such virtues as all men possess in less degrees;
namely, by punctuality, by personal attention, by courage,
and thoroughness."

Similarly, the most hardened reactionary could not quar-
rel with Emerson's *laissez-faire* conviction that "wealth
brings with it its own checks and balances" or that the
government should not "meddle" with business or seek
through legislation to regulate it or check its excesses. Emerson's espousal of such pious nonsense, despite the gross

suffering experienced by the nineteenth-century factory worker and despite the corruption of American urban life by slums and other injustices bred by poverty and class conflict, shows an undeniable and unbecoming insensitivity in the Sage. Again, it must be observed that an often strident elitism sullies Emerson's work. To the poet-philosopher who celebrates the sanctity of humanity, men in the mass are "imbeciles," the "uninventive or accepting class." Theirs is to follow the light at the end of the cave, as Emerson's beloved Plato suggested, the new priesthood: the poets, the seers of Transcendentalism, the scholars.

But these lapses of humanity are not representative of the heart of Emerson's philosophic message. In them Emerson succumbs momentarily to the prejudices of his class, but only momentarily. For when all objections have been made and all contradictions noted, Emerson remains a prime exponent of human freedom. More effectively, more consistently than any philosopher before or after him he affirmed man's ability to improve himself and his world through the unfettered use of creative intelligence. In an age of greed and materialism he affirmed the sovereignty of the human mind. In an age of heartless industrialism, in which size was confused with worth, he recalled men to the simple splendor of the flower, the pond, the bird in winter. In an age of strutting nationalism he saluted a cosmic Soul that held all men, all nations, and all ages in its unity. Then, and now, Ralph Waldo Emerson, in Matthew Arnold's words, was "the friend and aider of all who would live in the spirit." "He called one of his poems 'Sursum Corda,' lift up your hearts;" writes Dr. Waggoner, "the title points to the intention behind all his thinking."

For the muddying business of politics Emerson had little

use. On the great issues, however, he spoke out strongly. He opposed the annexation of Texas as a slave state. He favored the abolition of slavery and championed John Brown. And when the Civil War broke out, this gentle spokesman for the "Over-Soul" could say, "Sometimes gunpowder smells good."

After the war Harvard lifted its interdict on the Sage of Concord, named him an overseer of the college and awarded him an honorary LL.D. degree. Emerson continued to meet with old friends in Boston's famed Saturday Club for dinner and good talk—with the doctor-poet and wit Oliver Wendell Holmes, with Longfellow of Cambridge, with Hawthorne. But Emerson's powers were failing. He knew that his best years and best work were behind him. His lectures, which once excited audiences, now seemed repetitive, stale, and innocuous. "It is time to be old, / " he had written in his poem "Terminus," "To take in sail:—/ The God of bounds, / Who sets to seas a shore, / Came to me in his fatal rounds, / And said: 'No more! / No farther shoot / Thy broad ambitious branches, and thy root. . . .' "

The burning of his beloved home in Concord in 1872 greatly distressed the philosopher. His grief was softened by a visit to Europe, where he once again saw his old friend Carlyle, and by a hearty welcome home from friends and neighbors in Concord who had raised money to rebuild his home and ease the burden of his lecture tours. But Emerson's powers continued to fail, more noticeably now. A visitor to his home in 1875, struck by the silence of the philosopher who had once charmed guests with his eloquence, noticed a strange forgetfulness in Emerson. "He remembered the realities and uses of things when he could not recall their names. He would describe what he wanted or thought of; when he could not recall 'chair' he could speak of that which supports the human frame, and 'the implement that cultivates the soil' must do for plough." At Longfellow's funeral, his friend Oliver Wendell Holmes recalled, Emerson "rose, and going to the side of the coffin, looked intently upon the face of the dead poet. A few minutes later he rose again and looked once more on the familiar features, not apparently remembering that he had just done so." At the close of the funeral service Emerson turned to his daughter Ellen: "The gentleman we have just been burying," he assured her, "was a sweet and beautiful soul; but I forget his name."

One month later, on April 27, 1882, Emerson himself was dead. He was buried on a hill in Concord's Sleepy Hollow Cemetery near the grave of his young friend and protégé, Henry Thoreau. "In the woods . . ." Emerson had written, "all mean egotism vanishes. I become a transparent eyeball; I am nothing; I see all; the currents of the Universal Being circulate through me; I am part or particle of God." Now he was back to stay, the record of his thought complete, his fame secure. John Greenleaf Whittier confidently predicted that Emerson was "the one American who is sure of being remembered a thousand years." And in our time, the poet Robert Frost calmly ranked him with Washington, Jefferson, and Lincoln as one of "my four greatest Americans."

HENRY DAVID THOREAU

HE HEARD A DIFFERENT DRUMMER

"To go into solitude," Emerson wrote in *Nature*, "a man needs to retire as much from his chamber as from society. I am not solitary whilst I read and write, though nobody is with me. But if a man would be alone, let him look at the stars."

More often than the Sage of Concord, his patron and friend, Henry David Thoreau retired from his chamber and looked at the stars. The differences between Thoreau and the man whom Oliver Wendell Holmes dubbed "the Buddha of the West" can be exaggerated. Both men, after all, defied old dogmas, dared to trust their own minds and devise new creeds. Both men loved Nature in the raw, as much for what they considered its moral instruction as for its esthetic or factual interest. Thoreau had thrilled to Emerson's *Nature*, which he purchased with no little financial sacrifice at Harvard. He shared Emerson's teaching that "each particle is a microcosm, and faithfully renders the likeness of the world." And Thoreau, for all his scientific approach to field and stream, could declare at twenty: "How indispensable to a correct study of Nature is a perception of her true meaning. The fact will one day flower out into a truth. . . . Mere accumulators of facts . . . are like those plants growing in dark forests, which 'put forth only leaves instead of blossoms.'" So high did Emerson rank in Thoreau's esteem that young Henry, fourteen years Emerson's junior, walked the eighteen miles from Concord to Boston— and back—to hear a single lecture by the Sage. It is not too much to say, most notably in his formative years, that Thoreau created a life-style out of Emerson's philosophy, a style modified by Thoreau's own as he matured, to be sure, but a style influenced from first to last by Emerson's mysticism and Transcendentalist language.

But there were great differences between these men, too, despite their lifelong if sometimes strained friendship. A polished, propertied man of the world, at ease in the finest homes and clubs, a master of the lecture hall and literary salon, Emerson was content to celebrate Nature, one concludes, chiefly from his study window or on stately walks. It is difficult to imagine Emerson scaling Mount Katahdin, as Thoreau did, or "conversing" with woodchucks, measuring snow storms, surveying land, counting the rings on trees, standing in water for hours to watch fish eggs hatch, or lying on a Concord hill, drenched and ecstatic in the falling rain. The man who confessed to his *Journal* that he considered "the whole of nature [as] a metaphor of the human mind" could not have shared Thoreau's special brand of delight. "Would it not be a luxury," Henry wrote in his *Journal*, "to stand up to one's chin in some retired swamp for a whole summer's day, scenting the sweet fern . . . and lulled by the minstrelsy of gnats and mosquitoes? . . . Say twelve hours of genial and familiar converse with the leopard frog. . . . Surely one may as profitably be soaked in the juices of a marsh for one day, as pick his way dry-shod over sand. . . ."

Thoreau reveled in the sheer physical wildness of nature, as Emerson did not, and on at least one occasion permitted himself to defect from Transcendentalism itself: "The moral aspect of nature," he wrote in his *Journal*, "is a jaundice reflected from man." Emerson himself recognized their differences: If God had intended Thoreau to live in a swamp, he once told his protégé, he would have made him a frog, lamenting on another occasion that "instead of being the head of American engineers [Thoreau] is captain of a huckleberry party." Less harshly, Emerson con-

ceded: "In reading Thoreau, I find the same thoughts, the
same spirit that is in me; but he takes a step beyond, and
illustrates by excellent images, that which I should have
conveyed by a sleepy generalization. . . . 'Tis as if I went
into a gymnasium, and saw youths leap and climb and
swing . . . though their feats are only a continuation of my
initial grapplings and jumps."

Shy, bumbling, blunt, and aloof—Emerson avowed that
he'd sooner take an elm by the arm than take Thoreau's—
Henry was more at home with farmers and Indian hunting
guides than with fellow writers at high literary teas. He
abhorred pretentious chatter. "It takes a man," he declared
at twenty-one, "to make a room silent." And though an
avid reader—and translator—of the classics, he was wary of
education, because often, he believed, "it makes a straight-
cut ditch of a free, meandering brook." Henry was a loner.
Men cared too much for the good opinion of others, he
believed. As for himself, he said, "If I were confined to a
garret all my days, like a spider, the world would be just as
large to me while I had my thoughts."

"To be a philosopher," Thoreau concluded in *Walden*,
"is not merely to have subtle thoughts . . . but so to love
wisdom as to live according to its dictates, a life of simplicity, magnanimity and trust." Such a life could not be lived
among men lusting for money and social power, or among
scholars and writers whose success, as Thoreau saw it, was
more "courtier-like than kingly." For visionary reform
movements like that of Bronson Alcott, he had no use
at all. "I came into this world," he wrote, "not chiefly to
make this a good place to live in, but to live in it, be it
good or bad." To live fully in the present moment, to know
Nature, Thoreau decided, one must abandon mere nouns

and verbs and become totally conscious of man's oneness with all things, the fox racing in the snow, the titmouse in the poplar, the screaming eagle in flight. One must be blown on like a sail "by God's breath . . . flutter and flap and fill gently out with the breeze," confronting Nature unscarred by man, "pure Nature . . . savage, and awful, though beautiful," as on a high mountain. "Talk of mysteries! Think of our life in Nature,—daily to be shown matter, to come in contact with it,—rocks, trees, wind on our cheeks! the solid earth! . . ."

On July 4, 1845, Henry David Thoreau put these ideas to a historic test. As a boy he had scoured Concord's woods, swum naked and joyous in its rivers and ponds, known its birds, rocks, and trees as he knew his name. Now he declared an independence of his own and took a walk that would one day make him world famous. He turned his back on his town, went into the woods, and began life anew in a cabin he had built on the side of a hill by the edge of a pond named Walden. There he lived for twenty-six months, farming, fishing, reading, writing, baking his own bread, storing up notes for a book in which he hoped to share the insights and joys of life in the woods. He would call this book *Walden*, a testament of human independence that would move men's hearts on all continents and assure Thoreau's place in the pantheon of American folk heroes.

"I went to the woods," Thoreau said, "because I wished to live deliberately, to front only the essential facts of life, and see if I could not learn what it had to teach, and not when I came to die discover that I had not lived." He wanted, he explained, to "drive life into a corner, and reduce it to its lowest terms, and, if it proved to be mean, why then to get the whole and genuine meanness of it, and publish its meanness to the world; or if it were sublime, to know it by experience, and be able to give a true account of it in my next excursion." He no longer wished to "play" at life, or study it abstractly, but "earnestly *live* it from beginning to end," to "explore the private sea" of his own being, to discover who he truly was, what he was meant to do, and to seek out and obey "more sacred laws" than those made by man.

Thoreau's independence was nurtured not only by Emerson's philosophy and friendship but by his own family heritage. In every sense, he never truly left home. Born David Henry Thoreau (he himself reversed the order of his names) in Concord, Massachusetts, July 12, 1817, Henry was the son of an unsuccessful farmer and storekeeper turned pencil-maker named John. Henry's father traced his ancestry to doughty sailing Protestants on the Isle of Jersey in the English Channel and remotely to Tours, France. His mother, Cynthia (Dunbar), a no-nonsense Scot from Keene, New Hampshire, shared Thoreau's love of nature if not his religious skepticism, and was known for her active tongue no less than for her hospitable if somewhat austere table. Henry had an older sister, Helen, a specially loved older brother, John, who shared his youthful exploits and early professional ventures. A younger sister, Sophia, would also prove a close and reliable companion, assisting in the preparation of Thoreau's works for publication when illness confined him to bed at last and death claimed him.

Nicknamed "Judge" because of his gravity of manner, Thoreau did the chores expected of a boy in nineteenth-century rural New England. He drove cows to pasture, took on odd jobs, and helped out in his father's pencil factory on Concord's Main Street as he would intermittently throughout life, finally taking charge himself. And he hunted and fished, and searched the woods for Indian arrowheads, and rowed his boat with his brother John up the Concord River.

After some schooling in Boston, Henry entered Concord Academy, where in a heavily classical curriculum he studied Latin and Greek in which he became proficient. Perhaps there, too, he learned to play the flute, which would prove to be of lifelong pleasure to him. Emerson helped Thoreau get a scholarship to Harvard, which Henry entered in August, 1833.

At Harvard, Thoreau frankly preferred private reading to formal courses; Henry Wadsworth Longfellow's rambling lectures on German literature, for example, biographer August Derleth says, "very probably left [him] cold." He was intellectually happiest in the college library, which he used throughout life, poking into Virgil, Seneca, the poet Donne, Euripides, Homer, and Carlyle. Some biographers insist that Thoreau showed early evidence of his defiance of social amenities by wearing a green jacket to Harvard's compulsory chapel services when the rules rigidly required black. The consensus seems to be, however, that Henry simply couldn't afford to buy a black one, even with the money he received from his devoted family and from between-term teaching in Canton, Massachusetts, where he lived with the reforming Unitarian clergyman Orestes Brownson.

In a posthumous biographical sketch of Thoreau, Emerson makes the uncharitable statement that Thoreau wrote a scholastic record at Harvard "without any literary distinction." To be sure, Thoreau's adolescent style can be pompous and shows little of the purity and concision of line that distinguished *Walden* or the on-target imagery of his best journal entries in later life. But even in his college essays Thoreau defines at least three of the concerns that would absorb him throughout life: the pitfalls of conformity; the nature of sound writing; and the need for a genuinely *American* literature. "The fear of displeasing the world," he declared solemnly, "ought not in the least to influence my actions." Guided by Edward Tyrrel Channing, professor of rhetoric, he developed a sense of effective literary style he would never lose. "If we would aim at perfection in anything," Henry wrote, "simplicity must not be overlooked." He was determined to "omit all superfluous ornament," which, he believed, only distracted the reader's mind. Words must never be used to impress or obscure but to communicate and clarify. Good English was like the Roman toga, at once elegant and unadorned. Like the best of the Bible and of Shakespeare, he concluded, "the most sublime and noble precepts may be conveyed in a plain and simple strain," in what Thoreau called a "union of wisdom and simplicity."

In calling for a truly national literature in 1835, Thoreau suggested: "We are, as it were, but colonies" of England. "[T]hough we have rejected her tea, she still supplies us with food for the mind. . . . Our respect for what is foreign . . . has a tendency to render us blind to native merit, and lead us into a servile adoration of imported genius." He appealed for an end to affected foreignisms, an end to writers unaware that they would outlive the fashions they mimicked, to writers who "mistake the profitable for the useful" in trying to please a fickle public. And, most characteristically for the prose-poet of Walden Pond, Thoreau demanded an end to odes to imagined "skylarks and nightingales perched on [English] hedges, to the neglect of the homely robin red-breast, and the straggling rail-fence of their own native land."

At Harvard, Thoreau made no lasting friendships, except perhaps with Charles Stearns Wheeler, with whom he camped near a pond. Wheeler, indeed, might have given Thoreau the initial inspiration for the Walden experiment. As to Thoreau's social conduct, a not unfriendly classmate later observed: "We could sympathize with his tranquil indifference to college honors, but we did not suspect the fine genius that was developing under that impassive demeanor. . . . But he passed for nothing, it is suspected, with most of us; for he was cold and unimpressible. The touch of his hand was moist and indifferent. . . . He did not care for people; his classmates seemed very remote. . . . Thought had not yet awakened his countenance; it was serene, but rather dull, rather plodding." The same observer found "almost a look of smug satisfaction lurking 'round . . . [the] corners" of Thoreau's lips. And, noting that "Indian stride" that carried young Henry through Harvard Yard no less than through Concord woods, his classmate added that Thoreau's eyes "were sometimes searching, as if he had dropped, or expected to find something." In any case, he concluded, Thoreau "had no animal spirits for our sport or mischief," nor, it might be added, for college receptions and teas.

Henry graduated from Harvard in August, 1837, "close," writes biographer August Derleth, "to the top of his class." His rank was high enough to warrant a letter of reference from Harvard's President Josiah Quincy, attesting to

Henry's qualifications "as an instructor, for employment in any public or private school or private family." In a commencement address Thoreau characteristically assailed "the commercial spirit" for making wealth the end rather than the means of existence. He returned to Concord with plans no more romantic than teaching school or less commercial than making pencils.

Thoreau's first teaching assignment lasted two weeks. Corporal punishment of misbehaving students, normally with a ferrule, was the order of the day in this era. But Thoreau refused to substitute the rod for reason in the discipline of students. Ordered to crack the whip by school authorities, he decided to obey, but only to show the absurdity of the practice. For no reason at all he whipped six students at random, resigned his position, and returned to his father's pencil shop. But, impatient for a more creative life, he joined his beloved brother John in opening a private school, first in the Thoreau house in 1838, later in the old rented-out Concord Academy building. John was in charge. Henry taught Greek, French and mathematics, and, indulging both his students' love of the outdoors and his own instincts as a naturalist, he guided his classes on scientific field trips through Concord's woods and fields, patiently explaining the way of the natural world to his delighted disciples.

In September, 1839, Henry and John made their celebrated thirteen-day journey down the Concord River, then up the Merrimack River to the vicinity of Hooksett, New Hampshire. At this point they moored their boat and took off on foot for a trek through New Hampshire and the White Mountains, where they climbed Mount Washington. Out of this excursion emerged Thoreau's first book,

A Week on the Concord and Merrimack Rivers. It was a rambling, uneven, often sententious work in which periodically acute descriptions of these beautiful rivers and nineteenth-century life in towns along their banks are eclipsed by pedantic Latin quotations, dissertations on Chaucer and Hindu scripture, and translations of Greek odes. Thoreau was a long way off from the salty, taut prose of *Cape Cod,* and the at times awesome thrust of *The Maine Woods.* When finally published in 1849 by the Boston firm of James Munroe—at Thoreau's expense—the book fared badly. Of 1,000 copies printed, 706 were sent back to Thoreau. This defeat earned Henry the derision of some townsmen, but it prompted Thoreau's classic sally of droll Yankee humor: "I have now a library of nearly nine hundred volumes, over seven hundred of which I wrote myself."

Love touched Henry and his brother simultaneously in the person of one Ellen Sewall of Scituate, Massachusetts. Ellen was a pupil in their school, sister of another pupil, Edmund, to whom Thoreau had written a poem, "Sympathy," containing what Thoreau's finest biographer, Walter Harding, calls "to modern eyes at least—quite androgynous overtones." In his *Journals* Thoreau hailed young Edmund's innocence, his "pure uncompromising spirit," one "impossible not to love." And in "Sympathy," after one of Edmund's departures for home, he added: "Yet now [I] am forced to know, though hard it is, /I might have loved him, had I loved him less." In any event, Thoreau and his brother were soon irretrievably in love with Ellen, taking turns not only in courting her, but in proposing marriage. John was refused her hand. When Henry was rejected in 1840, he wrote dramatically: "To sigh under the cold, cold moon for a love unrequited is but a slight on nature; the natural remedy would be to fall in love with the moon and the night and find our love requited." Ultimately, Thoreau settled for the moon and the night, remaining a systematic bachelor throughout life.

The Thoreau brothers' school fared badly, too, closing down in 1841 when John fell ill, probably with tuberculosis. When John died of tetanus resulting from a shaving cut, in January, 1842, Thoreau, at least in a letter to Emerson, appeared reconciled, noting philosophically that death no less than life was a natural part of the cosmic cycle. But on the same day he wrote to his old friend, he gave way to his grief in solitude: "My life, my life! why will you linger? . . . Can God afford that I should forget him? . . . Why, God, did you include me in your great scheme? Will you not make me a partner at last?"

Lonely and still grieving, Thoreau moved into the home of Ralph and Lidian Emerson, who had themselves just lost little Waldo. Henry had impressed Concord's Sage as having "as free and erect a mind as any I have ever met," and in asking Henry to live in his home, Emerson clearly intended to assist him in the development of his intellect and writing style. For in this great house, Thoreau served not only as gardener and handyman and, during Emerson's absence abroad, as resident protector of his wife and children, but as Emerson's protégé. He was introduced to the bright lights of Transcendentalism, including Alcott and Margaret Fuller, who published comparatively inconsequential pieces by Thoreau in the *Dial*. In 1843 Emerson also arranged for Thoreau to teach his brother William's son on Staten Island, hoping at the same time that Thoreau might curry acquaintances in the

New York publishing world. Thoreau enjoyed meeting the crusading New York *Tribune* editor Horace Greeley, who would remain Thoreau's lifelong friend, publishing large portions of his works in his newspaper to bring them to a wider circle of readers. Thoreau met Henry James the elder, too, father of the great American novelist.

As a tutor, Thoreau fared well enough, but he was happiest by the sea, taking full advantage of this first opportunity to live by it, spending many hours watching vessels of commerce passing around Sandy Hook. Of New York City itself, Henry had little good to say: "I don't like the city better, the more I see it, but worse. I am ashamed of my eyes that behold it. It is a thousand times meaner than I could have imagined. . . . When will the world learn that a million men are of no importance compared with one man?" By mid-December, 1843, Henry was back in Concord to stay, except for short visits to Cape Cod, Maine, the Midwest and the homes of friends.

Muscular, lean, and of average height for his time, Henry had the strong hands of a laborer and long arms. For most of his life he wore no beard. His friend William Ellery Channing the younger, nephew of the great Unitarian clergyman—and Ellery Channing for short—left this deft description of his hiking companion: "His face, once seen, could not be forgotten. The features were quite marked: the nose aquiline or very Roman, like one of the portraits of Caesar (more like a beak, as was said); large, overhanging brows above the deepest-set blue eyes that could be seen, in certain lights, and in others gray,—eyes expressive of all shades of feeling, but never weak or nearsighted; the forehead not unusually broad or high . . . the mouth with prominent lips. . . . His hair was a dark brown, exceedingly abundant, fine and soft. . . . His whole figure had an active earnestness, as if he had no moment to waste. The clenched hand betokened purpose. In walking he made a short cut if he could, and when sitting in the shade or by the wallside seemed merely the clearer to look into the next piece of activity. Even in the boat he had a wary, transitory air, his eyes on the outlook,—perhaps there might be ducks . . . or an otter, or sparrow."

Nathaniel Hawthorne, after a visit by Thoreau to the Old Manse for dinner, found him "a singular character; a young man with much of wild original Nature still remaining in him; and so far as he was sophisticated, it is in a way and method of his own. He is as ugly as sin; long-nosed, queer-mouthed, and with uncouth and rustic manners,—But his ugliness is of an honest and agreeable fashion, and becomes him much better than beauty." Thoreau, Hawthorne complained, had "repudiated all regular means of getting a living," such as normal college-bred men pursued, "and [seemed] inclined to lead a sort of Indian life," except for serving as a gardener for Emerson. Hawthorne, nonetheless, lauded Thoreau as "a genuine observer of Nature" even a keen and delicate observer," one "on intimate terms with the clouds," no less than with herbs, fish and fowl. Even Emerson, while praising Thoreau's "incorruptible integrity" and his "great ability and industry" saw something of the poseur in Henry's manners: ". . . [W]e shall yet hear much more of him," the Sage declared. "But he affects manners rather brusque . . . is pugnacious about trifles; likes to contradict, likes to say No, and to be on the other side. You cannot always tell what will please him. He was ill, and I sent him a bottle of wine, which I doubt if he ever tasted. I regret these oddities. He needs to fall in love, to sweeten and straighten him."

As for Thoreau himself, he cared not a hoot for such judgments, or did not appear to. He was more than a loner. He had contempt for most means of making a living as degrading to a man, even those that the world held in greatest esteem. He had contempt for money, as such, and for wasting one more minute than he had to in obtaining it. "The cost of a thing," he believed, "is the amount of what I will call life which is required to be exchanged for it." And life as most men lived and paid for it, he decided, simply wasn't worth the cost. To live the life he truly wanted, Thoreau concluded, he must learn, in the words of biographer Joseph Wood Krutch, "simply to need less, rather than get more." So he went to his woods, his cabin, and his pond.

Thoreau's decision to live in the woods was neither sudden nor, in a strict sense, original. As we know, he stayed with his friend Stearns Wheeler in Wheeler's cabin at Sandy Pond in the neighboring town of Lincoln. And it was Sandy Pond, not Walden to which he referred in his *Journals* in December, 1841: "I want to go soon and live away by the pond, where I shall hear only the wind whispering among the reeds. It will be a success if I shall have left myself behind." His request to build a cabin at the pond, however, was denied by the owners of the land around it.

By March, 1845, however, Thoreau concluded a bargain with Emerson. Henry agreed to clear a brier patch on a plot owned by Emerson on the northwest shore of Walden Pond, in exchange for the right to squat on the property rent-free and to build the cabin of his dreams. Emerson agreed. On July 4, the cabin was ready and Thoreau settled in. No longer, he exulted, would he march in step with the crowd, as if he ever had! No longer would he be caught like a butterfly in a spider's web, in the "restless, nervous, bustling, trivial Nineteenth Century, but stand or sit thoughtfully while it [went] by."

As for his old neighbors, he said, he wouldn't miss them a bit. "The mass of men," he declared in *Walden*, "lead lives of quiet desperation." They are desperate to succeed, desperate to possess money and property, and in their desperation are driven into "incessant anxiety and strain," making themselves sick in their efforts to save money against a sick day. The world, he said, cared more for appearances than reality, considered fashionable clothes more important than a sound conscience. Men's houses were needlessly complex, filled with useless knickknacks, and looked more like museums and prisons than like homes. What men called progress was both silly and cruel. "We are in great haste," he observed, "to construct a magnetic telegraph from Maine to Texas; but Maine and Texas, it may be, have nothing important to communicate." Worst of all, men had become victims of their own machines, "tools of their tools," financial slaves of their own mortgaged properties. "We do not ride on the railroad," he declared, "it rides upon us." Even the farmer's cattle are freer than he.

As for our great new factories, Thoreau believed, they had brought a new form of slavery to America and trade had cursed everything it touched. New industries cost more in the degradation of human lives than they gave, as seen in the filthy shanty huts of immigrant Irishmen stretched on the beds of our shiny new railroads. "The principal object [of industry]," he wrote, "is not that mankind may be well and honestly clad, but unquestionably, that the corporations may be enriched." One man's wealth requires another man's poverty and so was a hateful thing. And Thoreau likened the nineteenth-century worker in America to the Egyptian slave who spent his life building the pointless pyramid tombs of vain Pharaohs and yet had no tomb of his own.

America, Thoreau taught, has lost its original spirit. It was crippled by "young men who had ceased to be young," and by old men who "would not go a-huckleberrying without a medicine chest." Most men were half asleep, digging their graves as they lived, held down by a faceless conformity to tyrannical customs, their opinions ready-made by the penny press. The average man's conversation and thought, he said, were "on a very low level, worthy only of pygmies and mannikins." Imprisoned within their petty villages, men had gotten too far from their original nature. They knew the bread on their table, but not the grain in the field. They had built a microscope, but had forgotten how to use their naked eye. And as for so-called modern social conveniences, Thoreau claimed, "I could easily do without the post office. . . . I never received more than one or two letters in my life that were worth the postage." The whole of what men called "society," Henry Thoreau decided in words still used by his Yankee kin, costs more than it comes to, and he wasn't buying.

Was there an alternative to this foolish, futile life? Yes, Thoreau cried, there *was* a way to beat it. And that was to separate frills from necessities. "Simplify, simplify," he wrote. "Let your affairs be as two or three, and not a hundred or a thousand; instead of a million count half a dozen, and keep your accounts on your thumb nail." Eat less; wash fewer dishes. Own less, dust less. "[A]nd reduce other things in proportion." Life need not be a hardship if men reduce their wants and live as innocently as nature. "A man is rich in proportion to the number of things he can afford to let alone." And in the solitude of his cabin, Thoreau was as good as his word. The average daily cost of his life there, it has been estimated, was twenty-seven cents. He succeeded in his determination to "front only the essential facts of life," to live without frills, without pretense or social hypocrisy. As for what other people thought of his way of life, he reasoned, why that was their business, not his. A man must be himself. "If a man does not keep pace with his companions," Thoreau declared proudly, "perhaps it is because he hears a different drummer. Let him dance to the music which he hears, however measured or far away."

Despite the evidence in *Walden*, the image persists of Thoreau as a hermit turning his back upon a world that rejected him, a world to which he no longer had anything to say. But Thoreau made it clear that he went into the woods not to brood in ascetic melancholy, but to cry like a rooster, to wake his neighbors up, to *show* them, if they cared to see, that an honest, simple life was possible, to prove that a home was made beautiful not by its furnishings or façade but by the quality of human life within it.

The small forest home—Channing called it "a sentry box in the shore"—stood on an eleven-acre plot of hickories and pines, a mile from the nearest neighbor, and about sixty yards from the deep glacial pond itself. "It was not a lonely spot," writes Thoreau's most exhaustive biographer, Walter Harding. "The well-traveled Concord-Lincoln road was within sight across the field. The Fitchburg Railroad steamed regularly past the opposite end of the pond. Concord village was less than two miles away, and the [Thoreau family] house was less than that along the railroad right-of-way." Henry made frequent visits home and enjoyed visits to his cabin by his mother and sisters bearing home-baked food. The Emersons and Alcotts still had him to dinner. Channing stayed with him at the cabin for two weeks, sleeping near Henry's cot on the cabin floor. Thoreau visited Concord village "every day or two," to fetch rice or gossip, enjoyed frequent callers—including runaway slaves whom he helped "forward to the north star"—and he claimed to have entertained as many as twenty-five to thirty visitors in his cabin at one time, including Emerson and Hawthorne. Louisa May Alcott, then a child, recalled his visits to Concord. Thoreau, she said, "used to come smiling up to his neighbors, to announce that the blueberries had arrived, with as much interest in the fact as other men take in messages by the Atlantic cable. . . . He gravely informed us once that frogs were much more confiding in the spring." Thoreau left his cabin even to lecture at the Concord Lyceum. In addition, idealism bought little Indian meal. There was a living to make. "While I lived in the woods," Thoreau freely admitted, "I did jobs about town,—fence-building, painting, gardening, carpentering, etc. . . ." Nor had he lost his Yankee acumen in his retreat to Walden. Once, he boasted, he built "a woodshed of no mean size for exactly six dollars; and I cleared half of that by a close calculation and swift working," proudly adding that any wood or nails left over were taken back to the cabin.

The cabin itself was almost primitively simple, in his own words "a sort of porch at the entrance of a burrow." Thoreau reveled in the thrill of building his own home, with his own hands, to his own taste. He himself hewed its timbers, rafters, and studs. He bought the boards for its walls from an Irishman on the move from his shanty. The cabin measured ten feet wide and fifteen feet long. Shingled and plastered, it boasted only one door, two windows, a brick hearth, a garret, a closet, and two trap doors leading to a sandy earthen cellar where food could be preserved. The total cost of the cabin, built at a time when a "thick coat" cost $5, Thoreau announced proudly, was precisely $28.12½.

Thoreau's cabin furnishings were equally plain, reduced to his simplest needs. He had made many of them himself. He had a bed, a table, a desk, three chairs, a looking glass three inches in diameter, a pair of tongs, andirons, a kettle, a skillet and frying pan, a dipper, a washbowl, two knives and forks, three plates, one cup, one spoon, a jug for oil, a jug for molasses, and a lamp. "The more you have of such things," he explained, "the poorer you are." The cabin had no curtains, "for I have no gazers to shut out but the sun and moon," no carpet to fade, no meat to taint. The cabin had no locks, except on its master's desk, because there was nothing worth stealing.

Walden Pond itself, one hundred and two feet at its greatest depth, was for Thoreau "a clear and deep green well," half a mile wide and a mile and three-quarters in circumference. Its surrounding hills rise sharply from its shores to heights of eighty to one hundred and fifty feet. In its total effect, it seemed to Thoreau "earth's eye."

In and outside of his cabin Thoreau practiced the

simplicity he preached. Up at dawn for a bath in the pond, he hoed his beans—he estimated the length of their rows to be seven miles—until noon. "Making the earth say beans instead of grass," he wrote, "—this was my daily work." He planted two and one-half acres of vegetables, potatoes, and corn, in addition to beans, peas, and turnips. And he cleared a profit on his crop the very first year. He got wood for his fireplace from old stumps, and he was proud of his initiative and self-reliance. "I have as many trades as fingers," he boasted. But his greatest skill, he insisted, was wanting little.

Thoreau was freer at Walden for the exercise of his intellect, too, because he had reduced his physical needs to the point where work was necessary, he said, only thirty or forty days in the year. Thus he was free for writing. He worked on *A Week on the Concord and Merrimack Rivers*. He took raw notes as he walked through the woods, refined them into clean hard prose as he transferred them to his *Journals*. And from these entries would emerge *Walden*: from seed, to blossom, to flower. He was free for reading, too, sustaining, no doubt, the pattern of his reading throughout life: Homer's *Iliad* in the original Greek; the Bhagavad-Gita, India's sacred book; Confucius; and no doubt the New Testament, for he loved Jesus, and therefore, he reasoned, he could not like the church that dared to misinterpret what He had said so plainly. The written word was for Thoreau "the choicest of relics . . . the work of art nearest to life itself," man's noblest legacy, raising us "out of the trivialities of the street." At Walden, too, Henry wrote articles for his ever loyal champion Horace Greeley in New York. And after hoeing and reading, hiking and writing, he would again bathe and swim in his pond.

Thoreau ate simply too: vegetables, rice, water, fresh fish, a little salt pork. He baked an unleavened bread of rye and Indian meal, made his own molasses of pumpkins and beets. He could make a joyous supper of blueberries or huckleberries alone. He ate meat at the pond only once— woodchuck—and found it musky and impure. He concluded that in man's march toward full civility he would abandon meat-eating completely. No liquor touched his lips, nor would he think, he said, of "dashing the hopes of a morning" with coffee, or of an evening with tea.

In the village Henry traded his beans for rice and meal. But "the true harvest" of his day, he wrote, was "a little star-dust caught, a segment of the rainbow which I have clutched." And the image of star-dust caught is not even slightly strained. It is not too much, and perhaps not enough to say that Henry David Thoreau's experience at Walden Pond, his intimate communion with Nature in all its seasons and forms, assumes the character of a profoundly mystical, a profoundly spiritual experience. Thoreau himself might denigrate that experience; at one point he tells his *Journals* dourly: "If I am not quite right here, I am less wrong than before. . . ." But it is difficult to read *Walden*, to sense its rhythms, to be stunned by its sudden and unaffected insights and not believe that Thoreau's life near "earth's eye" was an interlude of positive searching and philosophical serenity that few men know. Thoreau lived in Nature as wordlessly as the pine and sparrow, delighting in the cry of the nighthawk, the song of the woodthrush, the "lisp" of the chickadee, the pompous croaking of frogs, the screech of the midnight owl, and he treasured them all. He could hear the universe in the hum of the mosquito, translate the message of the wind, exult in the shimmering gold and emerald of the pickerel in Walden's rich blue waters, and he cherished the weed as the food of birds. He could rise at 2:00 A.M. to watch fog, or wait for the triumph of sunrise. He was soothed by long rains pounding the roof and walls of his tiny house, and loved even the "black kernel of night."

In Henry's theology, heaven knew no geography. It was as much below a man's feet as above his head. All life was sacred. For Thoreau, the only time man truly owned or could truly grasp was the present moment. He lived at the pond, he said, like the Puri Indians, who have but a single word for "yesterday," "today," and "tomorrow." Not even the searing scream of the locomotive could shatter the silence of his woods; didn't the train bear all the riches of the world?

Nature, Henry said, took on almost human form for him. "Every little pine needle expanded and swelled with sympathy and befriended me." And why not? Wasn't he "partly leaves and vegetable mould" himself? Indeed, there was much of the animal in Thoreau, too, much of the wild nature Hawthorne had seen in him. He ranged through the woods once or twice, as he himself put it, "like a half-starved hound," could watch with savage fascination a war to the death between red and black ants. For all his classical scholarship, Thoreau, as Emerson observed, "knew the country like a fox or a bird, and passed through it as freely by paths of his own." On one occasion, Thoreau writes, "as I came home through the woods with my string of fish, trailing my pole, it being now quite dark, I caught a glimpse of a woodchuck stealing across my path, and felt a strange thrill of savage delight, and was strongly tempted to seize and devour him raw; not that I was hun-

gry then, except for that wildness which he represented."
On other occasions, he reports, he walked the woods "with
a strange abandonment, seeking some kind of venison
which I might devour, and no morsel could have been too
savage for me." "I found in myself, and still find," he confessed, "an instinct toward a higher, or, as it is named,
spiritual life, as do most men, and another toward a primitive rank and savage one, and I reverence them both. I
love the wild no less than the good. . . . I like sometimes
to take rank hold of life and spend my days more as the
animals do." Again he explained: "We need the tonic of
wildness," for in the pampered life of civilized luxury we
risk emasculation.

At Walden, however, Thoreau's life was more serene
than wild, as he sought his goal: to "be nature looking
into nature with such easy sympathy as the blue-eyed grass
in the meadow looks in the face of the sky." At Walden,
Thoreau achieved a sense of oneness with Nature, if any
man has, encountering the world as if the creation were
yesterday, "in undisturbed solitude and stillness," charming
the perch to his boat with his flute in the silent evening,
growing in those seasons, he wrote, "like corn in the night."
"My days were not days of the week . . . nor were they
minced into hours and fretted by the ticking of a clock.
. . . This was sheer idleness to my fellow-townsmen, no
doubt; but if the birds and flowers had tried me by their
standard, I should not have been found wanting."

Was he ever lonely in his forest retreat? "Why should
I be?" he asked. "Is not our planet in the Milky Way?"
Is the south wind lonely, or the January thaw? "No exertion
of the legs," he said, "can bring two minds much nearer
to one another." How then could he miss his neighbors?

"We are for the most part more lonely when we go abroad among men, than when we stay in our chambers. . . . The value of a man is not in his skin, that we should touch him." His thoughts kept him company. Even in the deepest snow he lived "as snug as a meadow mouse" and happily tramped eight or ten miles, as he put it, to keep an appointment with a beech tree. After all, wasn't the village just as far from him as he from it? Besides, he said, he occasionally had the privilege of welcoming on long winter evenings "the old settler and original proprietor who is reported to have dug Walden pond." And if the Settler did not come, hadn't his poet friend John Donne assured him that "love . . . makes one little room an everywhere?"

Though passionately committed to his independent mode of life, Thoreau refused to advise others to adopt it as a general principle. "I desire," he said, "that there be as many different persons in the world as possible." He declined the role of crusader. Reformers, he thought, assume that because *they* have a stomach ache the world has been eating green apples. Thoreau asked only that every man follow *his own* way and not slavishly adopt someone else's, that every man face up to the world not as he would like it to be but as it is: a world in which "the perch swallows the grub worm, the pickerel swallows the perch, and the fisherman swallows the pickerel; and so all the chinks in the scale of being are filled." And he urged men to remember their cosmic place, too. Just as a man watches an insect, he said, a Higher Being watches man.

Thoreau's twenty-six months in the woods were not wholly tranquil. They were interrupted by two events of continuing importance. First, he went on an excursion in the wilds of Maine that would contribute to his classic account of mountain-climbing, camping, hunting, and boating, *The Maine Woods*. This book is unforgettably awesome alone for Thoreau's chapter on Mount Katahdin, and his confrontation with a "vast, Titanic" Nature he had not known in the idyllic woods of Concord. It was Nature "savage and awful though beautiful," which certainly humbled him, perhaps even frightened him as he made his way toward Katahdin's summit, the highest point in Maine, through swirling clouds.

Henry's sojourn at the pond was interrupted by the incident in his life for which he is remembered almost as much as for *Walden*. Like Abraham Lincoln who opposed it as a congressman, and General Ulysses S. Grant who fought in it but condemned it in his *Memoirs* for the intervention that it was, Thoreau opposed the Mexican War, as Emerson did, as outright American aggression. He saw it as a violation of America's own principles of independence and liberty. Accordingly, he refused to pay his poll tax, lest his money be used to kill a single innocent Mexican.

On his way into Concord village to pick up a mended shoe on an evening in late July, 1846, Henry was stopped by the local jailer and tax collector, Sam Staples, and asked to pay his tax. The story of Thoreau's jailing has been told in many inaccurate ways. It is told best by Thoreau's finest biographer, Walter Harding. According to Harding, Sam Staples was less than brutal in his approach to Henry: " 'I'll pay your tax, Henry, if you're hard up,' Staples said. He also offered to try to persuade the selectmen to reduce the tax if Thoreau thought it too harsh, but Thoreau replied that he had not paid it as a matter of principle and didn't intend to pay it now. When Staples asked what he could do about it, Thoreau suggested that if he didn't like it, he could resign his office. But Staples, not taking kindly to that suggestion, replied, 'Henry, if you don't pay, I shall have to lock you up pretty soon.' 'As well now as any time, Sam,' was the answer. 'Well, come along then,' said Staples, and took him to jail."

As word of Thoreau's less than heroic arrest spread to family and friends, according to one tradition, a heavily veiled person called at the jail and paid Thoreau's tax for him, that same night. Some like to think it was a disguised Emerson who paid it, despite the Sage's contemptuous dismissal of Thoreau's action as "mean and skulking, and in bad taste." But most likely, as Harding suggests, it was Thoreau's Aunt Maria. The tax paid or not, Sam Staples, who had taken off his boots for the night, was not about to rush things. He had tried to be reasonable. Thoreau, he decided, could just stay put for the night.

There is some question whether Thoreau took his imprisonment with the philosophical detachment with which he is often credited, and, indeed, credits himself. One biographer quotes Sam Staples as saying that Thoreau was "mad as the devil" when he was released in the morning, with the implicition that Henry thought he should have been released as soon as the tax had been paid. Despite the rather inglorious fact that someone paid Thoreau's tax for him, and so allowed Henry to have things both ways, no one disagrees about the historic outcome of that one night in Concord jail. In his nonviolent resistance to something he believed to be evil, Thoreau set an example, a style of political protest that inspired generations to come. For out of that experience would emerge Thoreau's eloquent essay "On the Duty of Civil Disobedience," which would inspire and comfort no lesser men than Mahatma Gandhi in his struggle for Indian independence and Martin Luther King, Jr., in his struggle for racial justice. It would give heart to hundreds of thousands of Americans in opposing their country's twentieth-century war in Vietnam through nonviolent demonstrations.

"Civil Disobedience" is a powerful work. No American, Thoreau declared, could associate himself with the American government in the Mexican war without disgrace. Americans, he said, would not have approved the war if they had been consulted. The true patriot does not remain silent; he speaks out when his government does wrong. "If the injustice . . . is of such a nature that it requires you to be the agent of injustice to another," Thoreau declared, "then I say break the law." Constitutional remedies, he argued, "take too much time, and a man's life will be gone," before justice can be secured. The only effective form of protest, in Thoreau's opinion, is to withhold one's physical support at the only point where the individual meets his government face to face: at the tax counter. If enough citizens refuse to pay their taxes to an unjust government, that government must back down. Imprisonment? He did not fear it, said Thoreau, for a jail is "the only house in a slave state in which a free man can abide with honor."

In Concord jail—a formidable county building—Thoreau saw how foolish the government was to believe that by imprisoning him physically it could stifle his thoughts. "I saw," Thoreau wrote, "that the State was half-witted, that it was as timid as a lone woman with her silver spoons, and that it did not know its friends from its foes, and I lost all my remaining respect for it and pitied it." Besides, Thoreau reasoned, once jailed a man can combat injustice more effectively because he has known it at first hand. Nor should the power of one man's individual courage in going to jail for his convictions be underestimated, "for it matters not how small the beginning may seem to be: what is once well done is done forever."

It was not the only time Thoreau spoke out against injustice. He despised the Fugitive Slave Act, which permitted Southern masters to hunt down their slaves in the North and force their return to peonage. When the runaway slave Anthony Burns was captured and returned, despite the efforts of his lawyer, the novelist Richard Henry Dana, Jr., Thoreau was angered: "What signifies the beauty of nature," he wrote, "when men are base? . . . Who can be serene in a country where both rulers and ruled are without principle? The remembrance of the baseness of politicians spoils my walks. My thoughts are murder to the State . . . my thoughts involuntarily go plotting against the State. I trust that all just men will conspire. . . . My advice to the State is simply this: to dissolve her union with the slaveholder instantly. . . . And to each inhabitant of Massachusetts, to dissolve his union with the State, as long as she hesitates to do her duty."

When word of John Brown's raid at Harpers Ferry ripped the nation and few dared speak up for him, Thoreau, undaunted, hailed Brown as a hero, a rare and courageous man who dared "to step between the oppressor and the oppressed," a man who dared practice what he preached. "I rejoice," Thoreau cried, "that I live in this age, and

that I am his contemporary." When Concord officials refused to ring the town bell announcing Thoreau's eloquent
speech at Town Hall in defense of Brown, Thoreau rang
it himself. Not everyone in Henry's staid audience approved his words, but Henry was unruffled. "No man has
appeared in America as yet," he announced, "who loved
his fellow-man so well and treated him so tenderly. He
lived for him. He took up his life and laid it down for him.
He has liberated many slaves, North and South." For
Thoreau knew that the enslavement of man by man existed as much in the mills of New England as in the cotton
fields of the South—indeed that there was a direct commercial relationship between them. Angered by those who
condemned Brown's insurrection as anarchy or treason,
Thoreau said he foresaw the time the painter would paint
this historic scene, "no longer going to Rome for a subject; the poet will sing it; the historian record it; and, with
the Landing of the Pilgrims and the Declaration of Independence, it will be the ornament of some future National
Gallery, when at least the present form of slavery shall be
no more here. We shall then be at liberty to weep for
Captain Brown. Then, and not till then, we will take our
revenge."

Thoreau left Walden Pond on September 6, 1847, "for as
good a reason," he explained, "as I went there. Perhaps it
seemed to me that I had several more lives to live and
could not spare any more time for that one." The routine
of life at Walden had itself become a rut almost as deep
as the one he had left behind in Concord village. But
Walden had taught him this, at least: "that if one advances
confidently in the direction of his dreams, and endeavors
to live the life which he has imagined, he will meet with a

success unexpected in common hours. . . . In proportion as
he simplifies his life the laws of the universe will appear
less complex, and solitude will not be solitude, nor poverty
poverty, nor weakness weakness. If you have built castles
in the air, your work need not be lost; that is where they
should be. Now put foundations under them." If he
seemed to boast of his success at Walden, Thoreau explained: "[M]y excuse is that I brag for humanity rather
than for myself . . ." adding for hundreds who would
doubt his experiment, "my shortcomings and incon-
sistencies do not affect the truth of my statement." They
did not and they do not.

The publication of *Walden* in 1854 brought Henry
Thoreau a measure of fame, but mixed critical reaction.
If Emerson, perhaps dutifully, could declare that "all
American kind are delighted with *Walden*," and if the
English novelist George Eliot could applaud Thoreau's
"deep poetic sensibility" and pronounce his mind "refined
as well as . . . hardy," and if others could express pleasure
over *Walden*'s "originality," "keenness of perception,"
and ruthless exposure of "shallow conventionalism," a
great many people were outraged by the book. Thoreau's
own family was incensed by Thoreau's religious "blas-
phemy," scolding Henry for "putting things into his book
that shouldn't be there." "It is a sorrowful surprise," the
Boston Atlas pontificated, "that a constant communion
with so much beauty and beneficence was not able to
kindle one spark of genial warmth in this would-be savage."
And from England, Nathaniel Hawthorne, newly and consciously affluent as United States consul in Liverpool, permitted himself to say: "Thoreau despises the world, and
all that it has to offer, and like other humorists is an intoler-

able bore. . . . He is not an agreeable person, and in his presence one feels ashamed of having any money, or a house to live in, or so much as two coats to wear, or having written a book that the public will read."

Despite such studied contempt, *Walden* brought Thoreau a degree of notoriety, new invitations to lecture, and immense personal satisfaction. But it was not, initially, the continuing success that it has become and will be, least of all financially. Only two thousand copies were sold, for one dollar apiece. It was not even reprinted until after Thoreau's death. Not until one hundred years after Henry Thoreau's death would a proper price be put on his classic by critics and readers who finally saw the book for the prophetic witness it was. "What in other men is religion," Thoreau said, "is in me love of nature." *Walden* proves that. In its highest reaches it has a Biblical serenity, a Psalmic purity. Its relevance is timeless. "The full significance of *Walden*," Henry Seidel Canby believes, "has never been felt until today. It is only in our generation that the industrial revolution has reached a point where man is in real danger of becoming a machine thinking like a machine," and, one might add, regimentation has virtually crushed the individualism and self-reliance that Thoreau, like his spiritual brother Emerson, so powerfully championed.

In Concord village again, Thoreau managed his father's pencil shop. He measured snow storms, deepened his study of nature. He toured Canada, Maine, Cape Cod, piling up data for books in which he shared his passionate love of Nature. He was a most careful note-taker, a most systematic writer: raw notes became journals, and journals books. And he was immensely conscious of his literary style. "Seldom," said one close associate, "have I known an author who made more drafts of what he might some time print, or more persistently revised what he had once composed." Naturalist Henry Beston is convinced that "Thoreau was the first American to write a completely modern prose," free of Victorian mannerisms and "the unctuous and moralistic fustian" New England had borrowed from the Old. In *Cape Cod*, for example, no less than in *Walden*, Thoreau writes with an immaculate hard line. There is no pretense, no word wasted, no word wanting. Breakers rolling in from the Atlantic are "droves of a thousand wild horses of Neptune, rushing to the shore with their white manes streaming far behind." Cape Cod is "the bared and bended arm of Massachusetts: the shoulder is at Buzzard's Bay; the elbow, or crazy-bone at Cape Mallebare; the wrist at Truro; and the sandy fist at Provincetown." The book *is* the Cape, saltier than its salt, or as salty, clarion of its thorn apple, beach plum, bayberry, shrub oak, sentinel of the tern, the plover, the ocean's incessant, eternal roar. Thoreau's chapters "The Wellfleet Oysterman" and "The Beach" would alone insure his place in anthologies, as would the Indian-haunted passages of *The Maine Woods*. And his *Journal* is a treasury of image and insight: "Some circumstantial evidence is very strong, as when you find a trout in the milk." And: "Nations! What are nations? . . . Like insects they swarm. The historian strives in vain to make them memorable. It is for want of a man that there are so many men. It is individuals that populate the world." January ice on forest leaves and twigs is "the wreck of jewels and the crash of gems." And always, Thoreau's vibrant trust in himself: "May I love and revere myself above all the gods that men have ever invented."

On March 1, 1861, Thoreau told visitors that his "pipes were not in good order." They were not. Henry was terminally ill with tuberculosis. A trip to Minnesota, for dryer air, did not help. He had caught cold on an old round, counting rings on a tree on a snowy day. At the end of September he made his last visit to Walden Pond, with his sister Sophia. And on November 3 he made his final journal entry. Considering the effect of a storm on gravel, he wrote what might have been his own epitaph as an acutely observant naturalist: "All this is perfectly distinct to an observant eye, and yet could easily pass unnoticed by most."

By mid-March, 1862, Thoreau could dictate to a friend: "I *suppose* that I have not many months to live; but of course, I know nothing about it. I may add that I am enjoying existence as much as ever, and regret nothing." Even on his deathbed, with Sophia at his side, Thoreau continued to work on his manuscripts for presentation to his publishers. Emerson stopped by to see him. And his old friend—and jailer—Sam Staples did, for he had come to respect Thoreau for his stubborn idealism. The Hawthornes stopped by too. They brought Henry the music box he had admired in their home. His Aunt Louisa asked him if he had made his peace with God, and Henry replied, "I did not know we had ever quarreled, Aunt." And as he lay in bed, disease seemed to him to have a natural beauty of its own, as natural as health.

By all accounts immensely at peace, Henry David Thoreau died on May 6, 1862, at the age of forty-two. Behind his coffin, over three hundred of Concord's four hundred school children walked in procession. He was buried on Authors' Ridge in Concord's Sleepy Hollow

Cemetery. Under shade trees, he lies there still, his grave marked with elegant simplicity, one foot high, "HENRY," near the graves of his brother John, of Emerson, of Hawthorne, of Louisa May Alcott. "Wherever there is knowledge, wherever there is virtue, wherever there is beauty," Emerson said at his coffin, "he will find a home."

Thoreau did not find a home until this century. He was ignored, condemned, or patronized. He remained unread. The literary bishops of his day shared editor James Russell Lowell's contempt for him. While conceding his obvious literary gifts, Lowell declared that Thoreau had "so high a conceit of himself that he accepted without questioning, and insisted upon our accepting, his defects and weakness of character as virtues and powers peculiar to himself." And on Thoreau's celebration of life in the woods Lowell poured contempt: "We look upon a great deal of the modern sentimentalism about Nature as a mark of disease. It is one more symptom of the general liver-complaint. To a man of wholesome constitution the wilderness is well enough for a mood or a vacation, but not for a habit of life."

Lowell's criticism was long in dying, if dead. If Thoreau is now widely praised as one of the noblest voices of American idealism and as the advocate of individualism against political tyranny, he has been condemned—and he is still condemned—as an impractical dreamer, a hypocrite who lived on his father's pencils while condemning industrialism, an unmannered dolt who appealed for civility, a bigot in reverse, a loner living on his family and friends.

But the evidence is in. All doubts aside, there can be no doubt of Henry Thoreau's pure, honest flame, his determination to live and think free, his wish to remind his countrymen of who they really were, where they came from and what they had to do to justify their birthright, what they must do to remain true to what he called the "higher laws" of existence, laws above any state, above any time or place. Thoreau can be inconsistent, didactic, even pious. But he came astonishingly close to realizing his vision of liberty. It is on this vision, not merely on his life, that he must—and will—be judged. The big thing, he taught and he knew, is to *aim* high, "to preserve," as he said, "the true course," no matter how distant the port, to shun all things that lure a man from justice. "I would rather sit on a pumpkin and have it all to myself," he said, "than be crowded on a velvet cushion." And so he sat.

NATHANIEL HAWTHORNE

HE SAW THE SECRET SIN

Even for Salem, Massachusetts—home of the witch trials and decaying, cursed Pilgrim mansions where unredeemed ghosts still walked at night—it was a strange thing to see.

For twelve years, the town gossips said, this handsome young man, home from college, had locked himself up in an attic room. He lived off his poor mother, had his meals left at his door. Only after twilight, they said, would he even budge from the house, then only for spectral, solitary walks. He was losing his mind, they whispered, had thought about suicide, had dreamed dreams and thought things no mortal should. And most shocking of all, he refused to go into business or a genteel profession as any God-fearing Christian man must.

What the gossips of Salem port could neither know nor understand was that during these twelve years of seclusion, young Nathaniel Hawthorne worked with single-minded devotion, day and night, to perfect his style as a writer, to deepen his knowledge of America and the American past and thus inform and enrich that style. What the whisperers could not grasp, in their dollars-and-cents view of the world, was that a life of trade, even what men called a "higher profession," was a life without meaning for a man like Nathaniel. "I do not want to be a doctor," he said, "and live by men's diseases, nor a minister to live by their sins, nor a lawyer and live by their quarrels." He wanted to be a writer of stories, despite little promise of financial success in commerce-centered nineteenth-century America. And he knew there was only one way to become a writer: to *write*, systematically pruning and honing his prose to a fine end, and to *work* and study, free as any man can be free of distraction and idle pleasure.

In those twelve years Hawthorne knew the moments of fear, of self-doubt, of despair that beset all serious writers. But emerging at last from his chamber under the eaves, he was well-nigh master of the literary technique that would one day produce the finest novel America had known until his day, a novel the world still honors and loves, *The Scarlet Letter*. In triumph he would look back on these lonely years and say with some justice: "In this dismal chamber FAME was won!"—fame not for *The Scarlet Letter*, which was several years away, but for the first of those beautifully wrought, haunting short stories that are the foundation of the house of his greater art.

Nathaniel Hawthorne was not only born in Salem, on July 4, 1804; he had Salem in his blood. The earliest of his forbidding Puritan ancestors, William Hathorne (Nathaniel changed the spelling) settled there in 1630 as judge and soldier. Judge William condemned the Quaker Ann Coleman to be whipped at the tail of a cart drawn through the streets. William's son John condemned "witches" in the infamous Salem trials of 1692. One of John's colleagues on the bench drew a "witch's curse" from a victim of that social insanity. Nathaniel recalled both of these ancestors with a sense of guilt, sensed a vague "curse" on his own family, and hoped that his art would help atone for their crimes. The sins of the fathers, he was persuaded, do in fact plague their sons. In one of his most touching stories, "The Gentle Boy," Hawthorne tells the story of an innocent Quaker lad almost torn apart by a mob for his beliefs. And in *The House of the Seven Gables*—a novel he considered better than *The Scarlet Letter*—he relates the fall of the once great Pyncheon family, condemned by a curse on its house.

In his grandfather Daniel, a Revolutionary War captain of derring-do, Nathaniel found more to admire, as he did in his father, Nathaniel, Sr., a hearty sea captain who died abroad when Nathaniel was only four.

Salem pulsed in the blood of Nathaniel's mother, too: Elizabeth Clarke Manning, who was descended from seventeenth-century Salem settlers. Her husband's death cast a new pall over her family, already diminished in wealth and position, but now thrown directly upon the charity of the Mannings. Once widowed, legend insists, Mrs. Hawthorne secluded herself in a private room, refusing even to eat with her children. The story, perhaps, is exaggerated, for there is evidence that Mrs. Hathorne later relented, until illness confined her totally to bed.

Nathaniel had two sisters—Elizabeth, two years older than he, and Maria Louisa, some four years younger. Throughout life, both would remain attentive, even devoted to him, and he to them. Elizabeth, bright and witty, assisted him editorially when, in 1836, he left his chamber for six months to put out the *American Magazine of Useful and Entertaining Knowledge,* a popular periodical of digests and excerpts. She scouted the Salem library for his books (he refused to enter the library himself), and kept a sharp ear attuned to fire alarms. "All his life," Elizabeth wrote, "he enjoyed a fire. . . . In Salem, he always went out when there was a fire; once or twice he was deluded by a false alarm; and after that he used to send me up to the top of the house to see if there was really a fire, and if it was well under weigh [*sic*] before he got up." Maria Louisa, cheerful and outgoing, lightened the gloomy atmosphere of the solemn old house. She assisted Nathaniel in the hand-printed publication of a family weekly "newspaper," the

Spectator, which contained family verse and essays in addition to a diverting satirical column, "Domestic Intelligence." In one of these, the young Hawthorne solemnly mocked the personal columns of contemporary newspapers: "The lady of Dr. Winthrop Brown, a son and Heir. Mrs. Hathorne's cat, Seven Kittens. We hear that both of the above ladies are in a state of convalescence."

When Nathaniel was nine he injured a foot playing ball and was forced to curb his activity, with the aid of crutches, for three years. The limitation, however, gave him more time to indulge a now firm habit of reading. Shakespeare and Milton were his old friends at fourteen. Among other favorites were Spenser's *The Faerie Queene*, from which he took the name of his first daughter, Una; the romances of Sir Walter Scott; and Bunyan's *Pilgrim's Progress*, which served as a model for his satirical tale, "The Celestial Railroad." Nathaniel's sister Elizabeth recalled that he would read half the afternoon, without speaking. His manner of study, however, does not appear to have carried over to formal education. "As a boy at school," Hawthorne's son Julian would recall, "my father learned his lessons easily, but was averse to schooling, and was irregular."

Nathaniel entered Bowdoin College in 1821, financed by his uncle Robert Manning. Even at college, Hawthorne maintained his intellectual independence, studying sporadically, but, rather like Thoreau, reading deeply only in subjects that struck his fancy. Among his classmates were Henry Wadsworth Longfellow, with whom he was less than intimate because they belonged to rival clubs, and Franklin "Frank" Pierce, later president of the United States. Frank, a fellow club member, would remain a lifelong friend to Hawthorne and Hawthorne to him.

Hawthorne the college man was less than a paragon of scholarship and deportment. He skipped classes and chapel services with the best of them, chewed his share of plug tobacco, showed no aversion to the local pub. On one occasion he was fined fifty cents for playing cards (a fellow student reveler was suspended for the offense). He explained the incident to his mother without contrition: "When the [college] President asked what we played for, I thought proper to inform him it was 50 cts., although it happened to be a Quart of Wine, but if I had told him of that he would probably have fined me for having a blow. There was no untruth in the case, as the wine cost 50 cts." Despite this triumph of hairsplitting, Nathaniel reformed. "I am very much afraid of being suspended," he explained, "if I continue any longer in my old courses." If relative poverty and dependence on his uncle troubled Hawthorne, he appears, at least in his senior year, to have overcome them, at least temporarily. "I have put on my gold watch-chain and purchased a cane," he wrote grandly home to Elizabeth, "so that, with the aid of my new white gloves, I flatter myself that I make a most splendid appearance in the eyes of the pestilent little freshmen."

But all was not fun and games at Bowdoin. For all his frivolity, Hawthorne was intermittently shy and withdrawn. He did feel the sting of dependence on the Mannings, the hurt pride of the only son of a family, which, if once of great status and substance, had been cheated by fate of its position. Even his closest friends found him hard to get to. One, Jonathan Cilley, observed: "I love Hawthorne, I admire him; but I do not know him. He lives in a mysterious world of thought and imagination which he never permits me to enter." Another intimate, Horatio Bridge, who would

remain Hawthorne's loyal benefactor in life and art, recalled: "He shrank habitually from the exhibition of his
own secret opinions." But if he said little, Hawthorne
thought much, notably of his future career: "How would
you like someday," he wrote to his mother, "to see a whole
shelf-full of books, written by your son, with 'Hawthorne's
Works' printed on their backs?" And, in fact, Hawthorne
began his abortive first novel, *Fanshawe*, at Bowdoin.

Graduating from college in 1825 at the undistinguished
middle of his class, Hawthorne returned home to Salem to
begin the secluded twelve-year apprenticeship as a writer
that would win the scorn and suspicion of his townsmen.
"I doubt whether so much as twenty people in the town
were aware of my existence," he announced. But his seclusion was neither as total nor as morbid as Salem—and at
least once—Hawthorne himself insisted. Hawthorne's finest
biographer, Randall Stewart, observes: "Although closely
occupied with literary tasks, Hawthorne found time for
diversion and recreation." While Nathaniel studied deeply
in the histories, diaries, newspapers, and court records of
colonial New England and wrote diligently, if sometimes
despairingly—as his story "The Devil in Manuscript" reveals—he also found time to visit relatives, take in the
theater, go dancing, and enjoy a regular round of cards
with cronies. And once a year, usually in the summer, he
would travel anonymously about New England, recording
in his journal the conversation, reminiscences, old tales,
and manners of New England's rugged folk: in the White
Mountains of New Hampshire, in the Berkshires of Massachusetts, on Martha's Vineyard and Nantucket at sea. His
social circle on these odysseys was scarcely polite. "He fell
in," writes Van Wyck Brooks, "with big-bellied black-

smiths, essence pedlars chattering about their trade, old men sitting at railway stations, . . . woodchoppers with their jugs and axes [and we may safely assume Hawthorne shared their libations] . . . conjurors, tombstone carvers, organ grinders." Or he would chat with a tavern keeper, all the while recording sights and sounds that would ring so true in future stories like "The Seven Vagabonds." Hawthorne seems to have had what the novelist Henry James had, too: an imagination upon which nothing was lost. "Think nothing too trifling to write down," Hawthorne told a friend about to travel, "so it be in the smallest degree characteristic. You will be surprised to find on reperusing your journal what an important and graphic power these little particulars assume." It is the synthesis of "these little particulars," both historical and observed, with narrative fantasy that informs Hawthorne's finest work.

With this said, however, it must be added that if Hawthorne moved happily about the real world of his time, he lived more compulsively in the imagined world of the colonial past. He faced and solved a problem that would plague American writers well into the twentieth century. To excite and hold interest, literature requires a strong— and shared—historical tradition, dramatic conflict, and an element of mystery, what Hawthorne called a "picturesque and gloomy wrong." Hawthorne's nineteenth-century America, basking, as he put it, in the "broad and simple daylight" of commercial prosperity, and persuaded, with Emerson, of its illimitable progress, lacked these essential elements of literature, as Europe, with its ageless legends and castles, did not. Hawthorne's literary solution to this problem, which would send many American writers abroad in search of richer dramatic material, including so mod-

ern a writer as Ernest Hemingway, was to turn his eyes
away both from contemporary America and, at least initially, from Europe. He looked back, deeply back into
America's Puritan past, the era of the New England
theocracy, when the conflict of good and evil, freedom and
tyranny, love and hatred was more explicit, more rigidly
defined, free of the ambiguities of an increasingly pluralistic
society, governed by a shared morality. In looking back,
and in building his great stories on what he saw, he did
more than re-create the past; he was not merely a literary
historian. He transcended his material, building out of it
a literature that speaks no less relevantly to the human
condition in our day than in his. If the test of a classic *is*
its timeless relevance to the human condition, much of
what Hawthorne wrote is classic indeed.

In his attic chamber, to be sure, Hawthorne sometimes
felt "like a person talking to himself in a dark room." The
gloom, the guilt, the self-deprecation, the fear that dominate his works were not merely imagined; they were felt.
As he submitted his first stories to publishers, failure followed failure as publishers turned him down out of hand.
Hawthorne destroyed rejected manuscripts "in a mood half-
savage, half-despairing." The few stories he did get published appeared anonymously in obscure periodicals for
little or no money. In this period, too, Hawthorne faced
the fact that his first novel, *Fanshawe*, published anonymously in 1828 at his own expense, was unworthy of him.
A shallow romance, based on his life at Bowdoin, it was
so bad that Hawthorne recalled and destroyed every copy
he could get his hands on, including his sister Elizabeth's,
which, she was convinced, he "no doubt burned." His close
friend Bridge, at Hawthorne's request, also destroyed the

book. And not even Hawthorne's wife Sophia would learn of its existence. Hawthorne lacked the confidence even to sign his early efforts, hiding behind such contrived pseudonyms as "Ashley Allen Royce," or publishing such excellent tales as "Roger Malvin's Burial" and "My Kinsman, Major Molineux," among his very best tales, anonymously.

The young author was profoundly despondent. Bridge feared that Nathaniel might be "too good a subject for suicide." Still Hawthorne retained his belief that one day he would prevail in his art. While he might deride himself as "the obscurest man of letters in America," his faith in the absolute necessity of creative solitude was unshaken: "If I had sooner made my escape into the world," he declared somewhat archly, in view of his social excursions, "I should have grown hard and rough . . . and my heart might have become callous by rude encounters with the multitude. . . . But living in solitude till the fullness of time was come, I still kept the dew of my youth with the freshness of my heart."

Nathaniel Hawthorne stood five feet, ten and one-half inches tall, unusually tall for his day. His first publisher, Samuel Griswold Goodrich, found him to be "of a rather sturdy form, his hair dark and bushy . . . his brow thick, his mouth sarcastic, his complexion stony, his whole aspect cold, moody, distrustful. He stood aloof," Goodrich added, "and surveyed the world from shy and sheltered positions." A lady admirer found Hawthorne handsome in a classic, even "angelic" way, while the English novelist Anthony Trollope pronounced him simply "the handsomest Yankee that ever walked the planet." Henry James's father, however, found him roguish, and another detected something demonic in his character. There seems to be no question, however, that Hawthorne's eyes were among his most powerful features. Of their precise color, there remains some question. They were probably blue to steel-gray, although the English author Charles Reade said he had an eye "like a violet with a soul in it." Of the penetrating effect of Hawthorne's eyes on many who met him there is no question. In the words of one observer, his eyes seemed less to see than to understand, as he understood the wretched creatures who haunt his pages. Looking out at the world from his study window, or roaming the streets in his long, navy-blue cape coat—coming on, said his publisher and friend James T. Fields, less like an author than a field marshal—Hawthorne preferred to observe life rather than to live it, to hover "invisibly round man and woman, witnessing their deeds, searching into their hearts," as clinically as a surgeon plies his steel. He preferred silence to chatter, as Thoreau did. He listened, and watched, and learned. In his presence, Emerson admitted, he felt uncomfortable, silently observed. "Hawthorne," said Concord's Sage, "rides well his horse of the night."

With all his delicacy and grace of feature, Hawthorne was a strong and imposing man. He "could shovel snow and split wood without weariness," a biographer notes. "His hands were large and powerful, and he was skillful with tools. He was an accomplished walker, and he could leap as high as his own shoulder from a standing position."

Of his early stories, Hawthorne wrote: "They have the pale tint of flowers that bloomed in too retired a shade." He was too hard on himself, as the publication of his first collection of short stories, *Twice-Told Tales*, under his own name at last, revealed. Underwritten by the loyal Bridge, the volume appeared in 1837 and was hailed by Hawthorne's Bowdoin colleague and friend, Henry Wadsworth Longfellow: "Beautiful sketches are interspersed among the stories like green leaves among flowers. . . . To this little work we would say 'Live ever, sweet book.' . . . Like children, we say 'Tell us more.'" *Twice-Told Tales* brought Hawthorne a modest measure of success and confirmed him as a writer to be reckoned with. It contained "The Maypole of Merry Mount" (see pages 82–83); "Old Esther Dudley," an at once touching and chilling story of a British colonial grandame who, unaware that the American Revolution has occurred, lives on in a Massachusetts province house in royal array; "The Ambitious Guest," which relates a White Mountain family's ironic attempt to "escape" an avalanche descending on their land; "The Minister's Black Veil," in which a clergyman, engaged to be married, inexplicably hides his face from his neighbors, parishioners, and betrothed with tragic results; and "The Great Carbuncle," in which a band of adventurers, each with an irrational or venal motive, sets out up a mountain to find a reported giant ruby, or carbuncle. This last story would set the tone and the central theme of many to come: the triumph of realism and humility over illusion, greed, and, above all, pride.

If the publication of *Twice-Told Tales* brought Hawthorne only modest success and little money, it perhaps indirectly brought him a rare love and ultimately an admirable marriage. Among those who delighted at last to know the identity of the author of these excellent stories was Salem's Elizabeth Peabody, one of Dr. Nathaniel Peabody's three bright and progressive daughters. Elizabeth remembered playing with the Hawthornes as a child, when they were neighbors. She recalled Nathaniel as "a broad-shouldered little boy, with clustering locks, springing about the yard." Now her old playmate was an author, clearly unafraid of controversial issues like guilt-ridden clergymen, and Elizabeth Peabody, in one biographer's words "the very embodiment of Boston enlightenment and reforming zeal," was determined to meet him.

"It was a difficult matter to establish visiting relations with so eccentric a household," Elizabeth insisted, "and another year passed away before Mr. Hawthorne and his sisters called on us." The meeting finally took place in the spring of 1838. "It was in the evening," Elizabeth recalled. "I was alone in the drawing room; but Sophia [her sister] who was still an invalid, was in her chamber," suffering from chronic violent headaches and living in a kind of artistic seclusion of her own. "As soon as I could," Elizabeth wrote, "I ran upstairs to her and said, 'O Sophia, you must get up and dress and come down! The Hawthornes are here, and you never saw anything so splendid as he is— he is handsomer than Lord Byron!' She laughed, but refused to come, remarking that since he called once, he would call again."

Hawthorne did call again. Sophia, white-gowned and twenty-seven, "small, graceful, active, and beautifully formed," came down to meet him. As Nathaniel looked down at the delicate Sophia, Elizabeth recalled, his eyes were "like mountain lakes reflecting the sky." It was a classic love at first sight. Hawthorne's financial plight and Sophia's lingering illness would force postponement of their marriage for four years, but engagement followed and nothing dimmed the bright light of what all the evidence suggests was an exalted love. "What a beautiful smile he has, . . ." Sophia wrote of Nathaniel. "There is the innocence and purity and frankness of a child's soul in it. . . .

He has a celestial expression. It is the manifestation of the divine in human."

Hawthorne's debt to Elizabeth Peabody was great. He owed her his introduction to Sophia. Elizabeth also encouraged him in the writing and publication of his highly successful children's stories and joined his friends, on at least one occasion, in attempts to secure him a profitable political post. But there were limits to Hawthorne's gratitude. He would have his way with her as he had it with his sisters and mother, who were obedient to his every wish. When, after his marriage to Sophia, Elizabeth presumed to advise her sister on what seems to have been a critical matter, Hawthorne wrote acidly to his sister-in-law: "I sometimes feel as if I ought . . . to endeavor to enlighten you as to the relationship between husband and wife. . . . But the conjugal relation is one which God never meant you to share, and which therefore He apparently did not give you the instinct to understand; so there my labor would be lost."

Now that he and Sophia were engaged, Hawthorne set his mind to securing a position that would put their marriage on a sounder financial footing than that afforded by speculative writing. Through the influence of the famed historian and Democratic Party chieftain George Bancroft, then collector of the port of Boston, and the efforts of Bridge, Elizabeth Peabody, and Senator Franklin Pierce, Hawthorne was appointed in January, 1839, as a surveyor in the Boston Custom House. In his capacity as measurer of coal and salt, he was paid $1500 per year, three times what he had been earning as a writer. It was no cozy, inside job, however. As a surveyor on Long Wharf "on long winter days," a biographer writes, "he paced the icy decks of salt-ships and coal vessels, or fled the freezing north winds by climbing down into dirty little cabins to warm himself beside red-hot stoves."

On January 1, 1841, Hawthorne resigned his position, and in April invested his Custom House savings of $1,000 in the Reverend George Ripley's Utopian Brook Farm Community, an experiment in communal living in West Roxbury, Massachusetts. While Hawthorne was motivated less by idealism than by the hope, once more, that he could earn enough money to finance his marriage, he announced with some pomp that he went to Brook Farm to get away from "all the fopperies and flummeries which have their origin in a false state of society." But the princely young author who had secluded himself in Salem to avoid "rude encounters with the multitude" was no Thoreau. To be sure Sophia's "blue-eyed darling" donned workman's clothes at Brook Farm, slipped into cowhide boots, and abandoned pride to shovel manure and farm. He ate at a common table, slept in a common dormitory, and, in fact, seems to have given the thing a go. But by the end of the year the adventure in back-to-nature had palled, both as an idealistic plunge and as a financial speculation, and Hawthorne pulled up stakes. "It is my opinion," he wrote his bride-to-be, "that a man's soul may be buried and perish under a dung heap or in a furrow of the field, just as well as under a pile of money. . . . The Real Me was never an associate of the community." "Is it praiseworthy," he added, "that I have spent five, golden months of my life providing food for cows and horses?"

As his marriage to Sophia approached, Hawthorne wrote her letters which, for the mid-nineteenth century, make surprisingly little pretense at concealing his physical need. He laments cold nights in bed without her "close into my bosom." His heart, he declared, was "thirsty" for her kisses. "My desire is full of warmth and hope; and though now I press my arms to my bosom and find thee not within them, yet I know that thou art destined there to be, and there to have thy abiding place." In the few separations they endured throughout married life his letters to Sophia lost none of their candid sexual ardor; it is impossible to doubt their heady attraction for each other.

Nathaniel and Sophia were at last joyously married on July 9, 1842, she approaching her thirty-third birthday, he just past thirty-eight. The newlyweds moved into the Old Manse in Concord, Massachusetts, the grand old home where Emerson had written *Nature*. Before they moved in, handyman Henry David Thoreau had planted a garden for their delight.

The Hawthornes' life at the Old Manse, framed by Concord's great old trees and the rural beauty of a town throbbing with history, was not, however, idyllic. They were burdened by virtual poverty. A bowl of chocolate was considered a luxury; Christmas dinner could be as humble as bread, milk, and preserved fruit. Hawthorne retired at dusk to save lamp oil. But their love again lifted them above adversity, their splendid love. The language of that love appears, perhaps, excessive to modern ears, but they meant it. For Sophia, Nathaniel was "the loveliest being who ever breathed life." She could wish, she said, for no broader region, "because I have as yet found no limit to this." Nathaniel was "completely pure from earthliness," she told her mother. He was an unequaled "union of power and gentleness, softness and spirit, passion and reason." "On the summery days of their honeymoon," writes R. V. Cassill, "they lay on a carpet of dried pine needles in the gloom of the shade around their house. 'There was no wind & the stillness was profound,' Sophia wrote. 'There seemed no movement in the world but that of our pulses.' " Nathaniel exulted, too: "I have married the Spring!" he cried. Sophia's love was as holy to him as the Bible. "We have soared into a region where we talk together in a language that can have no earthly echo." Sophia, he was convinced, had been "sent from heaven to show the possibilities of the human soul." Apart they were lonely and wretched; together they were minutely attentive to each other's needs. As debts piled up and they could no longer afford an Irish maid to "do" for Sophia, Hawthorne himself rolled up his sleeves, stoked the kitchen fires, even prepared meals; nor was Sophia above taking to the garden and raking leaves.

One critic said of Hawthorne that wherever he went "he carried the twilight with him," and Nathaniel himself, aware of his congenital gloominess, lamented: "I wish God had given me the faculty of writing a sunshiny book." But if Hawthorne wore a predominantly serious face in adult social life and in his books, he was sunshine itself to his three children: his first-born, Una, by turns his "Onion" and his "Little Tornado"; his only son, Julian, or "Bundle-breech," who would make something of a literary reputation for himself and would be his father's close companion in walks through the woods at home and in travel abroad; and his little Rose, or "Rose of Sharon." Hawthorne delighted in their company, joining in their games, making their toys by hand, reading to them aloud—and to Sophia —a lifelong practice that enthralled them all: reading from Shakespeare, Spenser, and Tennyson's *Knights of the Round Table*. They loved his funny nicknames for people; vegetarian Bronson Alcott was the "Sage at Apple-Slump,

/ Whose dinner never made him plump." They loved the games he cooked up to surprise them. He would have them all close their eyes until he said "Open!" And when they did, there Daddy would be high up in a tree laughing down. "He was capable of being the very gayest person I ever saw," Una recalled. "He was like a boy. Never was such a playmate as he in all the world." Nor was Hawthorne's athletic prowess confined to his home and fields. His daughter Rose left this priceless vignette of a Concord winter scene on the ice: Thoreau "an experienced skater—figuring dithyrambic dances and Bacchic leaps on the ice"; Hawthorne, "wrapped in his cloak, [moving] like a self-propelled Greek statue, stately and grave"; and Emerson, completing the trio, "too weary to hold himself erect, pitching head-foremost, half lying on the air."

Hawthorne's relationship with Emerson's Transcendentalist followers was polite but strained. He declined an invitation to meet Margaret Fuller, explaining to Sophia: "Providence had given me some business to do, for which I was very thankful." For in the tragic figure of this nineteenth-century feminist reformer, Hawthorne saw both naïvete and pretense. Not even Emerson, who by no means shared all of the Transcendentalists' fatuities, escaped Hawthorne's criticism. If he praised Emerson as "a poet of deep beauty and austere tenderness," he professed to find nothing in his philosophy. Only Thoreau of the Concord group, himself a loner, won Nathaniel's personal admiration. Talking with Henry, he said, was "like hearing the wind among the boughs of a forest tree; and with all his wild freedom, there is a high and classic cultivation in him, too." Once the two friends discarded all dignity and dared the elements by floating down the Concord River on an ice cake, towing their boat behind. But for the Concord reformers, afire with schemes and philosophical tracts, he had little use, particularly after Brook Farm. He had seen too much evil to share Emerson's bland assurance that "love and good are inevitable and in the course of things."

Reform, Hawthorne believed, must first exist in the individual human heart, where man had genuine power to nourish it. No act of will could effect it. And in two of his finest tales, and in a novel, Hawthorne pressed the point home. In the story "Earth's Holocaust," jubilant reformers celebrate the millennium by hurling the evidences of man's evil into a great fire: liquor, tobacco, weapons of war, emblems of nobility, even sacred books. But a "dark-complexioned personage" appears on the scene, warning that the reformers have made a fatal omission in feeding the fire of their Great New Day. They have failed to burn the human heart itself. Until that "foul cavern" is purified, he warns, "forth from it will reissue all the shapes of wrong and misery—the same old shapes or worse ones—which they have taken such a vast deal of trouble to consume to ashes. . . . Oh, take my word for it, it will be the old world yet!" For the reformers have confused the symptoms with the source of evil.

Similarly, in "The Celestial Railroad," Hawthorne satirizes the Utopian community as one governed by naïve and self-important "Mr. Smooth-It-Aways" who champion human rights in the abstract but ignore them in the concrete. He derides philanthropy as simply a more subtle form of egotism, motivated not by genuine concern for real people, but by vanity, a guilty conscience, or a less obvious form of commercial greed. Even the Celestial City, to which the train is transporting the hopeful pilgrims, turns out to be an illusion. Hawthorne returns to this theme in his novel *The Blithedale Romance,* inspired by his experience at Brook Farm. The novel's "hero," the vain and impersonal Hollingsworth, frustrates the credible loves and lives of real people in a fanatic pursuit of unreachable ideals.

Even on the issue of slavery, the dominant issue of his day, Hawthorne remained skeptical of reform. He opposed slavery on moral grounds. And once the Civil War broke out he supported the North. But he felt, first, that the Constitution had guaranteed Southern property rights in the slave; second, that the war, which he felt could have been avoided by rational men, would not remove slavery's sources in racism; and third, that emancipation would probably jeopardize rather than better the Negro's position. Hawthorne candidly placed the preservation of the Union above what he called "the mistiness of a philanthropic theory." Slavery, he concluded in his campaign biography of "Frank" Pierce—soon to be president—was "one of those evils which divine Providence does not leave to be remedied by human contrivances, but which, in its own good time, by some means impossible to be anticipated . . . it causes to vanish like a dream." Hawthorne found it difficult, too, to accept the patriotic fervor of his Concord neighbors at face value, and was unimpressed by the claims of both North and South to moral righteousness. Both, he reasoned, could not be right. "All," he said, "are thoroughly in earnest, and all pray for the blessing of Heaven to rest upon the enterprise. The appeals are so numerous, fervent, and yet so contradictory, that the Great Arbiter to whom they so piously and solemnly appeal must be sorely puzzled how to decide." To the end he remained loyal to Pierce and his conciliatory policies toward the South, even dedicating a book to him at the height of the controversy. Hundreds of Northern friends dropped from him, he said, "like autumn leaves."

Hawthorne's skepticism about human reform had its source not only in his own experience of life, but in elements he retained from his Puritan heritage. He was in no sense a churchman. Religion to him was neither ritual nor theology. It was very simply "the truth of the human heart," a truth which, as the Puritan fathers taught, embraced evil and depravity no less than goodness. Nor was man truly "free" and truly "perfectible." In Hawthorne's view, this essentially "religious" view did not presuppose supernaturalism as it was then understood by traditional "believers." "Man falls," as Hawthorne's most perceptive literary critic, Hyatt Waggoner, puts it, "whether Adam ever lived or not." "Hawthorne set himself against nineteenth-century progressivism," writes biographer Randall Stewart, "not because its utopian aims were not desirable but because . . . [too] often it ignored, he thought, the fallible, sinful nature of man, the life-and-death struggle between good and evil in human society and in the private beast, the inexorable influence of earlier modes and habits which form a predestinating chain of causality. . . . The evidence of history and of contemporary society appeared incompatible with the sudden metamorphosis of mankind."

Few of Hawthorne's stories illustrate his residual Puritanism more cogently than "The Maypole of Merry Mount." Merry Mount is a community of revelers and dancers, of "gay sinners" for whom "it was high treason to be sad" and for whom life is unrelieved Bacchanalian self-indulgence. We come upon the scene at a particularly jubilant moment. The Lord and Lady of the May, young, handsomely arrayed, are about to be married by an errant Anglican priest, whose religion itself is "pagan" to the stern Puritans of the outer commonwealth. Suddenly the festivities are halted by Governor Endicott, the arch-Puritan himself. The dancers are disbanded, their leaders arrested, and the maypole is cut down. But, apparently softening as he beholds the young Lord and Lady, frustrated in the moment of their highest expectation, Endicott bids them join the Puritan commonwealth, adopt a proper form of life, "valiant to fight, sober to toil, and pious to pray."

The resolution of this conflict seems at first harsh for the author of *The Scarlet Letter*. Even in "Maypole" Hawthorne condemns Endicott as an "immitigable zealot" and his followers as "grizzly saints" and "most dismal wretches." Hawthorne clearly despises their bigotry. But, "if forced to choose between the rival parties," as biographer Randall Stewart writes, "Hawthorne would go with Endicott, for life cannot be lived in wanton revelry." Hyatt Waggoner points out that "the young couple get married and go off to love and make love, with Hawthorne's blessing." They are shown that "between bestiality and ascetic repression . . . there is a middle ground where the phallic is not denied but hallowed." For his purposes, in short, Hawthorne has separated Puritanism's wheat from its chaff.

Mounting debts, inadequate compensation for published stories, and the demands of a growing family forced Hawthorne once more to seek a political appointment. Again through the efforts of Pierce and Bridge, he was appointed by President Polk on April 2, 1846 to a four-year term as surveyor of customs at the port of Salem, at a salary of $1,200. The new post not only rescued Hawthorne from near bankruptcy, but gave him a chance to go home again. For "though invariably happiest elsewhere," he confessed, "there is within me a feeling for old Salem, which, in lack of a better phrase, I must be content to call affection," for the dust of his ancestors nourished its soil.

Salem in 1846 was virtually dead as a port, giving way to the rising mercantile fortunes of New York, as Boston would soon after. But it retained much of its quaint old color. Salty merchant mariners swaggered through its streets, swapping yarns. Stately clipper ships lay anchored at its docks. And Surveyor Hawthorne, not unmindful of these charms, resigned himself to a new occupation. "No longer seeking or caring that my name should be emblazoned abroad on title pages," he wrote, "I smiled to think that it now had another kind of vogue. The Custom House marker imprinted it, with stencil and black paint, on pepper bags . . . and cigarettes, and bales of all kinds of dutiable merchandise, in testimony that the commodities had paid the impost, and gone regularly through the office."

The year 1846 also saw the publication of a second collection of Hawthorne's stories, *Mosses from an Old Manse*, which added luster to his reputation as a master of the psychological romance. "Every word *tells*," Edgar Allan Poe said of these stories, "and there is not a word that does not tell." The novelist Herman Melville, soon to be Hawthorne's friend, hailed *Mosses*, praising its "deep and noble nature," Hawthorne's "intricate, profound heart," and his insight into the evil men harbor behind the false veils of society. "Perhaps no writer," Melville concluded, "has ever wielded this terrific thought with greater terror." Hawthorne, he concluded, had mastered the "Great Art of Telling the Truth."

In *Mosses from an Old Manse,* Hawthorne's literary power is at its peak in "The Birthmark," which depicts the efforts of a deranged scientist to obtain total perfection in his beautiful wife by removing a small blemish from her face. In "Young Goodman Brown," which Melville found "as deep as Dante," a too curious Puritan husband leaves his happy wedding bed to attend a nighttime witches' sabbath in the Salem forest, and the results are shattering.

Nathaniel and Sophia, financially secure at last, faced a bitter reversal on June 8, 1849, when Hawthorne was dismissed from his Custom House post, the victim of the Democrats' defeat in the presidential election of 1848. Nathaniel was despondent. But again Sophia rose to comfort him. She had secretly saved money from her allowance, she told him, and he must take it. Sophia decorated lamp shades and hand screens to help make ends meet, too, and Hawthorne's friends, including Henry Longfellow, also came to his aid. "Now," Sophia said, "you can write your book," *The Scarlet Letter.*

There is evidence that Hawthorne first conceived of *The Scarlet Letter* as simply another short story and that his publisher, Fields, seeing its potential, urged him to expand it to novel length. In any case, as his mother lay dying on the floor below, and Salem sweltered in the summer heat, Nathaniel Hawthorne set to work on his masterpiece. These first weeks of labor were haunted, however, by Hawthorne's knowledge that his mother was not far from death. One touching visit to his mother's room, he wrote, "was surely the darkest hour I ever lived. And afterward, standing by the open window, the laughter of the children came up into the chamber from outside, and I saw my little Una of the golden locks looking beautiful, and so full of spirit and life that she was very life itself; and between her and my dying mother I seemed to see the whole of human existence at once. Just then, Una's voice came up, very clear and distinct. 'Yes, she is going to die!' " Hawthorne was almost frightened by his own child, uncertain, now, whether she was "elfish, or angelic or supernatural." It is difficult to reject the belief that Una was the model for the impishly ingenuous little Pearl Prynne in *The Scarlet Letter*.

Hawthorne's mother died on July 31, 1849. At her death-bed, despite the "sort of coldness" that had existed between them since he was a boy and the bitter years that had taught him not to cry, Nathaniel now "shook with sobs." He returned to his chamber to resume work on his master-piece. And on February 3, 1850 this incomparable book was finished. When he read the concluding pages to Sophia, Hawthorne wrote, "it broke her heart, and sent her to bed with a grievous headache, which I look upon as a trium-phant success."

The Scarlet Letter was greeted with critical and popular acclaim. Two thousand copies of the first edition were sold in ten days. To be sure, some, including the Reverend Orestes Brownson, with whom Thoreau had studied, de-nounced it as immoral, a scandalous defense of an indefen-sible evil. But most readers shared the prophetic reaction of the *Boston Transcript*, which saluted it as "one of the most powerful, original, and memorable books that America could boast." The novelist Henry James, himself forced abroad for fictional material, would praise its "indefinable purity," its "inexhaustible charm and mystery." And in our day a critic would say of it: "No novel so fine had appeared in America, and few so fine have appeared since." Though the book continued to sell well and received widespread attention, it brought Nathaniel and Sophia only $450 in its first two years. Three years later, however, Nathaniel could report $3,000 in investments.

The greatness of *The Scarlet Letter* lies not only in its sustained suspense and powerful imagery and symbolism, but in its gripping portrait of the psychological effects of a single momentary sin on four people—particularly how undisclosed guilt and the thirst for revenge can cripple and destroy the human mind and heart. As in his finest stories or tales, Hawthorne is interested not merely in telling a story—though he tells a devastating story indeed—but in using narrative as a means of teaching a moral truth. His characters, though entirely credible and real, become symbols of great forces and passions, instruments, in Hawthorne's words, of "an influence beyond our control [which] lays its strong hand on every deed we do, and weaves its consequences into an iron tissue of necessity." Over this novel there hangs a fatalism, a kind of inevitability, as if the final act of the human drama were written before man was born, woven into a hard, cold chain of cause and effect.

The story is as "simple" as it is awesome. A young woman of colonial Boston, Hester Prynne, whose husband, Roger Chillingworth, has long since stayed behind in England, gives birth to a child, Pearl. For her sin, Hester is condemned by church and state authorities, and sentenced to wear the scarlet letter "A"—for adultery—as a badge of shame for the rest of her life. Hester bravely accepts her punishment, but the father of the child does not come forward. Suddenly Chillingworth arrives from England and vows revenge on the guilty man. It becomes subtly and dramatically clear that the father of Hester's child is none other than the Reverend Arthur Dimmesdale, handsome and beloved pastor of Hester's church and one of the very authorities who condemned her.

With haunting suspense—until even the wind and the trees and the moonlight seem to whisper the minister's hypocrisy, weakness, and inner torture; Hester's heartache in a community that despises her; little Pearl's bewilderment and demonic taunting of her mother; and Chillingworth's crippling passion for vengeance—Hawthorne tells a powerful psychological story. He tells an astonishingly modern story, too—some critics maintain he anticipates Freud— and a courageous one. For in making Hester his heroine, even in making a novel of an incident many of his contemporaries would not discuss, Hawthorne defied the stifling moral code of his day, its prurient "taboos," its immature shame in sex, its vaulting hypocrisies. Hawthorne, indeed, goes further than that. If Hester has sinned, he seems to tell us, her sin was precisely that which Jesus forgave Mary Magdalene—the sin of having "loved much." Indeed, Hester goes to her grave, persuaded that the love she and her minister shared had "a consecration of its own," and thus, with Hawthorne's tacit approval, remains unrepentant for following the dictates of her heart.

Hester is unforgettably real. She is no drawing-room pawn of "masculine" dialogue, no over-idealized ethereal adornment. "She was the first important heroine in the American novel," writes critic Carl Van Doren, "which had neglected women, laughed at them, sentimentalized them, but never profoundly thought about them or greatly imagined any woman." Quite apart from the critical acclaim that greeted this book, Hawthorne received many letters from troubled people who poured their hearts out to him as one who would not judge them but understand their problems.

The Scarlet Letter's almost instant success confirmed Hawthorne's faith in his powers as a writer and gave birth to a three-year burst of literary creation perhaps without parallel in American letters: two distinguished novels, *The House of the Seven Gables* (1851) and *The Blithedale Romance* (1852); the still popular *A Wonder Book*, in which Hawthorne retold the classic myths in language children could understand (1852); a campaign biography of "Frank" Pierce, then making his successful bid for the presidency (1852); and *Tanglewood Tales,* a series of children's stories (1853).

Hawthorne wrote *The House of the Seven Gables* at Lenox in the Berkshires, where he and Sophia lived in bucolic joy from May, 1850, to November, 1851. There Hawthorne met the novelist Herman Melville, toasted his health, and struck up a lasting friendship with the author of *Moby Dick*, which, in fact, the two writers discussed in its preparation, and which Melville dedicated to Hawthorne. There in philosophic rambles, spiced by sherry, gin, champagne, and heady cigars, the two authors discussed their craft, the meaning of life, the nature of God, of goodness and evil. Hawthorne was deeply touched by Melville's intellectual intensity. Of a meeting later in England with Melville, Hawthorne would write perhaps the most penetrating, if brief, analysis of Melville's spiritual malaise, as Melville wandered, Hawthorne said, over the "dismal and monotonous" deserts of theology. Melville, Hawthorne concluded, "can neither believe, nor be comfortable in his unbelief." In a sense, as his own later life as an artist would prove, he might have said very much the same thing of himself.

In May, 1852, Nathaniel and Sophia settled down in their new home, the Wayside, which they had purchased from Alcott. There they looked forward to decorating their last home and to years of high joy and contentment. Nathaniel's success had thrust Sophia, she said, into "a blissful kind of confusion." They were clearly tasting the sweet fruit of success, so long denied them. But even with this productive period behind him, Hawthorne still felt the pinch of inadequate income. When Pierce proved victorious at the polls and moved into the White House, Hawthorne set his friends and allies systematically to work to secure a profitable political appointment from his old college chum. And in 1853 a grateful President Pierce appointed Hawthorne to the lucrative post of United States consul at Liverpool, England. This position, even after seven self-indulgent years abroad, not only in England but in a prolonged grand tour of the Continent, had netted Hawthorne $30,000 by his return to America.

In Europe, the once frugal Hawthorne satisfied repressed appetites for luxury. "I do not see how it will be possible for me to live, hereafter, on less than the interest of $40,000 . . . ," Hawthorne declared rather pretentiously. "It takes at least $100,000 to make a man comfortable." As a high American official in England, he was quite naturally wined and dined, at state dinners and in private homes, largely of the merchant aristocracy. Of one after-dinner speech, he wrote Bridge: "I had missed no opportunity of gulping down champagne, and so had got myself into that state of potvalor which (as you and Pierce know) is best adapted to bring out my heroic qualities."

Hawthorne enjoyed England immensely, visiting its literary shrines and cathedrals, the British Museum, the great galleries. But he wrote too. Some 300,000 words in his English journals would provide material for articles in the *Atlantic Monthly* on his return home, and for the book *Our Old Home*, described by biographer Stewart as having "a strong claim to the rank of one of its author's major works. No other American writer," Stewart declared in 1948, "has described England so vividly and completely or has comparatively weighed with so much care and insight the English and American cultures." If he found his consular duties predominantly tedious, Hawthorne gained much from his prolonged visit to England, which would have a decisive, if perhaps crippling effect on his future writing, for England had clearly gotten to him, reminding him of his origins, and he never got over its call to old family memories.

On the Continent, to which the Hawthornes repaired, after Nathaniel resigned his consular post in August, 1857, Hawthorne and Sophia, accompanied by their children, delighted in poking about the opulent museums, the classic ruins, the churches, and castles. In Italy, however, Hawthorne at least partially reverted to his ancestors' Puritan prudishness. He expressed shock at what seemed to him the gratuitous nudity of the great classic statues. "Man is no longer a naked animal," he pontificated, "his clothes are as natural to him as his skin and sculpture has no more right to undress him than to flay him." "Once more pagan than the Puritans," Mark Van Doren has observed, Hawthorne "was now more Puritan than the pagans," clearly taken aback by Renaissance man's delight in the aesthetically sensual and lack of proper Calvinist sexual inhibitions and the sense of carnal sin. At the same time, Hawthorne deepened his appreciation of art assiduously, and in his association with the expatriate American art colonies in Italy culled material for his last complete novel, *The Marble Faun,* which depicts the transformation of innocence into adulthood through its protagonist's awareness of man's basic evil in crime. Reviewing this novel, the poet James Russell Lowell declared: "Had [Hawthorne] been born without poetic imagination, he would have written treatises on the Origin of Evil," even as the colonial Puritan clergymen he had read in his attic room as a young man had written them.

Back in America in late June, 1860, Hawthorne tried unsuccessfully to complete another novel. "He had lived long with a premonition of early death," writes Hyatt Waggoner, "and now, with an increasing sense of urgency, he wanted both to make money to provide for his family after he was gone, and to say some things that he felt he had never yet succeeded in getting said. He failed miserably, desperately, shockingly," as though he had never written *The Scarlet Letter.* While he was able to write several articles for the *Atlantic Monthly* on his English sojourn, which were both well received and well paid for, Hawthorne in his last years was able to produce only fragmentary studies toward four novels, all uncompleted: *The Ancestral Footstep* and *Dr. Grimshawe's Secret,* both dealing with an American's claim to an English estate and reflecting Hawthorne's own sense of a lost homeland; and later, *Septimius Felton* and *The Dolliver Romance,* both concerned with an elixir of life and reflecting Hawthorne's own desolate fear of death, his sense of lost youth.

Hawthorne knew he had lost his power. The old images,

the old literary devices, the old Puritan polarities would not work. What had happened? Various explanations have been advanced to account for Hawthorne's artistic collapse: ill health, financial anxiety, indolence, immense sadness over the Civil War. Each, no doubt, was a factor, but none really accounts for the sudden defeat of so great a writer. One critic believes that after Hawthorne's return from England "some psychological factor . . . presumably the Oedipus situation," which had afflicted Hawthorne throughout adult life, led to renewed guilt feeling, exacerbated, again, by an obsession with death, and a "weakening of his religious views" and the literary motifs they had sustained. The psychological factor is emphasized most vividly by Frederick C. Crews, who describes Hawthorne in his life and in his art as a "self-examining neurotic," struggling in his stories to "universalize the results of introspection." In general, Crews is convinced, Hawthorne's fiction "depict[s] with incredible fidelity the results of unresolved Oedipal conflict," a continuing crisis created by "some clash between fantasy and fact," or, in Freud's definition of neurosis, by "abnormal attachment to the past." Melville had praised Hawthorne's mastery of the "Great Art of Telling the Truth," presumably about people and life as he saw them. What he perhaps did not know, and what makes Hawthorne's art great is that he told the truth about the only reality a man can know: himself. In his attempt to universalize his own experience, not to say his anticipation of Freud, Hawthorne created a literature of timeless relevance. If his style dates him, his insights into the human character do not and will not.

Hawthorne's despondence was heightened in the spring of 1864. He and his old publisher-friend, W. D. Ticknor,

who had done so much to promote his works, visited Philadelphia. Ticknor had hoped that the visit would shore
up Hawthorne's spirits. But it was not to be. Ticknor
himself was caught in a cold rain and Hawthorne saw his
friend die at the hands of an incompetent doctor. Badly
shaken, he returned to Sophia at the Wayside, "so haggard,
so white, so deeply scored with pain and fatigue," Sophia
remembered, that "I was frightened out of all knowledge
of myself." As she watched Hawthorne break down in
tears over the strain—a rare thing for Nathaniel—and saw
him failing daily, she begged him to see a doctor, to no
avail. At last, Nathaniel consented to see Dr. Oliver
Wendell Holmes, who observed, he said, "a marked loss
of weight, and an obvious depression." Holmes "confined
his treatment to words of encouragement . . . a sedative and
cordial."

Again, it was thought, a trip through the country
would do Nathaniel good, and so he and the always loyal
Frank Pierce traveled north. During the night of May 18–
19, 1864, in a hotel room in Plymouth, New Hampshire,
Nathaniel Hawthorne died quietly in his sleep.

Among Hawthorne's pallbearers at the church back
home in Concord were Emerson, Longfellow, Lowell, and
Holmes. Franklin Pierce sat with the family. Hawthorne's
body was borne to Sleepy Hollow Cemetery, Emerson
wrote, "in a pomp of sunshine and verdure." The Reverend
James Freeman Clarke, the same minister who had united
Sophia and Nathaniel in marriage over twenty-five years
before, now offered requiem words. Hawthorne, he said,
"had done more justice than any other to the shades of life,
shown a sympathy with the crime in our nature, and, like
Jesus, was the friend of sinners."

History's final judgment of Nathaniel Hawthorne as man and writer is yet to be made, but perhaps the broad lines of that judgment have been drawn. Many, including Emerson, have felt that except for *The Scarlet Letter,* Hawthorne wrote little in which he released his full powers as a writer. Others have complained of a certain passivity, narcissism, and plain laziness in his nature. It is difficult to reject the belief of Hyatt Waggoner, however, that before Hawthorne—and Poe—"there was nothing in American fiction that either writer could take very seriously," and that in turning to European fiction, especially to the Gothic tale, Hawthorne particularly "took what served his needs and transformed it, to create a form, a language and a meaning that had never before existed."

The knife of Hawthorne's art and imagination cut deeply into reality, exposing the joy in the heart of sorrow, the sorrow in joy, the good in what men call evil, the evil that men call righteousness. He was ever alert to what Henry James, who owed much to him, would call "the serpent in the bank of flowers," for what he himself called "the dark of intense brightness," "the deep, warm secret, the life within the life." Perhaps most important of all of Hawthorne's achievements, no less as a man than as an artist, is that he sought not to judge and condemn men, as his colonial ancestors had, but to understand and redeem them as an admired man of Galilee had. He sought, in Hamlet's telling words to his palace players, "to hold the mirror up to nature," and to report what he saw in that mirror—even his own veiled image—without distortion. "Life is made up," Hawthorne said, "of marble and mud." In the pages of his finest works, both marble and mud are held in a just, unique, and artistic balance.

RICHARD HENRY DANA, JR.

HERMAN MELVILLE

THEY LOOKED TO THE SEA

RICHARD HENRY DANA, JR.

Among New England's men of letters no two were less alike than the novelists Richard Henry Dana, Jr., and Herman Melville. Dana, a conservative, crusty Boston lawyer, the self-conscious scion of an eminent Yankee family, was coldly prim, aloof, and correct. Melville, the son of a New York merchant, was impish, outgoing, adventurous, a perennial adolescent, an incurable romantic. To be sure, one of his ancestors had donned an Indian costume in the Boston Tea Party and his family was as distinguished in its way as Dana's. But Melville had scant respect and less use for the pretensions of the well-born and mighty. In a visit to Windsor Castle he found the queen of England "an amiable domestic woman," but recommended to her in his journal that she try a special cosmetic for "clarifying the complexion." To Richard Henry Dana, Jr., such irreverence would constitute a form of heresy.

Despite such profound differences in their attitudes and style, Dana and Melville were to become almost one in the mind of America, united in literature by their common love of the sea—a love they poured out in America's two finest tales of adventure on the deep: Dana's powerfully realistic *Two Years Before the Mast* and Melville's roaring and salty allegorical legend, *Moby Dick*. The two men knew and helped each other. To Melville, Dana was no less than a "sea brother." In a letter to Dana of May 1, 1850—three months after Hawthorne completed *The Scarlet Letter*—Melville expressed "those strange, congenial feelings, with which after my first voyage, I for the first time read *Two Years Before the Mast*, and while so engaged was, as it were, tied & welded to you by a sort of Siamese link of affectionate sympathy. . . ." Dana, in turn, gave Melville a helping hand, writing at least one letter of introduction to a prospective publisher. Their names would be forever linked as symbols of a simpler, more heroic era, names virtually synonymous with the clipper ship plying ancient seas, weighing anchor in exotic ports, or riding out storms on the hill of titanic seas—a young man's wildest dreams come true.

If anyone had told Richard Henry Dana, Sr., that his son would one day sign up as a common sailor "before the mast," he would have laughed him out of the room. Richard, Jr., Dana's father was convinced, was "too sensitive for his own happiness." And while he praised his son as a lad of "excellent principles . . . generally cheerful and ready for play . . . a boy of true spirit," Dana's father concluded gloomily: "I never think of him without some touch of melancholy, and with an impression that if he lives he will not be happy; and so constant is this feeling in me whenever he comes before my mind that should he die early, tho' it would be a sad thing to part with him, my first and last thought of him would be, he has escaped the evil to come."

Richard Henry Dana, Jr., would in fact die an embittered, if most successful old man, but his father's prophecy was too forbidding. It was worthy of his ancestor Anne Bradstreet, the Puritan poet, who could ask divine forgiveness for expressing sorrow over the burning of her home, because her wealth did not "on earth abide." But his father's influence on him, chiefly negative, can scarcely be exaggerated. Born two years before the inauguration of President Washington, Dana's father was the heir of a family that had settled in colonial America by 1640—a distinguished family that had sent a son to the Continental Congress and boasted a succession of deacons, judges, and congressmen. The elder Dana was rigidly conservative in politics and religion, an unremitting Calvinist. "When you doubt the fitness of an act," he reasoned, "it is safest, first to ascertain what are your inclinations and next to decide against them." He was not without stature as a literary critic and essayist. As an editor of the influential *North American Review*, he helped to "discover" America's first great poet, William Cullen Bryant. But taken altogether, he was a diffident, ineffectual, excessively sensitive man, able to earn only $400 in thirty years of writing, unequal to the demands of four children upon his fatherhood. The death of his wife, Ruth Charlotte Smith, when Richard, Jr., was not yet seven, deepened his acute sense of futility.

Young Richard was born in Cambridge, Massachusetts, on August 1, 1815, during the presidency of James Madison and two years before Henry Thoreau first breathed life in nearby Concord. In Dana's boy's mind, the sloop *Harvard*, anchored in the Charles River, was a daring, mysterious Viking ship, and the placid Winthrop Duck Pond nothing less than the briny deep, a grand opportunity to practice "navigation." The year after his mother's death, young Dana, until then cared for by aunts, was sent to school in Cambridgeport, where he studied under a hard-nosed master named Samuel Barrett. Oliver Wendell Holmes, the great Boston poet, would remember Dana as "a little, rosy-faced, sturdy boy, piloting an atom of a lesser brother, Edmund, to and from the school-house."

Samuel Barrett's school was a dismal place, of the kind the English novelist Charles Dickens would expose and condemn in England, "a long, low dark room," Dana would recall, "with wooden benches well cut up, walls nearly black, and a close, hot atmosphere." Every infraction of the rules brought forth the punishment of flogging. "When the time came for dismissing school," Dana remembered, "the books were put away, the names of all the delinquents called over, the chest unlocked, and the long pine ferrule produced. How often did our hearts sicken at the sight. . . ! The boys were then called out, one at a time, and the blows given upon the flat of their hands, from two or four up to one or two dozen. . . ."

Another form of punishment was the practice of pulling students by their ears "across the school-room and over the benches." On one such occasion, Dana's ear was pulled so brutally it was partially torn from his head. When Dana's father protested to the school authorities, ear-pulling was abolished, but Dana was left with a passionate hatred of corporal punishment that would find its most powerful expression in his description of a flogging of two sailors by the infamous Captain Thompson in *Two Years Before the Mast*. The memory of such cruelty in school and at sea would inspire Dana to fight for the personal rights and dignity of oppressed seamen and other victims of social injustice.

Dana left the Cambridgeport school in 1825 to enroll in a private school administered in Cambridge by no less a personage than Ralph Waldo Emerson. Years later, Dana would praise the Sage of Concord, rather faintly, as "a very pleasant instructor . . . elevated in [his] habits of thought," but he would lament his lack of "system or discipline enough to insure regular and vigorous study." Despite at least one severe flogging at this school by another instructor, during which Dana refused repentance and, he writes, "could have gone to the stake for what I considered my honor," he remained there about four years until he enrolled in another dismal, flogging-bound boarding school, also in Cambridge, to prepare for college.

Young Dana entered Harvard in July, 1831, where he fared well in mathematics and stood high in his class. Before the end of his first year, however, his moral support of an insignificant student protest against the college authorities cost him a six-month suspension. He spent these six months pleasantly and profitably under the tutelage of the Reverend Leonard Woods of Andover (Massachusetts) Theological Seminary. Later president of Bowdoin College, where Hawthorne and Longfellow studied, Reverend Woods was a classical scholar of great erudition whose depth, intellectual fairness, and alertness to new ideas greatly impressed the young scholar.

Back at Harvard, Dana had just begun his junior year when he was struck down by an illness which, ironically, would immortalize him in American literature. He was stricken with the measles. The attack was not in itself severe, but it so weakened his eyes, writes Dana's chief biographer, Charles Francis Adams, that "for a while he could not endure the ordinary light of day, and, even when they grew better, any effort at reading caused intense pain." Young Dana had ophthalmia.

Forced to leave college, Dana made a decision that would lift him up out of the obscurity of a well-born aristocrat, following the prescribed paths and rules of a narrow society, into international acclaim. Aware that his father was neither able nor willing to send him to Europe for proper medical care, young Dana decided to go to sea. But he was determined not to make the voyage as most young

men of his social position would have made it—sitting in
a snug cabin reading and resting—but as a seaman. Spurn-
ing an offer of cabin space from one of Boston's prominent
merchant families, Dana rejected the idea of sailing "with
his gloves on," or as a gentleman or officer who associated
only with his equals and "hardly speaks to a sailor except
through a boatswain's mate." He would sail "before the
mast" as a common sailor, no better than any other, and
pulling his weight with the best of them.

Dana combed Boston's waterfront until at last he secured
a berth on the brig *Pilgrim*, bound for the California coast
to pick up a cargo of hides. On August 14, 1834, Dana left
Boston port on a voyage from which he would not return
for over two years. He sailed in search of adventure and
health, turning his back on the familiar faces and places
of home and looking hopefully to the sea, exchanging his
proper city clothes for "the white stockings and white
duck trousers, the blue jacket and the varnished hat and the
silk handkerchief flying from the outside pocket," that
marked the common tar. "But it is impossible to deceive
the practised eye in these matters," Dana wrote; "and while
I thought myself to be looking salt as Neptune himself, I
was, no doubt, known for a landsman by every one on
board as soon as I hove in sight." On board ship, in free
moments, under equatorial skies, rounding treacherous
Cape Horn, or sighting Monterey on the lovely California
coast, he was to keep a close journal of events and impressions on which he would base his masterpiece of the sea.

Conceding one minor exception, Dana in his preface
to *Two Years Before the Mast* noted that "all the books
professing to give life at sea have been written by persons
who have gained their experience as naval officers, or

passengers." He wanted his book to depict the sailor's life as written by a sailor, by "one who has been of them," speaking as "a voice from the forecastle," leaving polite romance behind, sticking closely to fact "in every particular." In addition to interesting the average reader, Dana hoped that his book would dramatize the plight of seamen in his day. And if it seemed also to "raise [seamen] in the rank of beings," he declared, "and to promote in any measure their religious and moral improvement, and diminish the hardships of their daily life, the end of its publication will be answered."

Richard Henry Dana, Jr., does not write with the supernal mystery of Joseph Conrad or with the mystical grandeur of his "sea brother," Herman Melville. But on every page he is true to his purpose of defining life at sea—"the light and the dark together"—with ruthless realism. On every page, in Dana's no-nonsense, hard-headed Yankee prose—as clean as the sun—the word becomes the thing. It is almost as if he had dipped his quill pen in salt water. We learn, in minute detail, how the sailor works, eats, sleeps, talks, thinks, walks, and dreams—even to the scream of his nightmare in the ocean stillness. The whole book is a giddy storm of halyards, gaff topsails, clew lines, rigged booms, reefing, spencer masts, skysails, slacked-up head-stays, gotten-up tackle, hauling, climbing, tarring, pulling, bowsing the rigging, furling the jib, hauling in weather braces. His book is as salty as his fellow sailors' beef, as intense as the hail, sleet, and rain that assault the ship as it slices through high seas, as mercilessly clear as the commanding cry of an angry first mate.

Dana has eyes and ears for beauty, too. A passing dolphin is "a stray beam from a rainbow." The sound of frogs and crickets assures his lonely mind of the nearness of land at last. His sense of drama is equally keen. Certainly his description of the rounding of treacherous Cape Horn equals any, his account of the loss of a man overboard is disquietingly eerie, and the scene in which a hysterically cruel Captain Thompson flogs two men beyond bearing ranks with anything in *Mutiny on the Bounty*. It was this spectacle, reminiscent of Dana's miserable school days in Cambridge, that made him vow that "if God should ever give me the means, I would do something to redress the grievances and relieve the sufferings of that class of beings with whom my lot had so long been cast," men like big John the Swede and his watchmate Harris, with whom, when all hands were asleep, he would discuss the problems of the universe, men he learned to admire in shared labor and suffering until his ship, sailing "gloriously on" to home and warm weather, brought him once more to the tolling of Boston's bells.

But out at sea, a great war raged within Dana's soul far removed from the drama and color of this splendid tale. Did he really want to go home, to Harvard, to his family's rigid ways, to a profession in which he really did not believe, to a society that had little time for Nature's great challenge except to exploit it for money and crush what was creative and daring in its young? "One year more or less," Dana wrote, "might be of small importance to others, but it was everything to me." A two-year voyage, he reasoned, "would be pretty long, but would not be fatal. . . . But one year more might settle the matter. I might be a sailor for life." The memory of Cambridge and the power of ancestral pride finally won this inner war. On September 22, 1836, after one year at sea and another gathering and curing hides in California, Dana returned to Boston on the ship *Alert*, healthy, bronzed, twenty-one, and strong.

At home he remained plagued by doubts as to the wisdom of his decision to return to his family and the genteel profession his social peers expected him to pursue. "How I loathe the business and petty things of the world," he wrote. "Yet I must give myself. Could it be possible that, if independent, I could lead a more satisfactory life, be open more to nature and art, and have my *soul* and my best affections and most elevated feelings more alive!"

Dana conquered these doubts. He did what was expected of him, falling once more into step on old, well-worn paths. Passing a special examination, he was admitted to Harvard's senior class. Like Emerson, Thoreau, Holmes, and the historian Francis Parkman, he profited much from the teaching of Professor Edward Tyrrel Channing, champion of a new, native American literature freed of stifling European forms, and advocate of a clean, strong writing style. Channing's influence on the renaissance in American literature that occurred chiefly in New England was decisive. He was that rare teacher and editor committed to awakening in his students a greater knowledge of their own powers and to pointing the way in which these powers might be realized.

At this time, young Dana appears to have experienced a religious deepening that resulted in his embrace of the Episcopal Church and was precipated by the death of a friend who had expressed concern over his spiritual welfare. In any case, Dana enrolled as a member of Beacon Hill's solemn old Church of the Advent, where he would remain a lifetime communicant. At Harvard he would head his class scholastically and win awards for English composition and elocution. But he had time, too, for the socially proper, less serious diversions of the well-born young Harvard swells: the snobbish Porcellian Club and the frivolously prestigious Hasty Pudding Institute. Dana had put on his frock coat again with a vengeance. After graduating in June, 1837, aware that he was succumbing to the tradition-bound Brahmins of Boston, who walked, he said, "in but one line from their cradles to their graves," he dutifully entered Harvard Law School, because law, after all, ran in the family line.

Erect, broad-shouldered, somewhat short, with exceptionally curly, long brown hair, Dana had an engaging smile and a strong Yankee mouth, together with a compelling boyish charm. If he had turned his back on the sea he had not forgotten it. While at the law school, he had the privilege of assisting Professor Channing as an instructor in elocution and, indeed, worked on his novel, no doubt with an occasional comment from Channing. When he finished *Two Years Before the Mast,* he read the manuscript to his father and to his uncle Washington Allston, the noted Boston painter and poet. Impressed, both men urged Dana to publish it, and Dana, anxious to marry and in need of money, agreed to try. Aware that the publicity attending publication of a book on the sea would increase his chances for a profitable mercantile legal practice, he sent his manuscript to William Cullen Bryant, then editor of the *New York Post.* Bryant, who had himself been given a literary leg up by Dana's father, who had recognized Bryant's "Thanatopsis" for the fine poem it is, returned the favor by sending young Dana's book on to Harper's. Bryant asked $500 for the manuscript, but Harper's, although it accepted the book for publication, refused to pay more than $250 for it—a sum low for its time. Dana ultimately accepted Harper's offer, plus twenty-four complimentary copies of the book, but he was denied any share in Harper's profits and the company did little to promote the book. Averse to haggling over money, which he considered beneath his station as a gentleman, Dana could take some comfort from the fact that a London publisher paid him a larger sum for a later British edition.

Indeed, in England Dana's book met with a heartier reception than in America. "In Liverpool," writes Van Wyck Brooks, "two thousand British sailors bought the book in a single day. . . . It was the real thing as the sailors knew, the first book written about the sea, not from the bridge or the cabin, but by one of the hands, one who had shared in the humblest form of sailing. . . ." It was one of those rare, great books that simultaneously told a good story and exposed institutional cruelty and injustice, a book destined to change men's minds and to force reform. "Everyone knew," Brooks continues, "that his book had done as much for the sailors as Dickens had done for the debtors and orphans of England and *Uncle Tom's Cabin* for the slaves." In the following year, Dana capped his service to seamen by publishing *The Seaman's Friend,* a manual explaining the law of the sea in clear terms, detailing sailors' rights and responsibilities. It sold well but necessarily to a limited readership.

Dana had, meanwhile, opened up his law office in Boston in September, 1840. His practice at first was not terribly profitable, for his clients were largely sailors who could scarcely afford normal legal fees. But this did not deter Dana from offering them his services. "His office," writes Charles Francis Adams, "was apt to be crowded with unkempt, roughly dressed seamen, and it smelled on such occasions much like a forecastle [*sic*]. . . ." By the end of 1842, however, Dana was doing well financially. His income, buttressed by fees for articles and lectures, approached $2,500 per year, a tidy sum for that day. Even at the end of his first year of practice, he found himself well enough paid to marry Miss Sarah Watson of Hartford, Connecticut, whose aunt was the daughter of a friend of the Dana family. The young couple had met at the Danas' Chestnut Street home in Boston, where Sarah and her aunt were welcome guests. Friendship became romance, and romance marriage in Hartford on August 25, 1841. Sarah would bear Dana six children.

Despite Dana's financial success in the practice of law—he handled many profitable admiralty cases—his heart was never wholly engaged by his work. His law partner, Francis Parker, found him "the steadiest of friends, the most indulgent and most affectionate of those whom he once honored with his friendship." But if genial and unruffled on the surface, Dana was impatient with the arid details of legal paper work about his office, was only fairly happy even at the bar, and detested the pettiness of most litigation. He longed, he said, for "at least one winter of leisure instead of wearing off the edge of being, in the small contests of a profession, the worth and attraction of which is past." If, in fact, Dana "battled like an avenging angel for the seaman's rights," to the point of alienating richer, paying clients and the "lords of the loom and the lash," he never seems to have been fully himself as a lawyer. After those two bracing years at sea in which the stinging salt air had filled his lungs and cleared his mind of all the hypocrisies and false pieties of society, life in Boston seemed pallid and stale. When run down by legal fatigue, he would always find solace and new health in traveling by sea. "No sooner had we got outside the lighthouse," he wrote on one trip from Boston to Halifax and England, "and the cool, salt night wind of ocean came over us than I felt myself a new creature."

Dana found a measure of relief from the humdrum practice of law in politics, more particularly in the antislavery movement then sweeping Boston and New England. Although no fire-eating Abolitionist like Wendell Phillips and William Lloyd Garrison, Dana was a cofounder of the Free-Soil Party, committed to the exclusion of slavery in newly settled territory. He attended the party's Buffalo convention in 1848 and actively campaigned for its cause, as he would campaign for the Republican Party in later years. Dana's allegiance to the free-soil cause precipitated a sharp break with what Lincoln would call the "silk-stocking Whiggery" of Boston. Massachusetts cotton-spinners enjoyed an unholy if profitable alliance with the cotton producers of the South, and when New England merchants and shipowners dropped Dana professionally and socially, he paid for his idealism by the loss of legal fees. But Dana was undaunted, and indeed hoisted the fat-cat merchants on their own petard. He explained his loyalty to the antislavery cause as he had justified his defense of oppressed seamen. It was the duty, precisely, of the upper class to lead the fight for social and economic justice. Now he declared his credo: "I am a Free-Soiler because I am (who should not say so?) of the stock of the old Northern gentry, and have a particular dislike to any subserviency on the part of our people to the slave-holding oligarchy." And with the New England patrician's contempt for trade, he added: "The spindles and the day-books are against us just now, for Free-Soilism goes to the wrong side of the ledger."

An active opponent of the Fugitive Slave Act under which runaway Southern slaves could be arrested and returned to their masters, Dana defended a slave known as Shadrach when the Negro was arrested in Boston in February, 1851, and imprisoned. Dana's efforts on behalf of Shadrach, as head of a vigilance committee, proved premature, however, for the slave was rescued by a mob of cheering Negroes who spirited the runaway off to Cambridge, moving, Dana observed, "like a black squall." Dana watched the rescue effort with jubilation. Again in 1854 Dana defied social ostracism on Beacon Hill to rise to the defense—this time unsuccessfully—of Anthony Burns, a runaway Negro slave who had found work in Boston as a tailor and had been thrown into jail to await return to slavery in Virginia.

Dana served as United States attorney for the district of Masschusetts from April, 1861, to September, 1866. As a United States counsel, he worked with William M. Evarts in the government's treason proceedings against former Confederate president Jefferson Davis. The trial was inconclusive.

In the rough-and-tumble world of politics, at its worst in the era of Ulysses S. Grant, the gentlemanly Dana met with continued misfortune. His difficulties, however, were caused not only by the crudeness and opportunism of his opponents but by his own haughty refusal to deal with realities and to make life's unavoidable compromises. In 1868, he failed utterly in his bid to unseat venal Congressman Benjamin Butler, polling only 1,811 out of over 20,000 votes cast, despite wealthy Republican backing. Butler, a crony of President Grant, whose administration was shot through with corruption and incompetence, was the stereotype of the backroom politician. In his element in shrill, rowdy public rallies, Butler found Dana an easy mark. He ridiculed Dana's clothing, his courtly manners, his aristocratic ancestry, to the delight of jeering crowds. As one scholar puts it, "it was like feeding raw meat to a lion." In defeat, an embittered Dana abandoned hopes of a career in Congress and returned to law practice.

If beaten at the polls, however, Dana remained hopeful that his legal ability might win him a diplomatic or political post. In 1872, his hopes neared fulfillment when President Grant nominated him as minister to the Court of Saint James, a position tailored to Dana's interests and tastes. But again the mendacious Butler rose to defeat him, blocking Senate ratification of the appointment by arranging false testimony against Dana's fitness for the post at secret hearings. Dana himself remained adamant. Summoned to Washington to appear before a Senate committee and refute the false charges against his name, Dana arrogantly declined. Unlike Hawthorne, an expert in lining up backroom support for his political ambitions, Dana refused to accept what he called "the humiliation of going before such a committee to vindicate my character against charges by Butler—a great office being the prize!" He explained his action with cold contempt: "I cannot do it; my father could not do it; my grandfather could not have done it; nor his father, and my son would not have done it." In short, Dana considered a summons from the nation's chief legislative body an affront to his own dignity and the traditions of his family. Predictably, the Senate was outraged by his disdain for its prerogatives, one senator roundly condemning him as "one of those damned literary fellows." Dana was denied the appointment.

Dana now plunged into scholarly work on a favorite subject, international law, only to face fourteen long years of legal controversy. Commissioned to write a more readable edition of Wheaton's celebrated *Elements of International Law,* Dana was unjustly charged with plagiarism and infringement of copyright by an earlier, less competent, and vindictive editor of this classic. Again, Dana refused to compromise with an adversary. The controversy was finally settled on Dana's terms, but its needlessly prolonged bitterness took its emotional toll on this proud, sensitive man.

Towering over all his frustrations and disappointments was Dana's continuing, haunting fear, in his own words, that he was "a failure compared with what I might and ought to have done." Should he have stayed, after all, at sea? Should he have come home? He felt that family tradition, perhaps snobbery and excessive class-consciousness, had cut him down, had prevented him from realizing his true ambition. More than that, more haunting still was his realization that despite his success at the bar, "my great success—my book—was a boy's work." And that pained him most of all. For only two years of his life had he felt wholly, creatively alive. He came to believe that he had been "made for the sea," that his life ashore had been "a mistake," and that far from being cut out to board the morning bus in Harvard Square for the wearisome ride to his stodgy Boston office, he had been "intended by nature for a general roamer."

But truth came to Richard Henry Dana, Jr., too late to reshape his life, and as age came upon him, his always aristocratic view of his social position hardened into an immature, overt contempt for those he considered inferior or coarse, and a stifling conservatism. He dismissed the novelist Charles Dickens during his charming visit to Boston as "a low-bred man," despite a "fascination," with "the true Cockney cut." Spitefully orthodox, he condemned Emerson and Carlyle for not attending church services while in Winchester, England, scolding them in his *Journal* for "lounging around the cathedral while service was going on inside."

An inveterate world traveler who had seen China, Egypt, and Japan, Dana wrote to his friend James Russell Lowell in August, 1878: "I have taken the great step of giving up my profession and my home to spend time enough in Europe to write a work of my own on international law." It was, he announced, to be his masterpiece—no more haggling now over copyrights or editing another man's work. But Dana, though in Europe, was to be denied this "masterpiece." On January 6, 1882, twenty-four days before the birth of a child much like him, named Franklin D. Roosevelt, Dana died of pleurisy and pneumonia. He was buried not in Cambridge, or in Boston, as he no doubt would have wished, but in Rome's Protestant Cemetery, near the graves of England's romantic poets Shelley and Keats. It was a fitting burial place for this Yankee romantic. For in a real sense Dana, like Keats, had died young. From the moment he stepped off the ship *Alert* on his return to Boston from his two-year voyage "before the mast" he ceased to be fully alive, fully himself. A star that would lighten the sky for generations of readers, young and old— Dana's one great book—would remain for Dana himself a short and haunting interlude in a gray and lonely life.

HERMAN MELVILLE

If an embittered Herman Melville, in his defiant later years, could dedicate his books to Mount Greylock and the Bunker Hill Monument—almost symbolizing his sense of withdrawal from society—a younger, eager Melville would honor a cherished friend on the title page of his masterpiece, *Moby Dick*: "In token of my admiration for his genius," he wrote, "this book is inscribed to Nathaniel Hawthorne."

The dedication was deserved. Melville wrote *Moby Dick* when his friendship with Hawthorne in the Berkshires was at its keenest. His debt to the author of *The Scarlet Letter*, both personally and professionally, was immense. Fifteen years Hawthorne's junior, Melville experienced a deepening of his intellectual and literary interests during their long philosophical dialogues and rambles in the Massachusetts mountains. In his celebrated essay "Hawthorne and His Mosses," Melville had hailed his friend's uncompromising portrait of the "blackness" in man, comparing Hawthorne's most powerful scenes with the "background against which Shakespeare plays his grandest conceits." Hawthorne, he added, appealed to "that Calvinistic sense of Innate Depravity and Original Sin, from whose visitations, in some shape or other, no deeply thinking mind is always and wholly free." In his own writing, Melville would be deeply governed by Hawthorne's insights and techniques; in the words of Harry Levin, the *Mosses* "provided examples for Melville . . . through their demonstration that tragic power lay within the grasp of native authorship."

But if Hawthorne knew great success in his own lifetime, Melville, despite an initial splash of notoriety, knew little. Even his great classic, *Moby Dick*, which has taken its high place among the world's greatest books, was a thundering failure in his lifetime, spurned·or ignored by a reading public that decried its obscurity and its symbolism. He was denounced for "word-mongering." His great tale of the sea and man's confrontation with God was dismissed as "sad stuff and dreary or ridiculous." After its publication, Melville's powers as a writer declined tragically. His old zest for life, his thirst, in the words of one of his characters in *Mardi,* for "the essence of things, the mystery that lieth beyond . . . that which is beneath the seeming," deserted him. This once passionate, life-loving, tempestuous man, whose own young life rivaled in drama any of his literary adventures, broke down mentally and retired, like a beaten dog, to almost twenty years of obscurity in a hack political post, "reconciled," he said, "to annihilation."

The critic Vernon Parrington concludes sadly: "There is no other tragedy in American letters comparable to the tragedy of Herman Melville." By contrast, he adds, "Hawthorne's gloom is no more than the skeptical questioning of life by a nature that knew no fierce storms." Melville differed from the Transcendentalists of Concord in temperament and intent. If he sounded much like Thoreau in declaring that life's major crime is for "a live man to vote himself dead," and that "all deep, earnest thinking is but the intrepid effort of the soul to keep the open independence of her sea" against the conspirators of the "slavish shore," he was congenitally discontent with projects of experimental rebellion like Thoreau's, the Olympian preaching of Emerson, even the cloistered contemplation of evil of his friend Hawthorne. He dared to confront no less than all the forces of heaven and hell, earth and sea that raged in the human heart and to depict these forces in a roaring, heaving ocean of words. He wished to wrestle with no less an adversary than "the angel, Art," and win. If Dana, secure in his Boston law office, could celebrate himself as one "intended by nature for a general roamer," Melville actually roamed the wide world in a search for excitement, truth, life, and love that would take him to the South Seas, to the Holy Land, around Cape Horn, "not so much bound to any haven ahead, as rushing from havens astern." His odyssey would culminate in that triumphal synthesis of literature and life called *Moby Dick*, as mountainous in its sweep and smashing pace as the greatest of Pacific waves. "Transcendentalism in Concord Village was one thing," Parrington adds. "But transcendentalism in the forecastle of [a] whaler . . . transcendentalism that drove fiercely into the blood-red sunsets of dwarfing seas, transcendentalism in the hot and passionate heart of a man whose vast dreams outran his feet—this was something very different from the gentle mysticism of cooler natures. . . ." Melville, in fact, was the Ishmael of his *Moby Dick*, the rejected wanderer, fleeing his prison of land, determined to find and cleanse his soul by hunting down every "watery part of the world."

Melville lived in New England for little more than fifteen of his seventy-two years. But he truly came alive there, inspired by Dana, Hawthorne, and Holmes to the realization of his finest powers as an artist. His masterpiece, which celebrates a saga of New Bedford whaling, is so quintessentially New England as to justify his inclusion in the ranks of New England men of letters. New York City, after the rural serenity of the Berkshires, would become for its native son a "Babylonish brick-kiln," its shrillness relieved only by retreat into his study.

Melville was born in New York City on August 1, 1819,

the son of Allan Melville, an importer of French silks and a conventional practical man of Scottish descent. Herman's mother was Maria Gansevoort, archly aware of her descent from New York's leading Dutch patroon families, the Van Rensselaers, Ten Broecks, and Van Schaicks. Young Herman, one of eight children, was a direct descendant of Lord John Melville, who was beheaded by Queen Mary I ("Bloody Mary"), "becaus," as the old record has it, "he was known to be one that unfainedlie favoured the truths." Both of Melville's grandfathers served with distinction in the Revolutionary War; his paternal grandfather, Major Thomas Melville, though later a conservative Federalist, took part—as we have seen—in the Boston Tea Party.

Allan Melville suffered business reverses caused by the scarcity of foreign exchange in the depression following the War of 1812. Ultimately forced into bankruptcy, he died when Herman was only twelve, leaving his family almost penniless. Nor could Herman find solace in his mother. Maria Melville, writes Herman's biographer Wheaton, was "a cold, proud woman, arrogant in the sense of her name, her blood, and the affluence of her forbears." Melville despised his mother's arid materialism, and she appears to have returned his hostility. "She hated me," Melville confessed in later life, and in the character of Mrs. Glendenning in his novel *Pierre*, he portrayed her without mercy as one who had driven him from home, "an infant Ishmael into the desert, with no maternal Hagar to accompany and comfort him."

Herman had no formal schooling after seventeen. Described by his father as "very backward in speech," "somewhat slow in comprehension," but "docile and amiable," he studied at the Albany Academy, where he seems to have fared well in writing. After leaving school, Melville was active in a young men's literary and debating society and contributed inconsequential pieces to a local newspaper. But there was little promise of that literary skill that would one day immortalize him. The year 1834 found him a clerk in a bank, after which he tried his hand at schoolteaching, farming, or helping out in his brother's fur and cap store.

At seventeen, Melville left home, signing on as a cabin boy on a ship bound for Liverpool. He explains this major decision through the lips of his hero in his novel *Redburn*, which was based on this voyage: "Sad disappointments in several plans which I had sketched for my future life, the necessity of doing something for myself, united to a naturally roving disposition, had now conspired within me, to send me to sea as a common sailor." Like Dana, Melville rejected the role of passenger, plagued by the tourist's seasickness, sleepless nights, and shipboard quarrels caused by boredom. "No, when I go to sea," Ishmael would explain in *Moby Dick*, "I go as a simple sailor, right before the mast, plumb down in the forecastle, aloft there to the royal masthead." Did he mind the incessant orders, the stern discipline, even the tyranny of a ship? Why should he, Melville replied, in an echo of Thoreau. Every man, high and low, has a master to obey; the common sailor is no more a slave to his captain than a rich man is to his wealth. Besides, only the sea, the monarch of Nature in all its primordial power and splendor, could relieve his "everlasting itch for things remote." Only in his final, lonely years would Melville lose that boundless love of the sea that enriches his works from *Typee* to *Billy Budd*. It was a challenge, a therapy: "Whenever I find myself growing grim about the mouth," Melville would write, "whenever it is

damp, drizzly November in my soul, whenever I find myself
involuntarily pausing before coffin warehouses, and bringing
up the rear of every funeral that I meet; and especially
when my hypos get such an upper hand of me, that it requires a strong moral principle to prevent me from deliberately stepping into the street, and methodically knocking people's hats off—then I account it high time to get
to sea as soon as I can." Life adrift brought perspective,
escape from trivia, a sense of one's place, for though sometimes longing for home, "you become identified with the
tempest, your significance is lost in the riot of the stormy
universe around."

After one month at sea and six weeks in Liverpool, young
Melville returned home, falling in line again as a school
teacher, trying his hand at lead-mining in Galena, Illinois,
failing as a scrivener in a New York law office because of
his atrocious handwriting. Life on land became increasingly
dull. The voyage to Liverpool had left him with an insatia-
ble hunger for the sea. On January 3, 1841, a rugged five
feet nine, blue-eyed, high-browed, wavy brown-haired, and
twenty-one, Herman Melville shipped out of Fairhaven,
opposite New Bedford, on the whaler *Acushnet* for an
eighteen-month voyage to the South Seas that would form
the basis of *Moby Dick*. He would pass Rio, round Cape
Horn, and sail up the South American coast to the Galapa-
gos Islands. It was a grand adventure. But all was not paradise aboard ship. Whaling was an occupation highly fancied by criminals and drifters and when conditions on the
Acushnet became unbearable, Melville and a shipmate,
"Toby"—Richard Tobias Greene—jumped ship in the
Marquesas Islands. They escaped, of all places, to the
valley of a cannibal tribe called the Typees, who made

their home, scenically at least, on an island paradise. Melville's adventures among the cannibals, who proved friendly but nonetheless held him captive, are recounted in *Typee*, as are his moments of joy with the charming native girl, Fayaway. Free of the false veils and inhibitions of a sin-conscious civilization in which sensual pleasures and beauty were allied with evil, Fayaway was, for Melville, a "beauteous nymph" with "the unstudied graces of a child of nature," dressed in "the primitive and summer garb of Eden," and "the very perfection of female grace and beauty." Far from being repelled by the Polynesians, Melville was captivated by their innocent olive beauty; they were "fresh," he wrote, "as at their first creation." By contrast, he wondered how Western man would look "stripped of the cunning artifices of the tailor." And his contempt for the intruding white man struck deeper, especially the missionaries who sought to impose their religion on a peaceful people, while greedy Western merchants were destroying island life.

If attracted by the innocence of native life, however, Melville became anxious to move on to other ports, even longed a bit for home. Despite tribal courtesies, he was keenly aware that he was being held by the Typees against his will. Most important, as F. O. Matthiessen writes, "he could never be a savage; his background of Presbyterian orthodoxy, though in abeyance now, was soon to reassert itself [after the publication of *Typee*] in his meditations on innate depravity." Once, he told Nathaniel Hawthorne, he had felt so much a part of the oneness of Nature that while he was lying on the grass his legs seemed to send shoots into the earth and his hair felt like leaves on his head, but despite such flashes of pantheism, he would remain entranced by the "fundamental questions in Puritan theology: what constituted original sin, to what extent could man's will be free?"

Melville escaped from the Typees and was rescued by an Australian whaler, the *Lucy Ann,* on which he again faced impossible conditions, this time a sick captain, a bibulous first mate, and a mutinous crew. Melville again jumped ship at Papeete, Tahiti, on September 9, 1842, where he earned his keep as a field laborer. In his novel *Omoo,* literally "roamer" and a sequel to *Typee,* he depicts life on Tahiti and tells the story of life on the *Lucy Ann,* which he renames the *Julia.* In Papeete, Melville was placed under shore arrest for jumping ship, but was allowed to escape when the *Lucy Ann* weighed anchor in mid-October. On a nearby island, he lived the life of a beachcomber for a month, then signed on as a harpooner on the *Charles and Henry.* He debarked in the Hawaiian Islands, where he made his way to Honolulu and a job as a clerk in a dry-goods store.

Anxious to get home now, Melville signed up for a year as an ordinary seaman on the frigate *United States* on a voyage retold in *White-Jacket: The World in a Man-of-War.* In this novel Melville exposes the wanton cruelty of navy discipline in his time, thus joining Dana in his successful campaign to urge Congress to abolish corporal punishment in the Navy. Indeed, in *White-Jacket* the narrator recounts a scene in which, threatened with flogging by a sadistic captain, he narrowly misses flinging the captain—and himself—overboard in a murder-suicide.

Home again on October 14, 1844, enriched by almost four years of travel, Melville, now twenty-five, set immediately to work writing *Typee.* He had written nothing of consequence before, but now, in F. O. Matthiessen's words, "the American with the richest natural gifts as a writer became one largely by accident," creating his novel not out of literary practice but out of the raw material of experience, becoming "aware of his talents through their exercise." And aware of his talents Melville certainly was. "From my twenty-fifth year," he wrote Hawthorne, "I date my life." And well he might. *Typee*, published in 1846, was "an instant success," so much so that to his disgust Melville himself was nicknamed "Typee" and was widely celebrated as the "man who lived among the cannibals." Evangelical churchmen were outraged by Melville's attacks on the missionaries; others doubted the credibility of his tale. But most shared the view of the critic who found *Typee* "lively and picturesque," and the book sold well to an enthusiastic public. The publication of *Omoo* the following year met with comparable acclaim. One enraged critic, to be sure, charged Melville with exciting "unchaste desires," and with viewing all women as "enchanting animal[s] fashioned for his pleasure." But in general readers welcomed its "direct, straight-forward air" and *Omoo*, like *Typee*, sold well.

On August 4, 1847, Melville was married to Elizabeth Shaw, daughter of Chief Justice Lemuel Shaw of Massachusetts. The newlyweds moved into 103 Fourth Avenue, in New York City. In this home, purchased on borrowed money, they were joined by Melville's entire family: his mother, his younger brother and his wife, four unmarried sisters, and a bachelor brother. And in February, 1849, Melville's first child joined the menage.

The New York years were productive ones for Melville. He wrote much and read deeply, discovering Shakespeare (whom he declared "another Messiah"), studying Dante, Seneca, Rabelais, Spenser, the German romantics, the Transcendentalists. Melville's reading and deepening interest in philosophy were reflected in his novel *Mardi*, published in 1849, a mystically religious and political allegory set, again, in the South Seas, a confused notebook of the often conflicting ideas swirling about in Melville's head. In his confusion about the meaning of life, Melville, in one critic's words, indeed reflected the ideological convulsions of the nineteenth century, the "tensions set up by the conflict between the will to believe and the need to be shown . . . between religion and science, between faith and skepticism." *Mardi* was a failure, artistically and financially. George Ripley, fresh from his own failure at Brook Farm, denounced Melville's "audacity" in attempting "such an experiment with the long-suffering of his readers." Melville's *Redburn*, a novel based on his first sea voyage in 1837, was more successful, confirming him in one critic's mind as "the most captivating of ocean authors." For Melville, who had disparaged the book to Dana as "a little nursery tale of mine," the book's public success was gratifying, for "it puts money," he said, "into an empty purse."

Melville visited England in October, 1849, to arrange better terms with his publishers. He recorded his impressions of England and the Continent in a revealing little book, *Journal of a Visit to London and the Continent*. Home again in February, 1850, he resumed his study of philosophy, especially Transcendentalism. He had met Emerson in Boston a year before, and if he would later condemn Emerson for "a defect in the region of the heart" and "a self-conceit so intensely intellectual that at first one hesitates to call it by its right name," he now hailed the

Sage of Concord as "a great man." He was not at all, Melville declared, "full of myths and oracular gibberish," as he had been told. Emerson was "elevated above mediocrity." "I love all men who dive," Melville added. "Any fish can swim near the surface, but it takes a great whale to go down stairs five miles or more. . . ." Melville had no use for the genial, yea-saying optimists of Concord and Boston, those whom he dismissed as "affirmers of perfection," despite the evidence of man's capacity for evil; they were "all cracked right across the brow." And it is certain that he considered Emerson's genius as somewhat tainted by this cosmic nonsense. But he had heard and obeyed Emerson's great call for a new, consciously native American literature. And if Emerson had had Melville specifically in mind as one of the great architects of this literature, when he proclaimed the American scholar, he could not have been more prophetic: "Not out of those on whom systems of education have exhausted their culture, comes the helpful giant to destroy the old or to build the new, but out of unhandselled savage nature." Like Hawthorne, Melville would defy precedent in the form and purposes of the novel, dare new directions, speak with courage not out of an ancient printed wisdom but out of his own vision of life.

In August, 1850, Melville bought a farm, Arrowhead, in the Berkshire mountain town of Pittsfield, Massachusetts. He would remain there for thirteen years. Hawthorne was there, at work on *The House of the Seven Gables*; so were great literary lights of the New England renaissance, including Oliver Wendell Holmes, exchanging ideas, roaming about, stopping by, and quaffing champagne during at least one "well-moistened" party. If he enjoyed the stimulating company of the *cognoscenti*, however, Melville had sought the peace of the mountains to complete his great work. He had already written to Dana in May that he was "half-way" in a book called "the whaling voyage." And in Pittsfield he became so immersed in the creation of *Moby Dick* that he wrote another friend: "My room seems a ship's cabin; and at nights when I wake up and hear the wind shrieking, I almost fancy there is too much sail on the house, and I had better go on the roof and rig in the chimney." To his English publisher, he described the work in progress. It would be, he explained, "a romance of adventure, founded upon certain wild legends in the Southern Sperm Whale Fisheries and illustrated by the author's own personal experience, of two years and more, as a harpooner." But *Moby Dick* is more than that. It is a powerful classic tale of the conflict between good and evil, as great in its way as Bunyan's *Pilgrim's Progress* and Milton's *Paradise Lost*. In its tone and thrust it is almost Shakespearean, almost Biblical, as vast, as sweeping as the sea itself in its torrent and fury. In Hyatt Waggoner's words, it is "passionately alive in every sentence, ambiguous to the end, vibrant with emotion . . . written by a man wholly committed to life and to his own insights and feeling." It is as plain as New England clam chowder, for which Melville includes the recipe, and as awesome as a tidal wave. If this work would be denounced in Melville's lifetime as artificial and bombastic "Bedlam literature," a penitent America would awake to its genius in the 1920s and salute it for the work of genius that it is.

On the surface, *Moby Dick* is an absorbing sea story drenched with nautical realism and legend, a story that reduces to a recounting of one man's maniacal lust for revenge. Captain Ahab, master of the whaling ship *Pequod*, has lost one leg to a notorious killer whale named Moby Dick, and bends his crew to his will to hunt down the ocean beast for the kill. With fanatical single-mindedness, Ahab at last confronts the mystical white whale and in the process sends himself and his crew to the bottom of the sea. Only the narrator, Ishmael—clearly Melville himself— is left to tell the tale.

Beneath the surface, *Moby Dick* is a profoundly philosophical inquiry into the nature of good and evil. The *Pequod* itself, with its exotic mixture of races and religions from the Polynesian prince Queequeg to Negroes and hard-bitten Yankee sailors, is a microcosm, a little world in itself. It is studded with long religious and philosophical discourses as enchanting as the salty story of whaling itself— Father Mapple's marvelously symbolic sermon at the book's start, the haunting chapter on the whiteness of the whale, Flask's sermon to the sharks, Melville's unforgettable description of the great Pacific. It is a splendid novel, which can be read on many levels, for adventure, for ideas, for the intellectual turmoil that marked the nineteenth century when the traditional answers to the question of the human condition were no longer enough.

Moby Dick was published in London on October 18, 1851, and in New York about one month later. It did not sell well. And, indeed, its completion marked the beginning of Melville's tragic decline as an artist. As he finished the manuscript, Melville himself seemed to feel his powers failing, fearful he said, "that I am now come to the inmost leaf of the bulb, and that shortly the flower must fall to the mould." He was right. *Pierre*, a heavy-handed story of a Hamlet-like idealist who leaves his country estate and family for truth in the big city with tragic consequences, sold fewer than three hundred copies in its first year. Discouraged and drained, Melville appealed to Hawthorne's friend President Franklin Pierce for a diplomatic post abroad; his request was denied. In February, 1853, he began contributing to magazines, including *Putnam's Monthly*, in which his short story "Bartleby, the Scrivener" first appeared and earned him the sum of eighty-five dollars. *Israel Potter*, the tale of an American Revolutionary private in exile in England, somewhat redeemed his reputation, but his best writing was behind him and he knew it. He was despondent. En route to the Holy Land in the spring of 1856, Melville visited Hawthorne at his Liverpool consulate, and Hawthorne noted in his journal that his friend appeared to have "made up his mind to be annihilated." Even in the Holy Land he would only find disenchantment. In his laboriously long and contrived metaphysical narrative poem, *Clarel*, which emerged from this journey in 1876, his pilgrim hero enters Jerusalem to find not the radiant solace of truth but an Arctic bleakness. His *Piazza Tales*, which appeared in 1856, and *The Confidence Man*, an uneven satire on the crass commercialism of his day, were the last prose works published in his lifetime and the last he would write for over thirty years.

To shore up his income, Melville turned in late 1857 to the lecture circuit, south to Tennessee and west to Chicago, discoursing on "Statues in Rome," "The South Seas," and "Traveling: Its Pleasures, Pains, and Profits." Of his treatment of the first subject, a critic in Charlestown, Massachusetts, declared: "One would hardly have guessed that he had ever been in Italy at all." Others complained that his voice was inaudible, that he spoke over the heads of his audiences, even that, of all things, he was "too uniformly excellent!" And if one critic could praise his "melodious cadences," "bold originality," and "greatness of vision"— qualities certainly more in character with the author of *Moby Dick*—Melville himself was revolted by the cheap compromises he was forced to make in pandering to the philistine taste of the general public. He was compelled to deliver lectures, tailored, in Morton Sealts's words, to "light entertainment and perhaps some utilitarian instruction, but less culture and nothing controversial," in short, what the public would buy. "Dollars damn me," Melville declared, and dollars would fail him, too. If Emerson could earn $1,700 in one year on the podium—then a tidy sum— Melville was able to gross only $1,273.50—less travel and living expenses—in *three* years.

When the Civil War broke out, Melville, just over forty, failed to obtain a naval commission. Selling his Pittsfield farm, which had paid its own way, Melville returned to New York City and turned, tragically, to poetry. His *Battle-Pieces and Aspects of the War*, published in 1866, contains moving pasages. In "A Meditation" Melville passionately condemns "Christian wars of natural brotherhood," laments the tragedy that "hands that fain had clasped again could slay," and sadly observes that former West Point comrades now shot each other down. But even these poems, in one critic's words, are "as cold as ice and as dead as the deaths they intend to commemorate." Melville himself said of these pieces: "I seem . . . to have but placed a harp in a window, and noted [sic] the contrasted airs which wayward winds have played upon the strings." He might have said this of most of his verse, including *John Marr and Other Sailors*, published in 1888, and the privately printed *Timoleon*, which appeared in 1891.

In 1866, Herman Melville, now honored among the world's greatest writers, was appointed an outdoor inspector in the New York Custom House. He performed his humdrum chores on the wharf at the foot of a street that bore—in bitter irony—his mother's maiden name, Gansevoort. In obscurity, in a kind of living death, Melville held this subordinate post for almost twenty years. Only in 1891 did he break through a pitiful anonymity to complete, or almost complete, another story, the enigmatic sea tale, *Billy Budd*, which would not be published until 1924. In this fine, brief novel some of the spark of *Moby Dick* enriches the strong, pure line of his narrative and Melville again does battle with the issue that most thoroughly gripped his Calvinist soul, in Willard Thorp's words, "the conflict between innocence and depravity, the 'mystery of iniquity,' the dilemma of the just man who had heavenly insights but must act in accord with earthly standards."

Three months after completing *Billy Budd*, Melville was dead. In a horrible gaffe, the *New York Times* obituary called him "Henry" Melville. Another observed: "If the truth were known, even his own generation has long thought him dead, so quiet have been the later years of his life." And he himself had said of all of his works that they were just "botches," just so much wood sawed for the fire.

The verdict of history would reverse the unkind judgments of both Melville and his critics. It would credit his achievement of a goal he had set early in his life: "We are the pioneers of the world," he had said of American writers, "the advance-guard, sent on through the wilderness of untried things, to break a path in the New World that is ours."

FRANCIS
PARKMAN

WILLIAM
HICKLING
PRESCOTT

THEY SAW HISTORY AS DRAMA

FRANCIS PARKMAN

In April, 1842, a distinguished professor of history at Harvard College named Jared Sparks received this note from one of his students: "Sir, I am desirous of studying the history of the Seven Years' War and find it difficult to discover authorities sufficiently minute to satisfy me. . . . Could you furnish me through the Post Office with the names of such authorities as you can immediately call to mind, you would do me a great kindness." The note was signed, "Yours with great respect, F. Parkman, Soph. Class."

It was no secret among Frank Parkman's classmates that the wealthy young swell from Beacon Hill had "Injuns on the brain." His note to Sparks, which was honored with a long list of books, was, however, perhaps the first formal indication of a plan of research long kept secret: Francis Parkman's intention to chronicle the epochal struggle between the empires of Britain and France for domination of the North American continent. Parkman's colossal labor in rewriting and illuminating the history of New World exploration and settlement and its decisive effect on United States history would lead to a still formidable classic, *France and England in North America*. His labor would lead, also, to a life of almost incredible pain and tragedy.

"His life," writes Parkman's eminent biographer, Mason Wade, "has been called the most heroic in the annals of literature, and with much justice." For Francis Parkman, impelled by a boyhood dream, would conquer near-blindness, a crippled body, and mental breakdown to write history as no American before him or after him has written it: history—like *The Oregon Trail*—whose color and drama still fire the imagination of readers, and whose painstaking accuracy still commands the respect of scholars.

Parkman's history rings with the warwhoops of Indians on the march, the stampede of buffaloes, the death cries of missionaries tortured to death by braves, the bright hope and pain of emigrant Americans in the nation's bold westward sweep, the rush of imperial armies through the wilderness and forest that Parkman had explored and loved as a boy.

Young Frank Parkman had hungered for a life of action, a life of hunting, exploring, daring, muscle, and grit, a life outdoors in total defiance of all danger and hardship. He was forced by illness to live periodically confined to dimly lit homes as a semi-invalid, pathetically dependent on his mother and sisters, frequently incapable of the slightest conversation, restricted to a wheelchair, or groping about in the twilight of his study. But in the hour of his greatest extremity, when he was physically and mentally beaten totally down, he remained determined to conquer his "Enemy." "If by God's mercy," he said, "a single finger is unloosed, its feeble strength will not lie idle."

Francis Parkman would never wholly conquer his "Enemy," as he called his mental illness. But he would prove to himself and many who faced comparable challenges that, again in Mason Wade's moving words, "a life lived largely in the study may be as adventurous and colorful as a life of action and in the end far more important in the history of mankind. The captains and the kings depart," Wade adds, "once they have fulfilled their roles, and the memory of their deeds soon grows dim; but the scholars and the writers leave monuments of words, often more enduring than the lifeless brass and stone."

Francis Parkman was "born to the purple and with a golden spoon in his mouth," September 16, 1823, on

Boston's plush Beacon Hill, the scion of a wealthy and professionally eminent upper class—or Brahmin—family. Among his ancestors was no less than Cotton Mather, the famed Puritan preacher, the self-appointed Messiah of the New England commonwealth, given to angelic visions of religious grandeur. Parkman's great-grandfather, the Unitarian minister Edward Brooke, had slung a musket on his shoulder and marched to battle in Lexington on April 19, 1775, in no less than "his full-bottomed wig." And young Frank's grandfather, Samuel, son of a poor country minister, came to Boston to make his fortune in the China and India trade, amassing wealth that would simultaneously free Frank from the need to earn his own living and win his contempt as the fruit of what he considered crass commercialism. Grandfather Samuel cut a colorful figure— a "merchant prince and Federalist grandee . . . remembered as a man of courtly presence and manners, faultlessly dressed in a brass-buttoned blue coat, a diamond on his ruffled shirt front."

Frank's father, the Reverend Dr. Francis Parkman, was the archetype of what biographer Howard Doughty calls "mild, decorous, rational and respectable Unitarianism." Properly Federalist, patronizingly philanthropic, and inescapably a Harvard overseer, Dr. Parkman served as pastor of Boston's socially correct New North Church from 1813 until a few years before his death in 1852. Sedulously ministerial, he delighted in socializing and in publishing shallow little homilies on morals and theology that troubled no one. In his son Francis, he inspired only contempt, for Frank detested "sweet, mild, unctuous smoothness." Of a boy later named after him the younger Parkman would observe: "I hope the youngster will do honor to the name.

He should be brought up to some respectable calling and not allowed to become a minister." This descendant of Cotton Mather bluntly dismissed the clergy as "vermin."

For all his apparent dignified calm and cheer—he was dubbed "the clerical humorist"—Dr. Parkman was subject to seizures of melancholia, had a distinct "manic-depressive tendency," and experienced a nervous breakdown that forced him abroad. It was a harbinger of the deeper affliction that would befall his son.

Frank's sister Eliza concluded that "whatever characteristics [he] inherited from his parents" came from his mother, Caroline Hall, who could trace her own forbears to the earliest settlers of the Massachusetts Bay and Plymouth colonies. Caroline Hall emerges in the biographies as practical, socially retiring, and outwardly reserved, despite deep inner feelings—and indeed Parkman was all of these things.

Parkman was the eldest son of Dr. Parkman's five children by Caroline Hall, including a brother John Eliot and three sisters—Caroline, Mary, and Eliza—who like their mother virtually worshiped Frank throughout their lives, attending to his slightest—or greatest—need.

Francis Parkman's boyhood appeared normal enough, despite the severe "head pains" that both he and his brother Jack endured. He tinkered with chemistry—most unscientifically—in experiments which, he observed in a disquieting third-person autobiographical letter many years later, "served little other purpose than injuring him by confinement, poisoning him with noxious gases, and occasionally scorching him with some ill-starred explosion." He had a normal boy's penchant for pranks. In one family procession from church, solemnly headed by his father bedecked in his minister's gown, young Frank brought up the rear impishly holding up a dead rat at arm's length. In one family move to a new home, Frank packed his belongings on a sled, and notwithstanding the snowless April, carted his goods along the sidewalk.

A strong touch of the ham propelled Frank into two years of amateur matinee stage productions in what he called the Star Theater, housed in Reverend Parkman's unused coachhouse. Rounding up would-be Thespians in the neighborhood, Frank supervised the action from stage-setting to direction, and, in his high-pitched voice, played Shakespearean female parts, did pantomime, and performed chemical tricks with side-show bravado.

Off-stage, the boy Parkman read avidly in Shakespeare, Milton, and the wandering romantic, Lord Byron. He was much taken, too, by Sir Walter Scott's novels of knightly adventure and by James Fenimore Cooper's tales of pioneers and Indians. But already the mental imbalance that would shatter Parkman's adult life cast its shadows on his boyhood. In his eighth year his parents considered his condition serious enough to send him eight miles from the city to a less complex life on his Grandfather Hall's farm, near the Five Mile Woods in the Middlesex Fells, Medford. At that time the Fells were a wilderness and the boy Parkman at once began his lifelong love affair with the forest, through which he roamed "untrammeled and at large; exploring its alluring recesses; collecting eggs, insects, and minerals; trapping squirrels and woodchucks; stalking birds with a bow and arrow. . . ." In Medford, Parkman attended Mr. Angiers' highly regarded school, declared it overrated, and learned, he said, little.

At thirteen, Parkman returned home to Boston and was

enrolled in Gideon Thayer's academy for young gentlemen, later known as Chauncey Place School, to prepare, of course, for Harvard. At the academy he did passably well in Greek and Latin but excelled in English. In later life he would acknowledge his debt to his teacher in the "rhetorical department," one William Russell, "a teacher," Parkman wrote, "of excellent literary tastes and acquirements," whose "constant care" was "to teach the boys of his class to write good and easy English . . . criticizing in his gentle way anything flowery or bombastic." Russell also encouraged his students to translate Virgil and Homer into idiomatic English. To the end of his life Parkman retained in his memory, verbatim, entire passages from the classics.

Parkman entered Harvard in the fall of 1840. Like most of his social class, he belonged to the right clubs, including Hasty Pudding. With gentlemanly disdain for amenities, he lost credits for tardiness, and while his father was overseer of Harvard, was reprimanded by a faculty committee for "excessive absences from compulsory prayers and recitations." Young Parkman drank his share of ale and wine and crossed the Charles River frequently to attend Boston theaters and dances. He rebelled against Harvard's old regimen of recitation by rote. "Whatever he liked," his cousin and classmate George Parkman observed, "he would take hold of with the utmost energy; what he did not like he would not touch," with the result that he failed mathematics in his freshman year.

Still, it was precisely this selective approach to learning that distinguished Parkman from his tradition-bound, toe-the-mark classmates. Far from shirking the life of the mind, he read voraciously the great historical works in Harvard's library, vast even then, poring over Gibbon's *Decline and*

Fall, over the American historian Bancroft, and the great French historian Michelet—history in the grand manner, as he wished to write it. For at age nineteen, in his sophomore year, as we have seen, he knew precisely what he wanted to do with his life. He would write the great forest drama of the French and English battle for an American dominion. And, in his own words, he "slighted all college studies which could not promote [this objective] and pursued with avidity, such as had a bearing on it, however indirect."

Parkman was blessed, as Thoreau and Dana had been blessed, by the tutelage of Edward Tyrrel Channing, professor of rhetoric, who taught him the elements of a purer and sharper style of writing. Under Professor Jared Sparks, whose appointment to Harvard marked the recognition of American history as a legitimate subject of study, Parkman learned to respect primary sources, original documents, rather than mere commentary on these sources two or three times removed. With Sparks's assistance, he sought and gained access to documents on the Anglo-French conflict in foreign archives and hired copyists to supply him with these documents. Nor was Parkman content with translations. In his junior and senior years, to assure his intimacy with original documents, he was taking four languages simultaneously: Latin, Greek, French, and Italian, and he would pick Spanish up later. He excelled in languages to the point at which he could read both Machiavelli and Voltaire in the original.

With all of this erudition, Parkman was no closet scholar. He scorned "that pallid and emasculate scholarship of which New England has had too many examples." Accordingly, he reasoned, his reliance, at least initially in his project, should be "less on books, than on such personal experience as should, in some sense, identify him with his theme." He would saturate his mind with a personal, first-hand knowledge of the very areas where the history he would write was made and "bring himself," he said, "as near as might be to the times with which he was to deal," following in the very footsteps of the great La Salle, of Frontenac, of Wolfe and Montcalm, and of Pontiac. And during his vacations from college, he did just that, visiting the Berkshires' historic Mohawk Valley, Lake George, Lake Champlain, Fort Ticonderoga, Montreal, the Penobscot Indians in Maine. And in the White Mountains of New Hampshire and the Green Mountains of lovely Vermont, he hunted moose, scaled great cliffs, rafted over rapids in the "howling wilderness," talked with crusty old Yankees who were alive when great history was being made, a snobbish Bostonian among provincial backwoodsmen and hunters, but now so tanned that he was taken at one point for an Indian.

Even in Cambridge, Parkman honed talents that would aid him in the outdoor aspect of his historical project. He rowed regularly on Fresh Pond, kept his hand in at rifle practice, took boxing lessons from a retired pugilist, and perfected his horsemanship under the guidance of a circus rider. Determined to keep himself in shape, ready for any contingency on the trail, and "cherishing," as he put it, "a sovereign scorn for every physical weakness or defect," young Parkman pushed himself with an almost frantic ruthlessness, rarely in his college room except to sleep, and "burning," as he put it, "his candle at both ends." Like Hawthorne he was generally a loner more comfortable listening than talking, a quality that won him the nickname "the Loquacious" from teasing classmates. All the while, he pursued his historical objective, he later explained, "with a pernicious intensity, keeping my plans and purposes to myself, while passing among my companions as an outspoken fellow."

So pernicious was Parkman's intensity that at the end of his junior year, from what appears to have been excessive gymnastic exercise, a fall from a trapeze, nervous exhaustion —or all three—he was forced to curtail his college career and embark on an eight-month grand tour of Europe. He sailed not as Dana had done but as a most proper Bostonian. But his descriptions of the sea rival Dana's best; he said of one violent storm: "We seemed imbedded among moving mountains." Abroad, Parkman poked about the great fort at Gibraltar, patronized poor Sicilians as "a gang of ragamuffins," explored the very crater of Vesuvius, toured Pompeii, went to Mass at Saint Peter's—deeply impressed, Yankee or not, by the power and pomp of the papacy— visited Virgil's tomb in Naples, marveled at the Rhine and the Alps, went trout-fishing in Scotland's Tweed River, made the Paris scene with his resident uncle, and, to deepen his understanding of the Catholic motives that governed imperial France's conduct in the New World, spent some time in a monastery in Italy. The trip did him good, got him out of himself. "Here in this old world," he confided to his diary, "I seem, thank heaven, to be carried about half a century backward in time." As the tour wore on, however, he would conclude: "Give me Lake George and the smell of the pine and fir!"

Parkman returned home in June, 1844, and reentered Harvard, from which he graduated Phi Beta Kappa and with "high distinction" in history in August, 1844. Obeying his father's request that he prepare himself for a career more esteemed in the eyes of reigning Bostonians than that of a mere writer, Parkman entered Harvard Law School. It is certain that at no point did Parkman even consider abandoning his objective as a historian, but, like a dutiful son, studied his Blackstone and made the social best of his law career with cavalier good cheer. "Here am I, down in Divinity Hall (!)," he wrote airily to a classmate visiting Europe, "enjoying to my heart's content that *otium cum dignitate* which you so affectionately admire; while you, poor devil, are being jolted in English coaches. . . . Do you not envy my literary ease?—a sea-coal fire—a dressing gown —slippers—a favorite author; all set off by an occasional bottle of champagne, or a bowl of stewed oysters at Washburn's? This is the cream of existence. To lay abed in the morning, till the sun has half melted away the [frost] on the window-panes, and Nigger Lewis's fire is almost burnt out, listening meanwhile to the starved Divinities as they rush shivering and panting to their prayers and recitations— then to get up to a fashionable breakfast at eleven—then go to a lecture—find it a little too late, and adjourn to Joe Peabody's room, for a novel, conversation, and a morning glass of Madeira. . . ." He enjoyed, too, at least one wild party with all of the Class of '44 alumni he could muster up that ended in a bottle-smashing war-dance on Cambridge Common.

Parkman's legal training—he won his law degree in January, 1846—had an ordering influence on his skill as a writer. As one biographer puts it, "his discreet reserves of judgment and timely skepticism are not unrelated to this part of his education," nor was his "lawyer's persistence in sifting facts."

May 5, 1846, found Parkman far removed from the sedate precincts of Boston and Cambridge, in Westport (now Kansas City) Kansas, after a long journey by "train, stage, flatboat, and steamboat." Westport was the jumping-off place to the West, and on May 9, Parkman and his cousin Quincy Adams Shaw embarked over the "great green ocean" of prairie for what Parkman modestly called "a tour of curiosity and amusement to the Rocky Mountains." It was, in fact, Parkman's unforgettable expedition along the Oregon Trail. Young Frank and Quincy were accompanied by the capable guide Henry Chatillon and a muleteer, and these four men, while they joined another expedition for part of their history-making trek, made most of their journey alone. Parkman later explained his purpose in making the trip, somewhat solemnly, as based on a determination to study the Sioux, one of the few tribes of Indians then still in their natural state, uncorrupted by the white man, again as preliminary research for his multi-volumed history *France and England in North America.* And, indeed, in Alvin Josephy's words, "Parkman's pictures of the Sioux [were] the first full treatment of Plains Indian life available to the average Eastern reader." In fact, the idea for the expedition was Quincy Shaw's and without doubt Parkman viewed the Western adventure as a romantic lark in the Byronic tradition. Certainly he could well afford it financially and must have welcomed this new release from the very private Yankee world of the mid-nineteenth century.

Now dressed in a red flannel shirt, buckskin trousers, and moccasins, after abandoning "the frock and trousers of civilization" en route, Parkman, astride his horse Pontiac, set out on the trail. Through the country of the

Delawares and the Shawnees, the party rode north to Fort
Leavenworth, west through the grasslands to the great
Platte River, and along the Platte to historic Fort Laramie,
Wyoming, a major post of settlement and supply, where
Frank and his party remained to rest for four days,
after their journey of thirteen hundred miles.

If the two Harvard men found "adventure" on the
trail, they found abundant hardship as well. Parkman's
weak eyes ached dreadfully in the glare of the merciless
sun. Stricken with dysentery, its effects perhaps worsened
by an unvaried diet of dried buffalo meat, Parkman could
hardly keep himself in the saddle and, dismounted, frequently staggered about, his "Enemy" ever lurking. All
around the young explorers were signs of suffering and
tragedy: graves dug up by buzzards, bleached carcasses of
cattle, the discarded city furniture of westward-bound emigrants forced to lighten their loads to survive. Vicious
prairie dogs—or rodents—roamed the plains, rattlers lay
in wait. And at night the silent air was torn by the "most
mournful and discordant howling" of wolves, who sometimes stole up to the very edge of their camp. On the way
home, Frank's and Quincy's thirst succumbed to mud
puddles. And most dangerous of all, as A. B. Guthrie, Jr.,
points out, the small Parkman party was "easy prey to any
[Indians] on the hunt for scalps. . . ." "In a region traveled
by bands and parties of half a dozen Indian nations,"
Guthrie observes, "the two easterners operated with what
might be regarded as a sublime confidence or a rash courage," although Parkman's defiant confrontation of treacherous Arapahoes along the trail was courage itself.

Nor did Parkman's ethnic haughtiness and class-con-
scious disdain toward traders, trappers, even emigrants

lighten his burden. Only his guide Henry Chatillon appears to have penetrated his thick Yankee sense of superiority. "I have never," he wrote, "in the city or in the wilderness, met a better man than my true-hearted friend, Henry Chatillon."

After a side trip by Parkman alone to the Medicine Bow country of the Sioux, whom he vainly hoped to join in a war expedition against the Crows and with whom he lived for a time, Parkman and his party left Fort Laramie for the long journey home, riding south to Bent's Fort (near the present La Junta, Colorado), and picking up the northern branch of the Santa Fe trail, pushed on to Independence, Missouri. On October 1, 1846, they boarded a steamer for St. Louis, and within the month were home in Boston again. Parkman had written to his father that "one season on the prairies will teach a man more than a half a dozen in the settlements." And as the expedition ended, he exulted: "I feel about ten years older than I did five months ago." He had tested, and confirmed his capacity for that self-reliance and resourcefulness that Emerson had preached. And if he had no use for what he crudely called the "she-philosophers of Brook Farm," he had proven their central thesis: that there were in fact greater worlds for a man of independence and nerve to conquer, and that the demeaning influence of industrialism had not snuffed out the fire of human daring and initiative.

In carefully recording his observations in three little notebooks along the trail, Parkman had proved another of Emerson's central instructions, that "every age must write its own books," that candid personal impressions and original study, not the crippling hand of past historians and philosophers, told the truest tale. For out of Parkman's notebooks emerged no less than *The Oregon Trail,* relating the adventures and insights of this awesome expedition. If not as sweeping in subject, if not as controlled and scholarly as Parkman's great *France and England in North America, The Oregon Trail* retains a hold on the popular imagination that only a work of realism and utter novelty can command. It is true that the book met severe criticism. Herman Melville was outraged by Parkman's blunt debunking of Cooper's myth of the "noble savage," for Parkman had found the heirs of the great Pontiac and Tecumseh, however gallant in war and splendid in physique, to be lewd beggars, deceptive, and effeminately helpless when even slightly ill—at times, he wrote, merely a "troublesome and dangerous species of wild beast." Other critics, to this day, condemn Parkman's preoccupation with the Indians and his exultation in the buffalo hunt as grossly myopic in a year in which the Western plains rang with the great continental migration, the American conquest and settlement of Oregon and California, the Mexican War, and the glory and growth of the Santa Fe Trail, bustling with traders, soldiers, settlers, and cowpunchers.

But Parkman had set himself his own private task; he had come to paint not a mural of the West, but a portrait of a people who would soon be lost to history, and with Yankee self-confidence he cared not a fig for the opinions of others. Dedicated to Quincy Shaw, *The Oregon Trail* was published serially in the *Knickerbocker* magazine, beginning in February, 1847, the same journal that had published Parkman's earlier accounts of his vacation adventures while a student at Harvard. Offered to the public first under the byline "A Bostonian," then under Parkman's own name, the work was published in book form in 1849 as

The California and Oregon Trail; the shorter title was adopted later. In a letter of praise, Frederic Remington, who would illustrate Parkman's book and win fame as the prime artist of the Old West, spoke the praise of generations of Americans: "I believe," he told Parkman, "that you have 'blazed a trail,' which will produce a romantic literature and an art in America."

The Oregon Trail is all the more remarkable in that it was dictated by Parkman to Shaw during the period of Parkman's total physical and mental breakdown that followed his return home. Parkman was plagued by dysentery, indigestion, insomnia, violent headaches, heart trouble, despondency, stoppage of circulation in the extremities, and semi-blindness, all exacerbated by marked hypochondria. "My eyes I don't mind," he wrote to a friend, "I can get along without them, but to have one's brain stirred up in a mush may be regarded as a decided obstacle to intellectual achievements." And, in fact, it was the "Enemy" that now struck Parkman down. The precise nature of Parkman's mental imbalance has been almost systematically obscured by his biographers. Wilbur Jacobs describes it candidly: "Seven modern physicians who have examined his life story, especially the relevant data in his letters, agree that his symptoms are indicative of an underlying neurosis. Unconsciously he created for himself what is called a 'struggle situation.' He forced himself to play the part of an exceedingly vigorous and aggressive man of action at the cost of tremendous physical and mental tension. Struggle became the keynote of his life, and through adherence to it he maintained his self-respect. He saw himself as forever battling a relentless foe, the illness which he personified as the 'Enemy.' "

"The most definite of the effects produced," Parkman wrote, "was one closely resembling the tension of an iron band, secured round the head and contracting with an extreme force. . . ." The most ordinary conversation became difficult for him as confused thoughts whirled through his brain. "The condition" and cause of his illness, Parkman concluded "was that of a rider whose horse runs headlong, the bit between his teeth, or of a locomotive, built of indifferent material, under a head of steam too great for its strength, hissing at a score of crevices, yet rushing on with accelerating speed to the inevitable smash."

Thus he who had had such contempt for physical weakness and had denounced "effete and futile scholasticism," became for life a semi-invalid, fearing and often facing "a weary death in life," angered by the physical limitations now imposed upon him—his inability, for example, to pack up and fight in the Mexican War. He became, in the words of his official biographer and secretary, Charles Haight Farnham, "a solitary, often a pathetic, figure in the silence and shadow of his study."

Assured by his doctors that the slightest effort to write was potentially suicidal, Parkman made a decision that saved his life. If a little work *might* kill him, he reasoned, total idleness *certainly* would kill him. He defied his doctors. He would work. He would study. He would write his "history of the American forest," no matter how much pain, how much time, how much illness it required. Half-blind, he set to work to devise a way to write. "He caused a wooden frame to be constructed," he wrote in his famous autobiographical letter to a friend, "of the size and shape of a sheet of letter-paper. Stout wires were fixed horizontally across it, half an inch apart, and a movable back of thick pasteboard fitted behind them. The paper for writing was placed between the pasteboard and the wires, guided by which, and using a black lead crayon, he could write not illegibly with closed eyes." His notes were then read back to him, after which he would dictate the text of his works, at the rate, at first, of about six lines a day.

For long periods, Parkman could not manage even this modicum of work. And his passionate commitment to examining original documents, through the paid services of copyists in foreign archives, complicated his staggering task even further. Despite these obstacles, *The History of the Conspiracy of Pontiac*, an account of the last great Indian uprising and the first of several projected volumes of his *France and England in North America*, begun in 1848, was published in 1851, and dedicated to his old professor and patron, Jared Sparks. Boston's eminent preacher Theodore Parker criticized the book for lack of unity and for Parkman's hostility to the Indians, whose treachery, Parker observed, was no worse than the white man's lechery with Indian women or his introduction of liquor. The bow and arrow, Parker declared, was no more evil than the white man's musket and powder. But the publication of *Pontiac*, still well regarded by scholars, was in itself a triumph. In Arthur Quinn's words, Parkman quite simply "saved himself from despair by hard work."

The shadow of illness gave way to light, too, in the person of Catherine Scollay Bigelow, daughter of Dr. Jacob Bigelow, a prominent Boston physician and a member of Harvard's medical faculty. Of Frank's engagement to Miss Bigelow his mother observed: "We are all much pleased, as we have good reason to be, it certainly is as good a connection as we could desire, & everyone says she is one of the finest girls . . . it makes Frank so happy & gives him something to do & think about. . . ." As for Parkman, his marriage on May 13, 1850 was, he said, like "a jump out of hellfire to the opposite extreme," and "a change from tempest to calm. Out of that tempest I saw a harbor of refuge, and looking for peace and rest, I found happiness."

Practical, lively, warm, and witty, "Kate" made the newlyweds' small home in Milton, just outside Boston, "snug and comfortable." She was at Parkman's side as a dutiful secretary while he was working on *Pontiac,* and on hand to comfort him in 1853, when a new nervous crisis forced him to put aside all historical work and restrict his writing to a highly revealing autobiographical novel, *Vassall Morton.* During this period, too, Parkman turned for diversion and solace to horticulture, won distinction for his nurture of roses, and published his *Book of Roses* in 1866. He would later teach horticulture at Harvard and head the Massachusetts Horticultural Society.

Even this relative happiness was shattered when Parkman's only son, Francis, born in 1854, died of scarlet fever in 1857. And Kate's death the following year thrust him again into acute mental disorder. His two daughters, Grace and Katherine, were sent to live with a relative and, again, Parkman sought relief in a trip abroad. "His brain was then in such a condition," Farnham writes, "that the most eminent specialists of Paris warned him against insanity and forbade him all literary labor. . . ." After his return to Boston in early 1859, Parkman disclosed, it was "about four years before the power of mental application was in the smallest degree restored."

After his return from Europe, Parkman lived with his

mother and sisters, Eliza—or "Lizzie"—and Mary, until 1865 at 8 Walnut Street and thereafter, until his death, at 50 Chestnut Street. He summered at his garden home at Jamaica Pond, just outside Boston, where he tended his flowers from a wheelchair. After Mary's death in 1866 and his mother's in 1871, he and Lizzie shared the Chestnut Street home alone. For Parkman, Lizzie, who subordinated her own life to his interests and health, as secretary, companion, and confidante, was "the *beau ideal* of sisterhood." Lizzie's touching devotion to her brother is, in itself, a kind of cameo classic of American literature.

With magnificent will, Parkman staged an intellectual, not to say mental comeback in the publication of his *France and England in North America,* volume by volume, confirming his reputation throughout the world as a historian of the first order. In 1865 he published *Pioneers of France in the New World,* an account of French exploration and settlement in North America. *The Jesuits in North America* appeared in 1867, portraying the suffering and zealous courage of the Canadian missionaries among the Iroquois. *The Discovery of the Great West* (1869) relates the exploits of the French explorer Robert Cavelier de La Salle, lauded by Parkman as "a statue cast in bronze," a conqueror on the classical scale, who, if he "dared too much, and often dared unwisely," was yet "a man of thought, trained amid arts and letters," and "no rude son of toil." The year 1874 saw *The Old Regime in Canada,* which studies French society in the New World during the seventeenth century. *Count Frontenac and New France Under Louis XIV* was published in 1877 and remains a telling, balanced portrait of France's celebrated, highly capable governor of Canada. *Montcalm and Wolfe* relates the struggle of the famed French and British generals in the Seven Years' War, culminating in Montcalm's defeat in the battle of Quebec. Published in 1884, it was hailed by no less a person than the expatriate American novelist Henry James as "a noble book" and a credit to American scholarship. With A *Half-Century of Conflict* (1892), Parkman brought to a close his heroic history, *France and England in North America.* What Oscar Handlin says of *Frontenac* can, on balance, be said of all of this great work: "It rests upon careful research, the results of which have been corrected in detail, but not superseded."

The history's unifying theme, if it has one, is perhaps best described by the novelist William Dean Howells. It is the moral lesson that "spiritual and political despotism is so bad for man that no zeal, or self-devotion, or heroism can overcome its evil effect." This is not to imply that Parkman, despite his own anticlerical bias, "took sides" as a historical writer between Protestant England and Catholic France. Throughout his work, Parkman sought to maintain the "judicial" rather than the "controversial," professed himself ever "ready to profit by honest criticism." "Provided I manage to tell things as they really happened," he said, "I do not care a farthing who is hit. . . ." Indeed, despite sharp differences of interpretation of the facts of the Anglo-French conflict, the Puritan Parkman maintained a warm and scholastically productive friendship with the Canadian Catholic historian Abbé Henri-Raymond Casgrain, and only extremist sectarian opposition thwarted Catholic Laval University's plans to award Parkman an honorary degree as Protestant McGill University had done.

Even in his later years, despite increasing illnesses—including water on the knee, arthritis, rheumatism, and gout—Parkman retained his passion for physical exercise, rowing precisely one hour a day on Jamaica Pond. Required to use crutches or a cane, he would descend stairs —to the delight of his grandchildren—by sliding down the bannister. He was systematically loyal to Harvard, interrupting vacations to attend commencements, serving first as an overseer and later as a member of the governing body. As late as 1883, at the age of sixty, he was up to riding horseback in his beloved White Mountains, and the year 1886 found him camping with his friend Charles Farnham in Canada.

Parkman was active, too, in the Saturday Club, where he sat at the same table with Emerson and Longfellow. He founded and was first president of the St. Botolph Club in which artists, writers, and other professional men gathered for good talk, and he contributed articles and reviews to such periodicals as the *Atlantic Monthly* and the *North American Review*. Parkman took immense pleasure in his grandchildren, writing to one in the mock language of his beloved cats: "My Deer Katy, Me and Creem are wel. We send u our luv. We do not fite now. . . . Yors till deth, Flora, her M [paw mark] ark." He inspired a generation of young Americans, including a young scholar named Teddy Roosevelt who dedicated his *Winning of the West* to him. And he had the pleasure of Henry Adams' ranking him in 1892 "at the head of our living historians."

In an age of national upheaval, however, Parkman remained strangely detached and insulated, the conservative opinions bred into him from birth basically unchanged. He detested democracy—or what he called "the unchecked rule of the masses," opposed woman suffrage as unnatural, and dismissed mass education as superficial, costly, and dangerous to the proper order of an elitist society. Parkman faced all but his own "class" as his hero, Count Louis Frontenac, had faced the Indians. He "conformed to their ways, borrowed their rhetoric, flattered them on occasion with great address, and yet constantly maintained towards them an attitude of paternal superiority. . . ."

Only the Civil War, like the Mexican War before it, appears to have roused Parkman to public passion, and then only because of his frustration in "holding the pen with the hand that should have grasped the sword." He hailed the "splendor and majesty" of American's civil conflict as greater than Marathon's. It was a holy war. "Conflict and endurance," Parkman proclaimed, "are necessary to both [nations and individuals] and without them both become emasculate." More than that, Parkman declared, the war was "like a clean, fresh breeze" that had stirred America's "clogged and humid atmosphere," polluted by upstart politicians and commercial materialism.

In the fall of 1893, Parkman celebrated his seventieth birthday and expressed the hope that he might attend the fiftieth reunion of his Harvard class. But he was ill. A few weeks after his seventieth birthday celebration, while returning from his daily row, he was stricken with appendicitis. Before an operation could be performed, peritonitis set in and on November 8, 1893, Francis Parkman died. Following a funeral at Boston's King's Chapel, where George Washington had worshiped, Parkman was buried at Mount Auburn Cemetery. The last book he read was Byron's *Childe Harold's Pilgrimage*. The last words he uttered related a dream of killing a bear.

WILLIAM HICKLING PRESCOTT

On Christmas morning, 1837, Professor Jared Sparks received another letter from a son of Harvard. Like Sparks's first letter from young Frank Parkman, it had to do with the writing of history—but this time not with exploratory plans for a great classic but with the joyous announcement that one had been born: "I have great pleasure at last," the letter read, "in sending you their Catholic Highnesses, who keep their Christmas in Boston; and a merry Christmas I hope it will prove to all concerned."

"Their Catholic Highnesses" were Ferdinand and Isabella of Spain. Sparks's young correspondent was the historian William Hickling Prescott, in expectant delight over the publication of his first book. And all concerned in the preparation and reception of this book, including Sparks, who had edited the manuscript, would spend a most merry Christmas indeed, exulting in a literary and historical classic that still enthralls readers the world over. And the forty-one-year-old writer who introduced the Spanish sovereigns in this elegant, new royal dress enjoyed the finest Christmas present of all: triumph over what had appeared an initial failure and a first, great, irreversible stride toward fame.

Like Frank Parkman, whose first great book *Pontiac* he would help to publish, Will Prescott was the wealthy, indulged, and princely scion of one of Boston's first families. Like Parkman, he had every advantage that "proper" origins, social status, and a classical Harvard education conferred in the mid-nineteenth century. Like Parkman, too, he would conquer a potentially disastrous illness—recurring blindness—and write, often in darkness, a kind of history that only Parkman himself rivaled for scholarly depth, drama, and power. The publication of *The History of the*

Reign of Ferdinand and Isabella the Catholic marked the end of a tortuous, often despairing ten-year road of study and struggle for William Hickling Prescott—a triumph of that diminishing commodity called character. From initial despondency, from an enforced physical seclusion in sunless rooms that would have beaten most men down to a crippling self-pity, escape into mindless frivolity, even suicide, Prescott emerged as a historical man of letters honored in royal capitals, universities, and the most distinguished learned societies throughout the world. For, in the tenderly accurate words of his biographer Rollo Ogden, Will Prescott, rising to courage, "turned from a dim world without to a radiant world within, took himself in hand, and forged laboriously in the dark the tempered weapon of his mind and heart."

William Hickling Prescott was born in Hawthorne's town of Salem, Massachusetts, the eldest of seven children—four of whom died in infancy—on May 4, 1796, a few months before George Washington completed his second term as a new nation's first president. Prescott looked at his own ancestors—among New England's earliest settlers—with justifiable pride. The earliest, John, was reputed to have "fought the Indians in a full coat of mail-armor,—helmet, cuirass, and gorget," and "struck to the savage foe by an appearance more frightful than their own." Prescott's paternal grandfather, cited by General Washington himself as "Prescott the Brave," held a command in the battle of Bunker or Breed's Hill, in which the Revolutionary rebels first showed their mettle to the arrogant soldiers of General Howe.

Young Will's father was Judge William Prescott, who, if Daniel Webster's accolade is to be taken as accurate, stood, "at the moment of his retirement from the bar of

Massachusetts . . . at its head for legal learning and attainments." A product of Governor Dummer Academy and Harvard, Judge Prescott served as a state senator and representative and was a delegate to the Hartford Convention of 1814, at which moderates prevented the secession of the New England states from the Union. The judge was regarded highly enough in his profession to be offered an appointment to the Massachusetts Supreme Court, which he declined. Enjoying a lucrative law practice, and practicing thrift and sound judgment in investments, Judge Prescott amassed money enough to free his son William from any need to work.

One biographer finds the judge "wise and noble-minded." For Will, his father was "counsellor, companion and friend from boyhood to the hour of his death," severe only to himself in his judgments, and possessed of "the qualities which command reverence without forfeiting love."

A "stay-at-home introvert," Prescott's mother, Catherine (Hickling), lived a less than epochal life. "My kind, invisible friend," to outgoing, travel-loving Anna Ticknor, wife of Prescott's intimate friend, the historian George Ticknor, Mrs. Prescott was an orthodox Episcopalian. Notwithstanding her husband's Unitarianism, she read the Scriptures in private and gave her time dutifully to Boston charities. In Will's words, she was endowed with "a warm and sympathetic nature," a "heart-full of love," and a capacity to "make sacrifice appear a pleasure to herself."

Taught first by his mother, Prescott was delivered to Miss Mehitabel Higginson, whose school catered to Salem's first families. At seven, Will was enrolled in the school of Jacob Newman Knapp, who recalled him with solemn candor as "a bright, merry boy, with an inquisitive mind, quick perceptions, and ready, retentive memory. His lessons were generally well learned; but he loved play better than books. . . . He never fancied rude or athletic sports, but amused himself with such boys of his own age as preferred games requiring no great physical strength." Will appears to have been fond of such practical jokes as sneaking up behind maids and saying boo.

When Judge Prescott moved his family to Boston in 1808, Will was enrolled in the home school of the Reverend Dr. John Gardiner, rector of Trinity (Episcopal) Church, whose splendid Romanesque architecture and cloistered passageways still grace Boston's elegant Copley Square. Prescott remained with Dr. Gardiner until 1811, beginning a friendship with his elder that would last through life, and striking up an acquaintance with George Ticknor, four years his senior, who would prove his friendship in a darker hour. Carefree, vivacious, popular without trying, Will learned more Greek and Latin under Dr. Gardiner, it was said, than most Harvard men knew upon graduation. But the truth is that Prescott simply did not distinguish himself intellectually, even under these ideal auspices. Again in Rollo Ogden's words: "There are no records of precocity— no vision splendid. The boy was but such as his fellows— a trifle gayer by nature perhaps, but mainly just the playful, prankish 'apple-eating animal' that we expect the normal male of twelve or fourteen to be."

Prescott, nevertheless, entered Harvard as a sophomore in August, 1811, occupying the same room as his father before him and his son after him. Again, his academic career fell short of excellence. "There was nothing discreditable about it," one biographer writes. "It was simply not distinguished." Even Prescott's most friendly—not to say pious—biographer, George Ticknor, concedes his friend's rather callow approach to his studies. "It was difficult for [Prescott] . . ." Ticknor observes, "to make the sacrifices indispensable to give him the position of a real scholar. He adopted, indeed, rules for the hours, and even the minutes, that he would devote to each particular study; but he was so careful never to exceed them, that it was plain that his heart was not in the matter." Like Parkman, Prescott, in his own words, "gave little attention to the mathematics and the sister sciences," and, like Parkman, he used his leisure as a gentleman-dilettante to read his favorite authors, the romantic Byron, Scott, Irving, Longfellow. "It was a matter of taste, with me," Prescott explained, "but considering my subsequent occupations, I have not found reason to regret it."

Prescott, in short, behaved at Harvard precisely as the canons of Brahmin Boston expected him to behave. He was "joyous and light-hearted," a classmate recalls, "without any enemies, with nothing but friends."

This idyllic interlude in the young patrician's life, however, was to be shattered in a Harvard dining hall. Leaving the table one day in the midst of a student melee, Prescott turned sharply around to see what prank was then being perpetrated by his fellow undergraduates, and he was struck in the left eye by a hard crust of bread thrown at him in fun. "The blow was a fearful one in its nervous effects," a biographer writes, "striking Prescott down as by a rifle bullet. No external mark, then or later, was left on the eye, but it was made instantly and incurably sightless." Prescott's retina was paralyzed, but, worse still, he would remain haunted throughout life by the fear that he would lose the sight of his right eye, too.

Absent from college for a while, Prescott returned to his books more mature and sober, and despite his grave disability, mustered the grit and self-discipline to study harder. On August 24, 1814, he graduated as a Harvard bachelor of arts, Phi Beta Kappa, and was feted by Judge Prescott, at a dinner for 500 guests held in a tent.

Judge Prescott had hoped that his son would do the gentlemanly thing and prepare for the bar, and Will dutifully began reading law. But in 1815, two years after his left eye had been struck blind, Prescott's *right* eye was stricken with acute inflammation, with awful consequences. Blind for days at a time, cut down by a potentially fatal fever, he endured one of the most critical hours of his life. "When at last he recovered," a biographer reports, "it was found that the cause of the trouble . . . was a form of acute rheumatism which permanently affected the retina. For periods of several years at a time no reading or writing was possible," and Prescott was what he had feared most, "sometimes totally blind." For the rest of his life, William Prescott would remain unable to use his one "good" eye except, in general, for a few to ten minutes at a time.

In search of relief, perhaps as much from Boston as from his affliction, Prescott sailed, in September, 1815, to the island of São Miguel in the Azores, where his maternal grandfather, Thomas Hickling, was United States consul. But again, in the relentless sunlight of the island, Prescott's eye became violently inflamed, and he fled into his grandfather's home, where for three months he was confined to a room, pacing about "in such total darkness," he wrote his parents, that "it was impossible to distinguish objects in the room." Once outside, he was forced to tie a handkerchief over a pair of goggles to preserve his health.

During these three lonely months, Prescott professed to have remained in good spirits, giving out in gay song and declaiming poetry. But the measure of his despair, despite his bravado, is surely taken in the solitary word that he entered in his diary in ninety days: "Darkness."

A visit to London's eminent oculist, Sir William Adams, in 1815, confirmed Prescott's case as hopeless. He confessed that he "could not bear candle light," and expressed the fear that as a result "I shall never be able to draw up my mind to any large amount." Undaunted still, Prescott visited Oxford and Cambridge, took in the debates in Parliament, and toured the Continent, meeting Lafayette in Paris. But they were bitter days for the young Bostonian. His friend Ticknor visited him in the French capital, offering comfort in distress. "It was in that dark room," Ticknor recalled, "that I first learned to know him, as I have never known any other person beyond the limits of my immediate family, and it was there that was first formed a mutual regard, over which, to the day of his death,—a period of above forty years—no cloud ever passed."

Home at twenty-one, Prescott enjoyed wide popularity as "a man-about-town . . . accepted in the best circles," including the White House of John Quincy Adams. His bright repartee and cavalier charm were not only welcomed, but sought out. To be sure, not everyone in Victorian Boston took kindly to his bantering gaiety. For Prescott's behavior at one social gathering, Richard Henry Dana, Jr., took him to task in his journal. "Prescott," Dana wrote, "found great fault with long hair, & blew up all persons who wear long hair. My hair was long, but P. always makes such mistakes & then is sorry for them. He is noted for it. . . ." And Dana added contemptuously: "If Prescott is not an ordinary man, I am no judge of cleverness. I did not know who he was until dinner was nearly over; & supposèd he was some ordinary mercantile man whom [his host] felt obliged to ask on account of some family connexion. This was not from his silence, but from the commonplace nature of his remarks." But most of Prescott's acquaintances enjoyed his "running over with animal spirits . . . his talking with joyous *abandon*," his "laughing at his own inconsequences." "If I were asked to name the man whom I have known whose coming was most sure to be hailed as a pleasant event by all whom he approached," Theophilus Parsons declared, "I should not only place Prescott at the head of the list, but I could not place any other man near him."

As for Prescott himself—ruddy, erect, handsome, brown-haired, and tall—he enjoyed to the teeth "jogging along" on what he called Boston's "old track—dinners, soirees, gossip—anything but hard study." At the same time to sustain what little vision he had left, he avoided late hours, watched his intake of wine (he abstained from liquor), observed a strict diet, and had no qualms about leaving social gatherings—even one he sponsored—to observe his scheduled bedtime. His most serious intellectual-social venture after his return from the Continent was the Tuesday evening Club, which he founded in June, 1818. The club issued an ingrown little publication called *The Club-Room*, to which members contributed politely. The magazine failed in a few years; the club persisted for over forty years.

On his twenty-fourth birthday, May 4, 1820, William Prescott was married to Susan Amory, daughter of a wealthy Boston merchant. Miss Amory, in addition, was the granddaughter of the British Captain Lindsay whose sloop *Falcon*, firing from the Charles River, had bombarded old

Colonel Prescott's position at Bunker Hill. The heirloom swords of colonel and captain were crossed in peace on the wall of the Prescott library.

The newlyweds lived at Judge Prescott's Bedford Street home until in 1845, after the judge's death, they moved into their new home at 55 Beacon Street overlooking Boston Common. They spent prolonged seasons out of town: at the ancestral estate of Colonel Prescott at Pepperell, at a cliff-side cottage virtually hanging over the sea at elite Nahant, and later at a more sedate shore home at Lynn Bay, all in Massachusetts.

Susan Prescott bore the historian four children: Catherine, or "Kitty," who died in her fifth year; William Gardiner; Elizabeth; and William Amory. The Prescott marriage, if like the Danas' scarcely euphoric, appears to have been a congenial one. After twenty-five years with Susan, Prescott could say: "Contrary to the assertion of La Bruyère— who somewhere says, that the most fortunate husband finds reason to regret his condition at least once in twenty-four hours,—I may truly say that I have found no such day in the quarter of a century that Providence has spared us to each other."

It is likely that marital responsibility, social appearances, and the Puritan concept of work as redemptive conspired to edge Prescott into writing. And the thoroughly gentlemanly thing to do, writing critical reviews for the socially proper—and intellectually powerful—*North American Review*, Prescott did. He dismissed it airily as "my annual peppercorn for the Old North," but his reviews marked his baptism as a serious writer. Defying medical advice— as Parkman defied it—that he must abandon literary work if he wished to retain his vision and health, Prescott began writing for the *Review* in 1821, determined, he wrote, to offer articles to this journal "no oftener than once in three Numbers . . . no *oftener*, and *print* only what I think will *add* to my reputation." To nourish this less than passionate commitment, Prescott planned a course of reading on a catholic scale, which was reflected in such articles as "Byron's Letter on Pope," his analyses of Italian poetry, Molière, and Scottish songs, and his review of Irving's *Conquest of Granada*. These articles and reviews would be bound together in 1845 and published as *Biographical and Critical Miscellanies*. Prescott's life of the novelist Charles Brockden Brown appeared in 1834 and is remembered principally for editor Jared Sparks's twitting comment to Prescott on its typographical errors: "All your dates are 1493, etc.," Sparks reminded him. "This shows your mind was running on the age of Ferdinand and Isabella." In general however, Prescott gave no public hint of his work in process on the Spanish empire. Outwardly, he remained the patrician dilettante, doing the "in" thing, and, above all, giving a wide berth to that devil's workshop called idleness.

Precisely when or how forcefully Prescott's interest in writing the history of the Spanish empire took final form is difficult to ascertain. We know that after hearing Professor Ticknor read his Harvard lectures on Spanish literature in 1824, Prescott studied Spanish, and that Ticknor had supplied him with lists of relevant books, which his family and friends and, later, paid secretaries read to him. But we also know that it was only the difficulty of reading Gothic script that kept him from pursuing Germanic studies, then held in high esteem. Indeed, as late as December, 1824, William Hickling Prescott said of Spanish in a letter to the historian George Bancroft: "I doubt whether there are many valuable things that the key of knowledge will unlock in that language!" In point of fact, as Stanley T. Williams reminds us, Prescott's initial approach to the colossal history of imperial Spain in the fifteenth and sixteenth centuries was "tentative, vacillating, almost accidental," and smacked of what Williams calls Brahmin Boston's "gentle aversion of the eyes from any ugliness in the American scene." Prescott's delay, in the opinion of Emerson and other critics, was due no more to intellectual doubt than to a congenital indecisiveness, or marginal laziness. Even when he first seriously "adopted" the Spanish subject in 1826, he deferred his final decision until 1829.

Once involved in his grand project, however, Prescott embraced it with a fervor that rivalled Parkman's pursuit of Frontenac and La Salle. Like Parkman, Prescott was determined to rescue history from the pedants and the preachers, to breathe drama, color, life, and relevance into history, to free it from dusty shelves, to lift it to a level of literature transcending the "dreary annals of blood and battle." He was determined both to entertain and to inform. Sound history, he believed, must be both factual and dramatic, moving to an ineluctable climax. It must bear scrutiny "both as respects its scientific results and its execution as a work of art." It must have Scott's "natural relish for gunpowder . . . his mettle roused, like that of a war horse at the sound of the trumpet." It must be embellished with "the graces of romance." And it must be objective, for truth knows no national boundaries. "If I am retained by the Spaniards," Prescott would say, "I shall lose my reputation with every other people." In addition, he said, with one eye on the super-moralizers of his day, he was interested less in "reflections" than in hard "facts."

Prescott assumed his great task with stoical courage. "Shut out from one sense," he said, "I was driven exclusively on another, and to make the ear do the work of the eye." Ironically, he had been inspired by Samuel Johnson's lament that it was virtually impossible for a writer like the blind Milton to work through another's eyes. Johnson's statement had been "discouraging at first," Prescott wrote, but "in the end stimulated the desire to overcome" what seemed like an insurmountable obstacle.

Using a "noctograph" or writing device much like Parkman's, which enabled him, Prescott said, to write "as well in the dark as in the light," Prescott proceeded apace, following the Italian motto *Rapido, ma rapido con leggi* ("Swiftly, but swiftly with laws"), or disciplined schedule. From ten in the morning until dinner at three, Prescott dictated notes on material as it was read to him, "marking" important passages. Next he would have his notes read back to him up to twelve times until he had assimilated them. Then, his data mentally organized, and ultimately extending to seventy-two pages, the nearly blind historian would sit at his noctograph, put his pencil between the wires of the device, one after another, and compose his great histories, as rapidly as one chapter in three days.

With astonishing petulance, Francis Parkman had complained that "Prescott could see a little—confound him he could even look over his proofs," adding that he—Parkman —was "no better off than an owl in the sunlight." But, Prescott, almost twenty-seven years Parkman's senior, had a slight advantage at best, for, as we have seen, he was often reduced to total blindness. When everything has been said, his achievement was stupendous. Not satisfied with secondary documents or with the preachy histories of his day, and determined to get every available book and document on his subject, Prescott would send literally to every corner of Europe and North America, buying up crates and cartons of research material, including "good, gossipping chronicle[s] and memoir[s]." He enlisted the good offices or paid services of a score of officials and friends: Alexander Hill Everett, United States minister to Spain; Ángel Calderón de la Barca, first Spanish minister to Mexico; the Spanish scholar Pascual de Gayangos, an invaluable assistant and great historian in his own right; and, of course, his good friends Sparks and Ticknor. With this assistance, in Stanley Williams' words, Prescott "riveted his story to truth through the most tyrannical scholarship, including a meticulous transcription of manuscripts, and a fanatical devotion to footnotes." He was aided, too, by a prodigious ability to retain facts and ideas. "His memory for quotations and illustration is a miracle—quite disconcerting," the British essayist Macaulay observed. "He comes to a talk like one specially crammed. Yet you may start the topic."

To inaugurate his great history of Spain in her two centuries of imperial grandeur, Prescott chose to tell the story of the brilliant reign of Ferdinand and Isabella—a "most important" reign, Prescott announced, "as containing the germs of the modern system of European politics." And though plagued by renewed inflammation of his right eye, forcing him into a four-month seclusion in a darkened room, he pushed himself onward, determined to finish his work on the Spanish monarchs in five or six years.

A more dramatic subject, or one of greater natural interest to American readers Prescott could not have chosen. During Isabella's reign America was discovered and colonized; Ponce de León claimed Florida; Balboa and Pizarro sighted the Pacific at Darien; the Spanish Moors were conquered; and, supremely, the kingdoms of Castile, Aragon, and Granada were united under a single crown. Spain embraced Naples, Navarre, Sicily, Sardinia, the Canaries, parts of Africa, and North and South America, aided—and frustrated—by Papal bulls. Under these monarchs, too, an imperial church exploited religious credulity to impose the tragic Inquisition, inspired and guided by the guileful Torquemada, who, in the age of faith, exploited the queen's. Under this otherwise brilliant queen, the Jews, envied by the incompetent and poor for their primacy in science and the humane arts, were expelled from Spain. "Alas!" Prescott concludes, "that such a blight should have fallen on so gallant and generous a people" as the Spanish, counterbalancing Isabella's achievement, and worse still, closing up "the fair buds of science and civilization ere they were fully opened," and staying "the proud march of human reason."

But *Ferdinand and Isabella* transcends conquest and chronology. It is human portraiture so telling, so incisive that it "vied successfully," in one critic's words, "with the novels of the day," and is more exciting than most in ours. Here, drawn with ruthless perception, is Ferdinand's continuing jealousy of Isabella's primacy and his initial intention to abandon her by returning to his duchy of Aragon; here is Isabella's acuity in government, Joan-of-Arc daring on the field of battle, and calculating generosity in death; here is the panicking cruelty of Torquemada, the obtuse genius of Cardinal Jiménez; here is the fatuous King Alfonso of Portugal who, in challenging the accession of the Spanish monarchs, managed only to unite them in purpose.

Published in America on December 25, 1837, and in London a few weeks later, *Ferdinand and Isabella* was an instant success, celebrated and cherished by critics and laymen the world over. It earned for Prescott, writes biographer C. Harvey Gardiner, "the first significant international reputation gained by an American historian." Bancroft hailed it in the *Democratic Review*. Ticknor unabashedly promoted it. The French historian de Tocqueville and the Swiss historian Sismondi, Prescott's idols, expressed approval. And perhaps most important to Prescott, a voice from Spain, that of the great scholar Gayangos, saluted the classic for its "exquisite erudition and . . . [its] freedom from all political as well as religious bias." From England, normally reserved in its judgment of American efforts, came unalloyed praise: Lord Holland declared *Ferdinand and Isabella* "the most important historical work since Gibbon." The historian Henry Milman pronounced it "the greatest work that had yet proceeded from America." And the trenchant historian-critic Richard Ford said outright: "I know of no modern author of greater perseverance, research, and accuracy, nor one possessing [Prescott's] talent of placing facts agreeably and truly before his reader." To be sure Prescott, like Parkman, incurred the pettifogging wrath of the Reverend Theodore Parker, who professed to find this work unparalleled as "a history in the English language, of any note, so entirely destitute of Philosophy," presumably Parker's own.

Few shared the clergyman's regret. Three-fifths of the first 500-copy, 3-volume edition—selling at an astonishing $7.50 in that era—was sold in Boston before a copy could be sent to New York, and the entire edition was exhausted in five weeks. England greeted it with comparable enthusiasm, and it was translated into German, Italian, French, Spanish, and Russian. Today, the work remains popular and respected after 147 printings, in at least six languages.

Intellectual honors crowned financial success, as *Ferdinand and Isabella* earned for Prescott membership in thirty-three learned societies at home and abroad: the Royal Academy of History at Madrid, which he especially cherished; the United States' oldest learned society, the American Philosophical Society; the Royal Academy of Science at Naples; London's Royal Society of Literature; and, in 1843, an honorary Harvard degree of Doctor of Laws.

Prescott wore his honors well, content, he wrote, that he had written "a book illustrating an unexplored and important period, from authentic materials," and "a plain, veracious record of facts," which "till someone else shall be found to make a better one, will fill up a gap in literature which, I should hope, will give it a permanent value." He had told Bancroft: "My object, you know, has not been gain, but an honest reputation." "Fortunately," he added, "I am not driven to write for *bread*; and I never will write for money." Indeed, he and Judge Prescott had spent $4,500 to defray the costs of printing, engraving, and publishing and research material for Prescott's first great work, or four and one-half times as much as the historian earned for the work in his first American contract. By March, 1844, however, affiliated with a new publisher, Prescott had realized some $7,000 on 4,500 of the books sold.

Prescott's achievement, at least in his own eyes, transcended both money and fame, sweet as they were. "Writing to me . . ." he said with Cicero, whose insight guided him, "is not so much for pleasure and glory, as for the enjoyment of study itself and the exercise of the mind, which nothing can snatch away from me." On a practical Yankee note, Prescott added, "If I be an ass of an historian, the public are greater asses to have endorsed me—that's some comfort."

Despite world acclaim, Prescott had concluded that *Ferdinand and Isabella* would be "the only civil history I shall ever attempt." Persuaded that his true interests lay in purely literary subjects, he contemplated writing a study of Molière, because, he reasoned rather frivolously, it "would make an agreeable book for the parlour table." But Prescott had been enthralled by the Spanish theme, and he now turned his eyes to Mexico, to the age of the *conquistadores*, a subject as grand as Isabella's imperial sway.

Published in America in October, 1843, the *History of the Conquest of Mexico*, relating the New World exploits of the great Hernando Cortés, confirmed Prescott's rank as a reigning historian in the epic voice. "It reads like a romance," George Ticknor told him. And to Prescott himself, the conquest of the Aztec overlords was "the most poetic subject ever offered to the pen of the historian," a story, he added, "too startling for the probabilities demanded by fiction, and without parallel in the pages of history."

The Conquest of Mexico is afire with Prescott's fervor as a scholar-adventurer: in the horror of the Aztecs' festive cannibalism and the ritual slaughter on their high pyramidal altars of countless thousands of human beings a year; in the gallantry and defiant daring of the 500 Spaniards, who, with twelve horses and ten brass guns, cultivated an alliance with oppressed Mexican natives to crush the empire of the mighty Montezuma and his hapless successor Guatemozin. In Prescott's stunning pages we relive the Spaniards' brazen seizure of Montezuma in his own palace in the presence of his guards, his subjects without; the storming of the great Aztec temple of Huitzilopochtli and the grisly battle at its altar summit, from which Cortés was almost thrown to his death; the Spanish conqueror's loving dependence on the bilingual Marina; Cortés' bitter, tearful retreat from the capital on the *Noche Triste,* or "Sorrowful Night," and his triumphant return to a three-day siege that brought the brave Aztecs to their knees.

Within a month of its publication, 4,000 copies of *The Conquest of Mexico* were sold. New honors came to the near-blind historian, still afflicted with pain—election to the *Institut de France* and to the Royal Academy of Berlin.

Prescott's *History of the Conquest of Peru,* depicting Francisco Pizarro's victory over the Inca empire, appeared in London in May and in New York in June, 1847. Five thousand copies were sold in America in five months and half as many more in Britain, translations appearing in German, French, Spanish, and Dutch. *The Conquest of Peru* does not equal the volume on Mexico in force or style, perhaps because Prescott lacked the empathy with Pizarro that he had with Cortés. But the passages describing the treacherous trek through the Andes, the confrontation with the Inca monarch Atahualpa, and the ghastly assassination of Pizarro, buried in his bloody shroud by dissident Spaniards, embody Prescott's best writing.

Depression followed Prescott's new success, for he was able to use his eyes, in mid-1848, for only ten minutes at a time and no longer than one hour a day, and was thus forced, as he put it, to "snail it along." "For a long time after the *Peru* was published," he confessed, "I hardly ventured to look into a book, and though I have grown bolder as I have advanced, my waning vision has warned me to manage my eye with much greater reserve than formerly." On his twenty-fifth wedding anniversary in 1845, to be sure, he expressed pleasure at the "sunny side" of his life, especially "a wife," he said, "who has shared my troubles real and imaginary, and my many blessings with the sympathy of another self." But as he reached forty-nine, he added: "I have many intimations that I am getting on the shady side of the hill, and as I go down, the shadows grow longer and darker." Prescott's melancholy note was brought on perhaps no less by his faltering vision than by the immense letdown an author feels after completing a work and confronting the disquieting loneliness that lies at the core of what men call success. Urged to write the history of the second "conquest" of Mexico—America's invasion of that country in 1848—Prescott discreetly declined: "I had rather not meddle," he said, "with heroes who have not been underground two centuries at least," adding later: "I belong to the sixteenth century, and am quite out of place when I sleep elsewhere."

The year 1850, however, was one to buoy Prescott's spirits. Early in the year he was the guest of President Zachary Taylor and Daniel Webster in Washington. And on May 22 he sailed from New York for a visit to England. It would be a much happier visit than that he had paid London thirty-four years before, when he was told that his left eye was incurable. No Herman Melville, however, Prescott found the voyage to Liverpool—a long siege of seasickness—beyond bearing. "Nothing," he said, "can redeem the utter wretchedness of a sea life—and never will I again put my foot in a steamer, except for Yankee land, and if I were not ashamed, should reembark in the Saturday steamer from Liverpool."

Prescott's malaise swiftly gave way to the splendid social and professional reception that awaited him in the land of his forbears. Oxford awarded him an honorary doctorate of civil law. He was presented at the Court of Saint James, he reported merrily, in "gold-laced coat, white inexpressibles, silk hose, gold-buckled patent slippers, sword and cha- peau. . . ." He dined with Queen Victoria, noting her prodigious appetite, chatted with Wellington, Peel, and Dis- raeli, and slept in eerie old castles. Macaulay paid him the backhanded compliment of asking how a man of his quali- ties could bring himself to go back to Boston.

After touring the Continent—excepting Spain!—Prescott set to work in Boston amassing and digesting the "370 vol- umes, fifteen thick folios of copies of manuscripts . . . plus the equivalent of eight or ten more volumes . . . bound and unbound" that would enrich his fourth major work, the *History of the Reign of Philip II*. Volumes one and two of this work appeared in America in December, 1855, vol- ume three in December, 1858.

Philip II was a massive undertaking—in effect the history of all Europe during the latter half of the sixteenth century, a burden made heavier by Prescott's steadily increasing dif- ficulties with his one good eye. Philip II headed what was then Europe's most formidable monarchy at the height of the Protestant Reformation. The study of Philip's inter- ventionist policies as the champion of established Cathol- icism forced Prescott, through his allies in research, into state archives in London, Belgium, Vienna, the Hague, Paris, Madrid, Simancas (Spain). His book, if less unified dramatically, less arresting in portraiture, and rather dis- connected in story line, nevertheless crowned Prescott's career as a historian in the epic dimension. What Gibbon had proved of the rise and fall of Rome, Prescott now proved of Spain's inexorable decline under the very mon- arch who wore her jewels most grandly. He saw in Philip's reign "already disclosed those germs of domestic corruption which gradually led to [the Spanish empire's] dismemberment and decay." Prescott's revised edition of William Robertson's *History of the Reign of the Emperor Charles V*, to which Prescott added a section on "The Life of Charles V After His Abdication," completed the historical cycle that began with Isabella's accession to the throne in 1479 and ended with Philip II's death in 1598, ten years after the disastrous defeat of the Spanish Armada.

"Your laurels are very green, and grow fast," Ticknor wrote Prescott from London in 1857. Indeed, as Irwin Blacker notes, Prescott became "the most frequently published and widely sold historian in America." In 1853 his net income, although derived largely from industrial investments, totalled $27,739, with expenses of $22,819.24. It was sheer luxury for Prescott's time, but it was shared wealth, too, for Prescott "tithed," giving one tenth of his income to a number of charities, notably Massachusetts' Perkins School for the Blind, which he helped to found.

Prescott practiced the most rigid economy, recording the minutest expenditure, and he left a larger estate than he inherited. He could be harsh in his treatment of members of what he called "the slippery trade," meaning the book business, once scolding his British publisher Richard Bentley for delay in acknowledging receipt of a manuscript: "You are a very bad Transatlantic correspondent, and fancy you are dealing with some North country squire whom you can answer by next post, if too late for this." No more gentle with his family in money matters, he once reprimanded his son William Gardiner for excessive spending and waste, announcing that he would make up the deficiency by taking the boy's cash birthday presents from his grandfather until the balance was paid.

Though he made most of his money from it, Prescott affected the Brahmin Bostonian's studied contempt for commerce, disparaging educated men who were satisfied with holding, as he put it, "the noble post of head of a cotton factory," and deploring the fact that the rush of business left America "no time to reflect—little to study— except as this last prepares us to act." "I wish," he said, "we had a little more of the liberal tastes shown by John Bull when his bags are well lined." Politically and religiously, Prescott toed the proper Bostonian mark. He was a conservative Whig, which is to say a Federalist, attended the Unitarian church and, no doubt because of his industrial interests, had no sympathy for the Abolitionists. During the Mexican War, he simply expressed the hope that advantage would be taken of America's occupation of Mexico City to encourage on-the-spot studies of Aztec sites and manuscripts. The war itself he dismissed as "most honorable to our arms, as all [*sic*] must admit, whatever one may think," he added in a clear reference to Democratic President James K. Polk, "of the counsels that rushed us into it." The French Revolution, by contrast, was "a lamentable comedy," as every good Federalist would agree.

Despite such limitations of class and time, Prescott emerges as a man of incalculable courage and rare humanity. He transformed what, in most instances, would have been a fatal liability into a talent for concentration, hard work, and self-discipline that few men have mastered. And he had no truck with self-pity. "I can't say that I like to be called blind," he said, though for long periods he was precisely that. "I have, it is true, but one eye; but that has done me some service, and, with fair usage, will, I trust, do me some more."

One's dominant impression of the man, apart from his

work, is one of cavalier gaiety and boyish charm, a man at ease with life's best—in one critic's words, "loyal to his club, an inveterate diner-out [at what he called his 'croney-ings'], a connoisseur of wines." By turns droll and in-genuous, Prescott "could be happy," a friend said, "in more ways and more happy in every one of them than any other person I have ever known." And this man, who, in Daniel Webster's words again, had "burst upon the world like a comet," was happiest, as he grew older, at his ancestral retreat at Pepperell. There he relished "the sweet sense of security from friends—the worst foes to time," and reveled in games, walks, family song, and story-telling, his grand-children in worshiping attendance.

While preparing the third volume of *Philip II* on Febru-ary 4, 1858, Prescott had sustained and recovered from an apoplectic stroke. On January 28, 1859, in bright spirits in his Beacon Street home, he was stricken again. Just a few years before, loyal George Ticknor had found him "as fresh as ever, with twenty good years of work in him." Now Prescott died, at work on a fourth volume on King Philip, at work on a revised edition of *The Conquest of Mexico*.

Three days before his death, discussing the passing of a relative with his son, William Amory, Prescott wrote: "The evening of life is coming over those of our generation, and we must be prepared to say farewell to one another." Now Boston said farewell to him—the well born, the learned, the poor he had aided, the blind he had inspired. A clause in his will, ordering that his major vein be severed to preclude his being buried alive, was honored. This done, he lay in state in his library among the books he loved, again as he had ordered. He was buried in the Prescott family crypt in Saint Paul's Episcopal Cathedral in the heart of Boston.

HENRY WADSWORTH LONGFELLOW

HE SAW THE "AUTUMN WITHIN"

Queen Victoria had seen nothing like it before. She had agreed to receive the American gentleman on no less than the Fourth of July. But this audience was extraordinary in another way. "I noticed an unusual interest among the attendants and servants," Victoria recalled. "I could scarcely credit that they so generally understood who he was. When he took leave, they concealed themselves in places from which they could get a good look at him as he passed. I have since inquired among them, and am surprised and pleased to find that many of his poems are familiar to them. No other distinguished person has come here that has excited so peculiar an interest. Such poets wear a crown that is imperishable."

To be sure, not everyone accepted the queen's coronation of Henry Wadsworth Longfellow, poet, of Cambridge, Massachusetts. Edgar Allan Poe, for one, dismissed Longfellow's conception of poetry as *all wrong* and accused him of plagiarism. Margaret Fuller, mother superior of the Concord Transcendentalists, considered him "artificial," given to metaphors both unoriginal and mixed, and found in his verse "a hollow, second-hand sound."

But most of the world, from Victoria's court to Victor Hugo, shared the queen's adulation. The brooding French poet Baudelaire, tending his "flowers of evil," acknowledged Longfellow's genius and influence. Over his teacups in Boston, Oliver Wendell Holmes saluted him as "our chief singer," a poet who "wins and warms . . . kindles, softens, cheers [and] calms the wildest woe and stays the bitterest tears!" On hearing "The Building of the Ship" and its famous line "Thou, too, sail on, O Ship of State!" President Lincoln wept, hailing Longfellow's "wonderful gift" of stirring men. Hawthorne lauded his first book of poems,

Voices of the Night: "Nothing equal to some of them," said the author of *The Scarlet Letter*, "was ever written in this world,—this western world, I mean; and it would not hurt my conscience much to include the other hemisphere."

Longfellow's popularity would grow to such proportions that criticizing him, as Bliss Perry puts it, would become an act as criminal as "carrying a rifle into a national park." His poetry, for good or ill, would touch the heart of Americans as none before it or since. "There was the little girl," one biographer recalls, "who, being asked in Sunday School to name the book that all good people loved to read, at once named Longfellow's poems." His rhyme and rhythm at once reflected and helped shape the American character, ideology, and language for over seventy-five years: The "pause in the day's occupation that is known as the children's hour"; the "midnight ride of Paul Revere"; the "village blacksmith" sweating in honest toil, in debt to no man; Priscilla Mullins' "Why don't you speak for yourself, John?"; "Life is real, life is earnest. . . .Let us then be up and doing"; even, perhaps, the charming doggerel about the little girl who "had a little curl right in the middle of her forehead."

To a nation sundered by Civil War, presidential assassination, the revelations of Darwinism, Reconstruction atrocities, political corruption, and massive immigration, Longfellow sang a sedative song of faith, trust, and optimism, re-creating in verse at once lucid and sentimental a purer, less frantic American past: the Indian Hiawatha, the noble Evangeline pathetically seeking her lost lover. Amid upheaval he preached serenity, telling his countrymen not, perhaps, what they had to hear, but what they wanted to hear, and telling it in language as plain as a chestnut tree.

In the shock and disillusion of world war, and as the style and purpose of poetry radically changed, Longfellow's reputation and influence, especially among academic critics, declined sharply. "Longfellow is to poetry," one critic declared in 1915, "what the barrel organ is to music." In the Depression of the 1930s, another said with contempt: "Who, except wretched schoolchildren, now reads Longfellow? . . . The thing to establish in America is not that Longfellow was a very small poet, but that he did not partake of the poetic character at all." Others derided the white-bearded poet as maudlin, preachy, repetitive, impervious to reality and the tempestuous changes about him. "Between him and the actual American scene," even a kindly biographer wrote, "there intervened an Indian summer haze, dreamily dim, which blurred and softened every hue and line and angle, hiding the coarse and the familiar, substituting the colors of the heart's desire."

But if once over-praised, Longfellow became, surely, over-abused. His poetry does not, to be sure, speak to the age of the Atom and of Freud. If we are to pronounce Shakespeare and Dante great, we cannot so honor Longfellow. But critical appraisal of his work is less harsh and more balanced than it was. His narrative power, notably in *Tales of a Wayside Inn*, is conceded. He is no longer blamed for not sharing the disillusions and conceits of hard-nosed "modern" poets who followed him, no longer subjected to what a critic has called "the vicious fashion of testing poets by single flashing lines or isolated passages," missing the gentle, nostalgic beauty of poems like "My Lost Youth." Nor is Longfellow judged by the canons of almost deliberately obscure modern poets, who, in the words of the German philosopher Friedrich Nietzsche, "muddy their water that it may appear deep." In the many-mansioned house of American poetry, Longfellow is granted his proper room, not as large as it was, but still tidy and warm. Biographer Newton Arvin speaks for the new critic, when he notes an occasional timelessness in Longfellow's best poetry and warns that "our literature is not so rich in writing of this kind that we can afford to discard any of it."

Equally important, the image of Longfellow as a bearded old man, looking down benignly from a thousand classroom walls, is a false image. Behind the beard lie the scars from the fire that killed his wife before his eyes. Behind the face of complacent old age lie bitter years of sexual torment, neurosis, and "moments of panic," and the memory of a schoolboy in Maine so sensitive to "rude excitements" and the taunts of rough-and-tumble classmates that he had to be taken home and sent to a private school. Behind the solemn portrait was a living man subject to the heartache and despair all men must face. If his poetry could be shallow and over-sweet, his life was not.

Henry Wadsworth Longfellow was born on February 27, 1807, in Portland, in what was then known as the District of Maine, then part of Massachusetts. Though still ringed by virgin forests, Portland was a thriving town enriched by clipper ship trade in fish, molasses, and rum, and by farming and logging. "Harry" was the second of eight children, of whom he and his brother, the Reverend Samuel, were the most distinguished.

Four years younger than Emerson, ten years older than Thoreau, Longfellow took pride in his paternal grandfather Stephen's descent from early New England settlers, his service in the Massachusetts legislature and as a judge in the Court of Common Pleas. Grandfather Stephen cut an arresting, if anachronistic figure, well into the nineteenth century, in colonial dress—"long-skirted waistcoat, small-clothes, and white-topped boots, his hair tied behind in a club, with a black ribbon." General Peleg Wadsworth, his mother's father, also traced his ancestry back to the New England pilgrims, to no less than John and Priscilla Alden, whom Longfellow would immortalize in *The Courtship of Miles Standish*. General Wadsworth commanded the entire eastern department of Maine in the Revolutionary War, kept a store, served in Congress, and in retirement kept his powder dry while drilling his neighborhood militia in readiness for any Indian attack.

Henry's Federalist father, Stephen, was a lawyer, "stately, grave, a little pompous, but generous, humane . . . and filled with a high sense of public responsibility." He, too, was a member of Congress, a founder of Bowdoin College, and president of the Maine Historical Society. There is no question of his affection for Henry, but his letters, like Prescott's father's, strike the modern ear as coldly impersonal and politely impatient with his son's literary ambitions. While he ultimately took great pride in his son's literary success, Stephen Longfellow, from the beginning, would have preferred that his son follow the time-honored path to financial and social success in the practice of law.

In his mother, Zilpah, Longfellow found an ally in his love of books. Zilpah's influence on her son, throughout life, was decisive. Though described as "a nervous invalid," she kindled and shared Henry's enthusiasm for reading—the *Arabian Nights, Don Quixote, Robinson Crusoe*—led the family in Bible readings on Sundays, and conducted a lifelong correspondence of ideas with her son. She loved music, too, accompanied her children in song on Portland's first known piano, and had Henry given lessons in singing, the piano, and the flute. The young boy preferred martial music.

If not wealthy, the Longfellows lived most comfortably in Portland's first brick house, in an atmosphere, writes biographer Edward Wagenknecht, of "Puritan highmindedness . . . shorn of all its early hardness and fanaticism." But the boy's life in Portland was scarcely tranquil. Off Casco Bay he could hear the naval gunfire of the War of 1812 and visits to the farm Grandfather Peleg ran in the forests of Hiram, Maine, offered challenge and adventure to an imaginative lad. But Henry, when all is said, was a nervous, sedentary child. The sound of Fourth of July fireworks so upset him that he "begged to have cotton put in his ears." Books were his deliverance, and he pored eagerly over the English nature poets, James Thomson and Oliver Goldsmith, and America's first great nature poet, William Cullen Bryant, to whom Longfellow later acknowledged a major debt. Washington Irving's *Sketch-Book* was a special favorite: "Every reader has his first book;" Longfellow recalled, "I mean to say, one book among all others which in early youth first fascinates his imagination and at once excites and satisfies the desires of the mind."

At Portland Academy, where he and his brother Stephen prepared for college, Longfellow was known as "a studious and conscientious, not a rebellious, small boy. He fared better in Latin grammar than boys twice his age and was at home with Cicero and Virgil. With his piano and flute teacher, Charles Nolcini—who would prove a decisive influence on his career as a linguist—Longfellow learned French.

Longfellow's first published poem, "The Battle of

Lovell's Pond," commemorating "a desperate [Patriot] encounter with the savages," appeared when he was thirteen in the *Portland Gazette*, after a rival newspaper declined to publish it and Henry demanded its return. After waiting in anguish for the appearance of his first poem, he cried himself to sleep when a family friend, not realizing that the poem, signed simply "Henry," was his, condemned it in his presence as "very stiff" and plagiarized.

Although Stephen Longfellow was a Harvard man, he was a trustee as well as a founder of Bowdoin College in Brunswick, Maine. This personal interest in Bowdoin, buttressed by Maine's new pride as an independent state, determined his choice of Bowdoin as the proper college for his son. Henry and Stephen Jr. were formally admitted to the school in 1821, but, judged too young to live alone in rural Brunswick, were required to study their first college year at Portland Academy. In 1822, the brothers entered the college as resident sophomores to pursue its Harvard-based curriculum of the classics, Holy Scripture, mathematics, philosophy, and natural science.

A classmate but not yet a friend of Hawthorne, Henry dutifully followed Bowdoin's Spartan regimen of compulsory six o'clock morning prayers, with his first class immediately following, and, only then, breakfast at the parson's. Longfellow studied at least hard enough, he said, not to be "more deficient than the rest of the class." And he appears to have been "normal" enough to defy evening curfew and fill his cup at nearby Ward's Tavern. In this regard, however, his conduct was more decorous than that of young Stephen, who was suspended for smuggling liquor into his dormitory in innocent-looking new kerosene cans. Henry showed a rather different form of independence in defying Bowdoin's stiff-necked Congregationalism to establish the college's first Unitarian society.

As an undergraduate, Longfellow contributed essays and poems to Portland papers, the *American Monthly Magazine*, and the *United States Literary Gazette*. Inspired by Professor Thomas Cogswell Upham, young champion of a native American literature free of obsequious imitation of European models, Longfellow wrote almost forty poems between January, 1824, in his junior year, and late 1825. The time was ripe, he thought, for a new American literature, and if his own literary skill fell far short of his mature work, he was already demonstrating a prodigious ambition and capacity for sustained work.

On December 5, 1824, Longfellow announced to his father: "The fact is,—and I will not disguise it in the least . . . I most eagerly aspire after future eminence in literature, my whole soul burns most ardently after it." In defiance of his father's wishes, he declared his unwillingness to enter the law. But Stephen Longfellow was immovable. He conceded his son's literary potential, even his "genius & taste," but he insisted that the United States had neither the wealth nor the will to support "merely literary men." At the same time, he granted Henry's request for one year of graduate study at Harvard to deepen his knowledge of French and Italian, before he began reading law. Henry deferred to his father's wishes with impudence: "I can be a lawyer," he told his father, "for some lawyers are mere simpletons. This will support my *real* existence, literature an *ideal* one."

Graduating fourth in a class of thirty-nine, in 1825, Longfellow delivered a memorable commencement address to an audience including young Hawthorne, soon to return to his lonely years in Salem. In his address, Longfellow called for an American poetry that was more than a pastime, urged his countrymen to give encouragement and financial patronage to native authors, to rise above Americans' "aversion to everything that is not practical. . . ." And he appealed to his fellow authors to cease thinking of literature as an avocation, to develop a "conviction of the glory of their calling," and to abandon all else in "a noble self-devotion to the cause of literature."

Longfellow found his own liberation from the practical world of law and profit-seeking when Bowdoin offered him its newly created post of professor of modern languages. There was one stipulation. While Henry's mastery of the classical languages—a decisive factor in his choice—was recognized, so was his deficiency in modern languages. Accordingly, his appointment was made contingent upon his studying abroad, at his own expense, before assuming his post. Longfellow was ecstatic. He had not only escaped a career of drudgery in the law. His dream of actually visiting romantic places he had merely read about in Irving, and Scott, and Cervantes was about to come true!

In the spring of 1826, despite his mother's fear of his "going into a thousand perils," he embarked for Europe and a tour of the continent from which he would not return for three years. To France and the Paris theater, to Spain and the Escorial, to Italy and the Roman carnival and the pomp of the Vatican, to Germany and Dresden coffee houses and Rhine castles, the fair-haired, blue-eyed Yankee wandered gayly off. Lieutenant Alexander Slidell, a traveling companion, leaves this picture of the romantic American Byron: "He was just from college, full of all the ardent feeling excited by classical pursuits, with health unbroken, hope that was a stranger to disappointment, curiosity that had never yet been fed to satiety."

To his sisters at home, young Henry wrote: "I assure you that by every language you learn, a new world is opened before you." He affirmed his increasing competence in French, Spanish, Portuguese, and German, insisting that he was taken for an Italian at a hotel until he presented his passport. On balance, however, Longfellow's grand tour of the continent was precisely that, impressive less for its scholastic commitment than for its all too human interludes of simple tourism, romantic flirtations—notably one rather torrid affair in Italy that seems to have aroused even Stephen Longfellow's suspicions—and Longfellow's disillusionment as he confronted the great historic sites of Europe, even lovely Florence. Except at Göttingen, where he studied German under the man who taught Ticknor and at Madrid where he employed an instructor, Longfellow never enrolled formally in any sustained course of study during his three years abroad, content with what linguistic skills he could acquire in lodging houses or on the road. His letters to his father are filled with transparent evasions concerning his academic progress and plans. Even his verse suffered, despite the challenge of Europe. "My poetic career is finished," he informed his sisters. "Since I left America, I have hardly put two lines together." He repeatedly begged for extensions of his time abroad until his father, exasperated by his dilettantism and delays, ordered him home.

Even at Bowdoin, after winning a battle with the trustees, who had sought to demote him to the role of instructor, the young professor was restless, despite every evidence of success. Between 1830 and 1832 he edited or translated six texts in French, Spanish, and Italian. He appears to have enjoyed teaching, at least juniors and seniors. In 1833, his first translation in book form, the *Coplas* [ballads] *de Jorge Manrique* appeared, and his second, *Outre-Mer*, an account of a pilgrim's travels and trials beyond the sea, was published in 1835. His students liked him, one lauding his "charming courtesy . . . his earnest and dignified demeanor . . ." adding that "a better teacher, a more sympathetic friend, never addressed a class of young men." Even his thirst for literary eminence was at least lessened by the publication of linguistic articles in the prestigious *North American Review*. And he experienced great happiness in his marriage on September 14, 1831, to Mary Storer Potter, daughter of a prominent Portland judge. An old classmate at Portland Academy, Mary was dark-haired and blue-eyed, and possessed "a sweet expression, and dignified though dainty bearing." She helped Henry directly in his work, even in writing his lectures, and appears to have borne patiently the burdens of life in rural Brunswick and marriage to an ill-paid young professor. "I have never seen a woman," Longfellow told Mary's father, "in whom every look and word, and action seemed to proceed from so gentle and innocent a spirit."

Still Longfellow was unhappy at Bowdoin, impatient with such details as correcting papers. "I hate the sight of pen, ink, and paper," he told a friend. "I do not believe that I was born for such a lot. I have aimed higher than this: and I cannot believe that all my aspirations are to terminate in the drudgery of a situation, which gives me no opportunity to distinguish myself, and in point of worldly gain, does not even pay me for my labor."

Rising above what he considered pointless drudgery,

Longfellow, while at Bowdoin—in a review of an American edition of Sir Philip Sidney's *Defence of Poesie*—would write a credo of American literary independence that still does credit to his insight and prophetic power. Five years before Emerson's "The American Scholar," while Thoreau, Melville, and Lowell were schoolboys, he attacked in the pages of the *North American Review* the heartless commercial spirit of his age. "We are swallowed up," he wrote, "in schemes for gain, and engrossed with contrivances for bodily enjoyments, as if this particle of dust were immortal, —as if the soul needed no aliment, and the mind no raiment." America was obsessed, he said, with territorial expansion and commercial profit, with the conquest of industry over nature. "Yet, the true glory of a nation," Longfellow declared, "consists not in the extent of its territory . . . the height of its mountains . . . but in the extent of its mental power . . . the height and depth and purity of its moral nature. It consists not in what nature has given to the body, but in what nature and education have given to the mind. . . ." Americans, Longfellow said, "are too apt to think that nothing is useful, but what is done with a noise, at noonday, and at the corners of streets; as if action and utility were synonymous, and it were not as useless to act without thinking, as it is to think without acting." It was time, Longfellow concluded, to end our fatuous equation of the arts with ornamental effeminacy, to realize that the state needs its writers and poets as much as its traders and bankers and diplomats, to recognize that art has its origin and justification in our authors' obedience to Sidney's command: "Look in thy heart and write."

It was a splendid credo, one that still gives life to the continuing dialogue on the American character and purpose. It was an angry Longfellow, a Longfellow demanding recognition of the arts. It was Thoreau before Thoreau, the cry of Ishmael for identity long before the *Pequod* sailed. And beyond its national import, it perhaps reflected, too, the loneliness and frustration of an ambitious, widely traveled young man in provincial Maine. In vain Longfellow had sought appointments at New York University, at the American legation in Madrid, at the University of Virginia. He was almost desperate for the world's esteem. "The only consolation I have," he told a friend, "is that at some future day I shall be forced to go back to Europe again for nobody in this part of the world pretends to speak anything but English—and some," he added with contempt, "might dispute them even that prerogative."

All the while, Longfellow had carefully maintained contact with friends in Cambridge, no doubt with the hope of a Harvard appointment. This was granted in 1835 in a letter from President Josiah Quincy offering him the position of Smith Professor of Modern Languages to succeed George Ticknor. In the same letter, Quincy advised Longfellow that a year in Europe to deepen the poet's knowledge of German was in order.

A delighted Longfellow, armed with letters of introduction from Emerson and Jared Sparks, was off again for the continent, accompanied by his wife. His second visit to Europe was more scholarly than his first. He enrolled at Heidelberg, immersing himself in the works of Goethe and Schiller and, traveling through northern Europe, acquiring skill in Dutch, Danish, Swedish, Finnish, Icelandic. He met bright lights of the romantic, post-Napoleonic Europe of the "medieval revival," including Carlyle, and was, again, happy in the role of wandering gentleman scholar.

Mary's death in Rotterdam, from an infection caused by a miscarriage, ended the poet's idyll in late November, 1835. Longfellow had his wife's body embalmed and shipped back to America for burial. He remained behind, attempting to seek solace in study. He failed. "One thought occupies me night and day," he wrote. "She is dead—she is dead! All day I am weary and sad—and at night I cry myself to sleep like a child. . . . Sometimes I think I am crazed— and then I rally and think it only nervous disability. . . ."

Weary of Heidelberg, he decided to go home in June, 1836, planning a visit en route to Italy. Passport difficulties precluded this visit, and Longfellow went instead to Switzerland, where, in July, 1836, he met—and fell in love with— Frances Appleton, daughter of a wealthy Boston industrialist. "Fanny" Appleton enjoyed Longfellow's German lessons and delighted in helping him translate romantic ballads, but she did not requite his love.

At Harvard in December, 1836, Longfellow assumed his new professorship in a manner so grand that he would be pronounced "the First Citizen of Cambridge." After a stint in a students' boarding house, he moved into the elegant Craigie House, Washington's Revolutionary headquarters in Cambridge. His day was predictable and pleasant: a hot cup of mocha, a walk at sunrise, a few lines of translation from Dante, then off to the lecture room, urbanely introducing undergraduates to the culture of Europe. His course in *Faust* was the first in any American college. His translations, in several languages, spanned the trivial to the *Divina Commedia*. "He could talk French with Frenchmen, Italian with Italians, and German with Germans," a student recalls, adding that while Longfellow could be so "very flowery and bombastical" as to be "out of taste," his "regular translation and explanation part of [a] lecture" was "very good."

At least once, Longfellow confessed his resentment at having his mind "constantly a playmate for boys," forced to adapt to their limited view rather than "stretching out and grappling with *men's* minds." He was, nonetheless, very popular with the students. They liked his cosmopolitan dash, his delight in the exotic, his ability to make literature come alive, the very fact that he had been in Europe. "His mind," writes Van Wyck Brooks, "was like a music-box, charged with all the poetry of the world. Students appreciated his precedent-shattering courtesy in calling them "Mr.," and during student demonstrations would listen to him as to no other.

But life in Cambridge for Henry Wadsworth Longfellow was not wholly academic. Although his alarming bright waistcoat gave way to Harvard's quiet black frock coat and cane, Longfellow cut a cavalier figure in the streets and salons of Cambridge—in Margaret Fuller's eyes, "a dandy Pindar." With Prescott and a law professor named Charles Sumner, he drank wine, sang German songs. He found joy in his lyre-shaped garden, in afternoon horseback rides, in dinner at Boston's chic Parker House. And he loved his comfort: "I think it exquisite," he said, "to read good novels in bed with wax lights and silver candlesticks." Life was good to him. "Longfellow," Hawthorne observed, "appears to be no more conscious of any earthly or spiritual trouble than a sunflower is—of which lovely bloom, he, I know not why, reminded me."

Longfellow's tranquility was superficial. At heart he was deeply troubled. Across the Charles River, in Boston, a disdainful Fanny Appleton still refused his love. Subject to "periods of neurotic depression with moments of panic," Longfellow was forced in 1842 to take a six-month leave of absence from Harvard for therapy at Marienberg, a health spa near the Rhine. But there was no getting over Fanny Appleton. Dickens might later anoint her as "a very beautiful and gentle creature . . . a proper love for a poet," but, for almost seven years, she offered scant hope to the lovesick poet, even expressing the wish that "the venerable gentleman" would not "pop in on us," after his return from Europe in 1836.

Fanny's "beauty and dignity," James Russell Lowell observed, "are worth five hundred treatises on the rights of women." And to Longfellow, she was "the stately dark Ladie," a woman of acute intellect, vivacity, and bright independence. But Fanny, unmoved by Longfellow's ardent proposals of marriage, and angered by the publication of *Hyperion* in 1839—a novel in which Longfellow almost autobiographically revealed his love for her—dismissed Longfellow's mind as "a thing of shreds and patches," declared herself "entirely disgusted with the honor" or the notoriety the Cambridge poet had given her, adding that he was "more of a mocking-bird than a nightingale."

Longfellow was undeterred. "I shall win this lady or I shall die," he declared. It was, he believed, a war of wills, and he meant to win it. "The lady says she *will not!* I say she *shall!* It is not pride but the madness of passion. I visit her; sometimes pass an evening alone with her. But not one word is ever spoken on a certain topic. No whining—no beseeching—but a steel-like silence. This *is* pride. So we both stand eyeing each other like lions."

Longfellow won the war. On May 10, 1843, Fanny accepted him. Exultant, Longfellow walked, he said, "with the speed of an arrow" from Cambridge over the bridge that spanned the Charles to Boston, "with my heart full of gladness and my eyes full of tears." He was "too restless to sit in a carriage—too impatient and fearful of encountering anyone!" For Fanny, their engagement was a "great, inexpressible great joy," "a *true dream*—brighter than all my fictitious ones," and the once mocked poet now became for her "a nature . . . noble and gifted and true," a being of whom she felt unworthy.

Henry and Fanny were married on July 13, 1843, and moved into Craigie House, given to them as a wedding present by Fanny's father. They were deeply in love, miserable in each other's absence. Once, Longfellow said, he went to a ball without Fanny. "The lights seemed dimmer, the music sadder, the flowers fewer, and the women less fair." Fanny felt "broken and incomplete when he [was] absent a moment," found "infinite peace and fulfillment" in his presence. She was impatient with housework, which she cheerfully left to servants, and Longfellow declared that he would rather not eat if Fanny cooked dinner. But she was a constant intellectual ally, shared her husband's interests, read to him as his eyes failed, bore him six children, with the distinction of being the first woman in the western world to bear a child under ether.

Longfellow's most productive period as a poet, 1843 to 1860, began with his marriage. To be sure, *Voices of the Night*, his first volume of poetry—including his most famous poem, "A Psalm of Life"—had appeared in 1839 and ran through six editions in its first two years. The celebrated "Psalm" ("Life is real, life is earnest") had been translated into fifteen languages, including Chinese and Sanskrit, and for better or worse, in Longfellow's brother

Samuel's words, had stirred depressed American hearts "as by a bugle summons." A Chinese mandarin inscribed it on an ivory fan. For despite what Hyatt Waggoner calls its "absolute incoherence," its fatuous doctrine of passive trust in undefined forces, and its astonishingly mixed metaphors, the "Psalm" had launched Longfellow on a wave of popularity that held its crest well into the twentieth century. Longfellow had also published *Ballads and Other Poems,* including "The Village Blacksmith," "The Wreck of the Hesperus," and the popular "Excelsior," in 1841. And his *Poems on Slavery,* including the moving "The Slave's Dream," had appeared in 1842, one of Longfellow's rare departures into controversial contemporary issues.

Still, his poetic output had been slim until in 1847, *Evangeline,* "the first important sustained poem by an American," was published, placing Longfellow, Hawthorne declared, "at the head of our list of native poets." It is a touching story of the dispersal of the French Acadians in 1755, of the search of Evangeline for her lost lover, Gabriel, and her service to the sick and poor in the manner of Hawthorne's Hester Prynne. Indeed, Hawthorne is said to have given the idea of the story to Longfellow. In 1850 *The Seaside and the Fireside* was published, a volume of poems including the poignant "The Building of the Ship" and the fine imagery of "The Fire of Drift Wood." *The Song of Hiawatha,* Longfellow's epic portrait of the American Indian, appeared in 1855. The story of John and Priscilla Alden was given to the world in *The Courtship of Miles Standish* in 1858. And what has been called Longfellow's masterpiece, *Tales of a Wayside Inn,* a series of narratives in the manner of Chaucer's *Canterbury Tales*— including Paul Revere's ride and the tale of the hated

Torquemada, leader of the Spanish Inquisition—was published in three parts in 1863, 1872, and 1874.

Of Longfellow's popular success little more need be said
than that *Miles Standish* sold five thousand copies on
publication day in Boston alone! For the relatively short
poem "The Hanging of the Crane" alone, Longfellow was
paid $4,000 by *Harper's Magazine*. At his death, his estate
was valued at $356,320, including an allowance of $75,000
for Craigie House. Fanny's wealth does not truly account
for his success. In the first ten years of his marriage, only
once did her income exceed his. In his best year, 1868, he
alone, from both writing and investments, earned over
$48,000. Ironically, his epic poem *Christus*, on which he
worked for twenty-three years, intended as "the really great
work of his life," and purporting to be an account of the
progress of Christianity from ancient hope through medieval faith and modern love, proved a failure.

Longfellow's poetry is dominated by a melancholy sense
of life's transience, of lost friends, lost faith, lost youth,
the "autumn within" the spring, the snow in the heart of
summer. His verse is a synthesis of sermon and song, reverence and romance, pathos and bathos. Essentially, as Hyatt
Waggoner again points out, "Longfellow had just one
thing to say, and he tried as best he could to deny it: that
time is inherently and inevitably man's enemy, bringing
only loss and nothingness. . . . He did what he could to
cheer himself and reassure his age by repeating the clichés
about Progress and Enlightenment."

It is never certain, however, that Longfellow himself was
impressed by these clichés. Even in the "Psalm of Life," in
which we are told that the grave is not life's goal—itself a
repudiation of orthodox religious teaching—we are also

told: "Time is fleeting, / And our hearts, though stout and brave, / Still, like muffled drums, are beating / Funeral marches to the grave." It is a distressing contradiction sustained in much of his poetry, which seems more concerned with the sentimental symptoms than with the emotional and intellectual sources of the human condition. There is little of the probing passion of a Shakespeare, a Goethe, even Hawthorne and Melville at their finest. Poet Howard Nemerov is correct in describing Longfellow as "a good minor poet," persuaded by popular acclaim that he was a major one, and, in any case, "stretching a relatively small gift over a very large frame." If, as has been suggested, Longfellow's mind was mellow before it was ripe, it is also true, as Howard Mumford Jones reminds us, that "there are surprises in Longfellow for anybody who will read him with impartial sympathetic eyes," for example, the haunting, isolated tragedy of "The Tide Rises, the Tide Falls," the apocalyptic vision of the end of the world in "Michael Angelo."

With their six children in Craigie House the Longfellows lived a placid life: Charles and Ernest romping about, and "grave Alice," laughing Annie Allegra, and "Edith with golden hair," heroines of "The Children's Hour." Their first daughter, Fanny, died in her second year.

Tragedy shattered the tranquil Longfellow home on July 9, 1861. Seated in the draft of an open window, Fanny was sealing packets of locks of her daughters' hair, when a lighted match, or hot wax, fell on her light summer dress, which burst into flames. In panic, she rushed into Longfellow's study, where the poet seized a rug, flung it around her to smother the flames, holding her close. In intense pain, Fanny was put to sleep with ether, and Longfellow himself was badly burned on his face and hands. Fanny awoke the next morning, drank some coffee, fell into a coma, and died. On July 13, the Longfellows' eighteenth anniversary, Fanny was buried at Mount Auburn Cemetery.

Longfellow hid his disfigured face in a beard. But he could not hide his profound grief. In the initial shock he thought he was going insane, and begged "not to be sent to an asylum." He lost interest in life, felt that he was "inwardly bleeding to death." Only eighteen years later did he give voice in public to his sorrow in "The Cross of Snow":

... There is a mountain in the distant West
    That, sun-defying, in its deep ravines
    Displays a cross of snow upon its side.
Such is the cross I wear upon my breast
    These eighteen years, through all the changing scenes
    And seasons, changeless since the day she died.

In the love and care of his children, Longfellow found great solace. "No matter who were the guests in the home at the time," his son-in-law, Richard Henry Dana III, recalled, "at the tinkle of a little silver bell, he would mount the stairs, hear their prayers, kiss them goodnight and return to his company." Of his children, Edith alone married and provided him with nine grandchildren, to his delight. His resignation from Harvard in 1854 had left him more time not only to poke around among what Walt Whitman rather caustically called "his plush and rosewood, and ground-glass lamps," or sit grandly before his "silver inkstand and scented paper," but for scholarly work, like his translation of Dante's *Divina Commedia*, which appeared between 1865 and 1867.

The poet could take comfort, too, from the mounting adulation of the public. Men uncovered their heads and offered him their seats on public street cars. Children followed him, Pied Piper-like, through the streets of Cambridge. When the city's famed chestnut tree—made a national monument in "The Village Blacksmith"—was cut down, the children of Cambridge raised money, had an armchair made of its wood, and presented it at Craigie House. Longfellow laid down the law that every child who wanted to see the chair was to be admitted without question. One little boy, appalled that Longfellow did not have a copy of *Jack and the Beanstalk* in what was reputed to be one of the richest libraries in America, went out and bought him one. From the schoolchildren of one city alone, sixty letters reached Longfellow's desk in one day.

Longfellow was not wholly immune to the crises of his time. His "Arsenal at Springfield," one of Fanny's favorites, is an effective antiwar poem, and Longfellow condemned the Mexican War as "disgraceful" and "shabby," denouncing the "intellectual legerdemain" which, in war, makes murder "glory instead of crime." In general, however, he took little or no active interest in political life. Content to call himself an "old Washington Federalist," he disapproved of Andrew Jackson's democracy, never made a public speech, considered politics unworthy of a gentleman, and expressed pain at the sight of Emerson reviled on the steps of Cambridge City Hall at the height of the furor over the Fugitive Slave Law. Mildly Unitarian, committed "not to any one sect but rather to the community of those free minds who loved the truth," he lived in the past—in the words of biographer Odell Shepard, "like an heir, living on the inherited capital of a great estate, adding little but managing well, with a deep sense of obligation to those who preceded him and to those who were to follow."

If Longfellow could assure his aging Bowdoin classmates at their fiftieth reunion in 1875 that "nothing is too late / Till the tired heart shall cease to palpitate," he himself was failing physically by the fall of 1881 when he suffered an attack of vertigo followed by nervous prostration, which confined him to bed for weeks. In late March, 1882, he took a chill, was stricken with peritonitis, and died on March 21, less than one month after his nationally celebrated birthday. "Under gently falling snow," his body was taken to Mount Auburn Cemetery.

JAMES
RUSSELL
LOWELL

HE SAW LITERATURE AS HOLIDAY

"Like a boy, I mistook my excitement for inspiration, and here am I in the mud." James Russell Lowell, forty-four, was despondent. "I did not make the hit I expected," he confessed, "and am ashamed at having been tempted again to think I could write *poetry*, a delusion from which I have been tolerably free these dozen years."

James Russell Lowell—poet, literary critic, and Longfellow's successor at Harvard—had shared a Cambridge platform with Emerson and the doctor-poet Oliver Wendell Holmes to honor Harvard's Civil War dead. He had put off the composition of his "Commemorative Ode" until the last possible moment, and now, eclipsed by the eloquence, by the very presence of the Sage of Concord on the same stage, he had failed in its presentation, and he knew it at once.

But in the very harshness—and acuity—of this self-appraisal Lowell revealed a sense of value and proportion and a balance of character for which, alone, he may be fondly remembered. Boston and Cambridge might lionize him and overrate his work in their ingrown, latter-day Federalist salons. The world at large—in Alfonso XII's glittering court in Madrid, in Victoria's grandest imperial hour—might celebrate him as the Yankee's Yankee, the bookman's bookman, the very paragon of the gentleman of letters. But there is little evidence that Lowell was taken in long, if at all, by the world's adulation. As a scholar, he was less interested in the good opinion of his contemporaries than in the judgment of history. He knew his Dante and his Virgil too well to believe, for a moment, that he was a poet of the first rank.

If James Russell Lowell stands rather low in the hierarchy of letters, he remains eminently secure in another, perhaps finer art: gentility. "Fine as is the written work of Lowell," a British editor wrote upon Lowell's departure from England as minister to the Court of Saint James, "his unwritten work is finer still." For in the art of personal grace, intellectual curiosity, and refinement of taste Lowell has had few peers in any culture. "It has long been fashionable," writes Lowell's most perceptive biographer, Martin Duberman, "to dismiss the 'Brahmins' as smug, limited men, ineffectual shadows of their Puritan forbears. . . . But the value of a life can be estimated by its style as much as by its events; by what it was rather than by what it did." Of Lowell, Duberman adds, "His deepest loyalties went to individuals, not ideas." Judged by strictly personal, human standards, this merely competent man of letters was an extraordinary man indeed: a most affectionate and loyal friend, a devoted husband, an indulgent father, and, within the often stultifying bounds of Brahmin Boston, remarkably free of dogma, remarkably openminded and independent.

To be sure, Lowell was capable of the petty bias that afflicted his class, even of social and ethnic pettiness. Henry James's sister Alice objected to Lowell's systematic snubbing of Dr. Holmes in the Saturday Club. Lowell has been patronized as "an unoriginal appreciator"; an obtuse Tory fighting the eight-hour day as "piratical"; a smug Bourbon determined to crush democracy and rebuild America's initial republic of the elite; a hopeless provincial, prone, in one critic's words, to viewing the Rue de Rivoli in Paris as "a mere continuation of Brattle Street," Cambridge; or an intellectual reactionary in maudlin opposition to science and its "erosive action upon religious belief." "His mind," Vernon Parrington writes, "was hopelessly bewildered by his own vast disorder . . . as cluttered as a garret, filled with an endless miscellany of odds and ends." In short, Lowell was more a dilettante than a scholar, more of a poetaster than a poet. And to still others, he seemed effete. "In later life," wrote one of his contemporaries, Lowell "got all barnacled with quotations and leisure," poking grandly about his estate at Elmwood in his elegant smoking jacket, idyllically pitching hay to the mental rhythms of Chaucer while the blood ran at Gettysburg. "He pulls out pocket-books and gold snuffboxes and carbuncled cigarette-cases," his critic adds, "and emerald eye-glasses, and curls and pomatums himself and looks in pocket looking glasses, and smooths his Van Dyke Beard and is a literary fop—f-o-p— fop. . . . His later prefaces are so expressive—O my! so expressive of hems and haws and creased literary trousers."

Lowell's judgment of other artists—even the greatest— was no less caustic and often outrageously blind. He dismissed Michelangelo, incredibly, as "the apostle of the exaggerated," mistaking, he declared, brawn for strength and attempted originality with artistic value. "I suppose," Lowell said of Emerson's poetry, "we must give it up." To the squire of Elmwood, Walt Whitman's *Leaves of Grass* was "solemn humbug," and Thoreau's "whole life . . . a search for the doctor."

Lowell's initial concept of his own worth was equally preposterous. "I am the first poet," he could say in 1849, "who has endeavored to express the American Idea, and I shall be popular by and by." But as his comprehension of great literature deepened and his awareness of his own slim potential and output became more acute, Lowell arrived at perhaps the most important decision of his life: he accepted himself with uncommon perspective and cheer.

If he could not write greatly, he would live greatly, reveling in good talk with good friends, savoring good wine, tending his garden, embracing the Gothic splendor of Chartres Cathedral, breathing in the sharp, salt air of the Massachusetts coast, and, in Van Wyck Brooks's memorable image, sitting in his study, "winter and summer, for years on end, feeding like a silkworm on his books, only stirring abroad for his daily walk." If he were an amateur, why so be it. "In my weaker moments," he confessed, "I revert with a sigh, half deprecation, half relief, to the old notion of literature as holiday, as 'the world's sweet inn from pain and wearisome turmoil.'" It was more than an echo of Longfellow's concept of literature as romantic escape. It was the candid credo of a man who had achieved what Goethe has defined as the beginning of wisdom: the simple recognition of one's limits and the determination to live as fully as possible within them.

James Russell Lowell, born in Cambridge, Massachusetts, on February 22, 1819, took pride in forbears as impeccably Yankee as Longfellow's, tracing their American roots to a British merchant named Percival Lowle, who settled in Newbury, Massachusetts, in 1639. James's paternal grandfather, John Lowell, was a member of the Continental Congress, a chief justice of the First Circuit Court, a fellow of Harvard, and a prime mover in the councils of Federalism. James's uncle John, splenetically anti-Jefferson and commercially opposed to "Mr. Madison's War" of 1812, was active with such reactionaries as Timothy Pickering in the abortive secessionist-minded Hartford Convention of New England states in 1815. Another uncle, Francis Cabot, a mill-owning entrepreneur, founded the city of Lowell, Massachusetts.

James's father, the Reverend Dr. Charles Lowell, "represented," in one biographer's words, "the best of a type—
the liberal New England minister, optimistic, benign, rational, moralistic." A Harvard graduate, he studied theology
at Edinburgh, but was less distinguished in that discipline
than in a rare stability and grace of character. Quietly
Federalist, he served for over fifty years as pastor of the
West Church (Unitarian) in Boston, remembered by
"Jemmy," his youngest son, as a man of unshakable "trust
in God and . . . sincere piety," a father "tender," Lowell
said, "to find excuses for him." "Never deeply concerned
about dogmas," writes biographer Ferris Greenslet, Dr.
Lowell "preached Grace and Good Works, and formed
friendships with those who achieved them." Shunning the
nit-picking sectarian squabbles of his day, Dr. Lowell advised James "not to become a partisan in theology, &, without calling yourself a trinitarian or unitarian, orthodox or
liberal, let it be your sole aim to be in truth *a christian.*
The faith of the *heart* is the only essential faith, & this may
be held by christians of every name." But Charles Lowell
was no quietist. He denounced slavery from his pulpit with
no deference to the Northern mill-owning "cotton Whigs,"
as a "monstrous iniquity," and championed not only
temperance but relief for orphans and refugees.

Jemmy's mother, Harriet Brackett Spence, was descended
on her father's side from the Highland Scots and on her
mother's side from Orkney Islanders. Diminutive, high-
strung, mystical, and Episcopalian, Harriet Lowell dis-
pensed poetry, ballads, and romantic tales of her native
land, not always with fidelity to factual detail. Mrs. Lowell,
never a stable personality, suffered a psychotic breakdown
in James's late twenties, dying of a stroke when he was

thirty-one. A member of the family concluded that Harriet's death was, in fact, anticlimactic: "The larger portion
of her mind had gone before. . . . There was some strange
derangement . . . a mystery that could not be fathomed."
Despite this tragedy, Lowell remembered his mother with
fond gratitude. Still "Babie Jamie" to his mother at six-
teen, Lowell wrote to her in Europe: "I am engaged in
several poetical effusions, one of which I have dedicated to
you, who have always been the patron and encourager of
my youthful muse." In a later poem, "The Darkened
Mind," distinguished for its emotional power among Lowell's generally arid and obscure verses, James would give
voice to the sorrow he felt as he watched his mother,
sitting in her "wonted corner," now wringing her hands,
now moaning, or staring blankly:

> We can touch thee, still we are no nearer;
> Gather round thee, still thou art alone;
> The wide chasm of reason is between us;
> Thou confutest kindness with a moan;
> We can speak to thee and thou canst answer,
> Like two prisoners through a wall of stone.

Jamie's Aunt Mary provided a measure of maternal care,
reading Shakespeare and Spenser to the lad, albeit often
to Lowell's drooping eyelids. It was, however, an informal
education well remembered. Lowell was first formally educated at Sophia Dana's school in Cambridge, where he
and his chum "Ned" Dana (the novelist) were the only
two boys in attendance. Resolved to avoid that stigma,
Lowell manfully discarded the gold-tasseled white hat in
which his mother had dressed him for school, and free
now of the risk of being called a sissy, applied himself to

the fundamentals of Latin and to children's stories in French. From ages eight to fourteen, Lowell attended Mr. William Wells's school in Cambridge, the same school recalled by Dana with such bitterness. Lowell appears to have gotten his share of the ferrule for what he proudly called "deviltry of all descriptions," but at the same time he received, in preparation for Harvard, adequate grounding in Greek, Latin, and mathematics.

As a boy, Lowell skated on Fresh Pond and pumped the bellows of Longfellow's chestnut-tree blacksmith with solemn delight, "as proud of the privilege," a biographer writes, "as he would have been of occupying a throne by permission of a king." Blue-eyed, golden-haired, short, stocky, muscular, and endowed with abundant "animal spirits and boyish charm," he could inspire mischief even in such staid adults as Richard Henry Dana, Sr., who, on one occasion, invited Jemmy and his Shetland pony through his front door and tried unsuccessfully to urge both pony and rider upstairs.

Lowell entered Harvard College at fifteen, his hair now reddish brown, his chin soon to bear a smart Van Dyke beard. In black jacket and lace collar, as one biographer notes, he looked indeed like "something more than a *reader* of Shakespeare" [Italics mine]. Now five feet eight inches tall and already affecting eight to ten cigars a day, Lowell took a less than intense interest in Harvard's dreary classical curriculum of Latin and Greek and rote recitations in English rhetoric, logic, mathematics, theology, and moral philosophy. In the cavalier fashion of his day, he would maintain a gentlemanly rank near the middle of his class, unmoved even by the genial lectures in language and literature by the man whom he would succeed.

Certainly, James was not without inducement to excel scholastically. "If you graduate one of the first five in your class," his father assured him, "I shall give you $100. . . . If one of the first ten, $75. If one of the first twelve, $50. If the first or second scholar, two hundred dollars. If you do not miss any exercises unexcused, you shall have Bryant's Mythology or any other book of equal value, unless it is one I may specially want." But Lowell was impervious to such blandishments. He was, in fact, a campus rebel, demonstrating that contempt for formalities and schedules expected of Harvard's well-born—at least by themselves. If he had deliberately set out to defy his father's strictures, he could not have done so more effectively. Even as a sophomore, despite three threats of dismissal from college, he was absent from compulsory chapel fourteen times and from classes fifty-six times, to the point of losing academic credits. In his senior year, now sporting white pantaloons and a black beaver hat, and exhilarated by such pranks as lopping the top off a post in Harvard Yard and flaunting rules by wearing a hat in chapel when he did go, young Lowell got his comeuppance. An editor and poetic contributor to the campus publication *Harvard-iana,* he already enjoyed some notoriety as a competent versifier and had been named class poet and scheduled to perform in Class Day exercises on July 17, 1838, when the bomb fell. On June 25, an annoyed college faculty brought him to book: "Voted," the officials announced, "that Lowell, Senior, on account of continued negligence in college duties be suspended till the Saturday before Commencement, to pursue his studies with the Revd. Mr. Frost of Concord, to recite to him twice a day, reviewing the whole of Locke's essay ["An Essay Concerning Human

Understanding"] and studying also McIntosh's Review of Ethical Philosophy, to be examined in both on his return and not to visit Cambridge during the period of his suspension."

Lowell was indignant. But notwithstanding a mass protest by loyal classmates, he was packed off in a buggy to Emerson's Athens, "damning everything and vowing that he would neither smoke nor shave so long as he remained in the wilds."

In Concord, the young cut-up had as little use for Barzailli Frost, who, he said, talked pontifically and too much and, in any case, chewed his food too loudly. He found Thoreau, just seven years before his departure for Walden, fawnishly imitative of Emerson. "With my eyes shut," Lowell insisted, "I shouldn't know them apart." As for the Sage of Concord himself, he conceded his good nature in taking walks with him and lending him books, but pronounced him affected in speech: "After all I'd heard of him, as an Eagle soaring in pride of place, I was surprised," Lowell declared, "to see a poor little hawk stooping at flies or at least sparrows and groundlings." It would not be the last time that he would dismiss as overrated a reputation of the first rank.

The Reverend Charles Lowell could pocket all of the prize gifts he had promised James upon his graduation from Harvard. Young Lowell was not only denied his Phi Beta Kappa key for nine years but graduated below the middle of his class. True to Brahmin tradition, he went on to Harvard's Dane Law School, winning his bachelor of laws degree in 1840, and two years later he was admitted to the bar. But neither his heart nor his head was in this profession, which competed every step of the way with

Lowell's passion for the courtly life of a man of letters. He considered preaching, but not even the placid dogmas of Unitarianism proved facile or liberal enough for his restless mind, impatient with fixed forms and ideas. It was, for the just graduated Harvard dandy, a period of nettling indecision, made more melancholy by the opposition of Abijah White, wealthy Watertown merchant, to Lowell's early marriage to his daughter Maria. Mr. White relented only enough to permit the young couple's engagement in the fall of 1840, insisting at the same time that Lowell must be gainfully employed before he would permit the marriage to occur.

A pupil of Margaret Fuller, and zealously caught up in all the "in" reform and antislavery movements of her day, Maria White, for all her ideological passion, exercised a restraining influence on the impulsive Lowell, who, during this period of doubt and delay, showed suicidal tendencies so pronounced that at one point he put a loaded, cocked gun to his forehead, dissuaded by fear from pulling the trigger. His deep love for Maria cannot be doubted. In "Irene," which appeared in his first book of poetry, *A Year's Life* (1841), and which, he said "owes all its beauty to her," he celebrated his bride-to-be, herself an amateur poet, as a woman "free without boldness, meek without fear," a woman of open heart and quiet charity, of intuitive and actively charitable rather than formal religious feeling, "her whole thought" almost seeming to be "how to make glad one lowly human hearth." More than that, Lowell said, Maria's "gentle & holy presence" had "set his spirit free," her "whiter & purer" soul had given him "all-embracing hope." Maria, he added, seemed "half of earth and more than half of Heaven." "In short," Lowell concluded, "I am *happy*. Maria *fills* my ideal and I satisfy hers. . . . She is every way noble." James and Maria were married, at last, on the night after Christmas in 1844; their life together was described by a friend as "the very picture of a True Marriage."

Despite his own later view that it contained "more of everybody else than of myself," and less than polished verse, Lowell's *A Year's Life* was received with unwonted praise, pleasing even Margaret Fuller and inspiring a now inconsequential critic to proclaim that Lowell had at last produced great American poetry "that shall silence the sneers of foreigners, and write [Lowell's] name among the stars of heaven." Sales were less brisk than criticism; only three hundred copies of the book were sold.

Lowell derived considerable benefit from the publication of his verse, however, in the form of invitations to write articles and poems for journals as respected and influential as the *North American Review, The United States Magazine and Democratic Review,* the *National Anti-Slavery Standard.* His critical essay series, *The Old English Dramatists,* appeared in *The Boston Miscellany* in 1842. And in 1843, in a venture more imaginative than practical, Lowell went into partnership with an expatriated Albany visionary named Robert Carter to publish a new magazine, the *Pioneer,* which, Lowell announced, would do no less than "furnish the intelligent and reflecting portion of the Reading Public with a rational substitute for the enormous quantity of thrice-diluted trash, in the shape of namby-pamby love tales and sketches, which is monthly poured out to them by many of our popular Magazines—and to offer . . . a healthy and manly Periodical Literature." And indeed, the first issue of the *Pioneer,* greeted with justified acclaim, could boast Poe's classic, "The Tell-Tale Heart" and poetry by no less a personage than Elizabeth Barrett of England. But Lowell's publishing venture was fatally jeopardized by an eye disease, probably brought on from excessive editorial work, that forced him to go to New York to see the same doctor who attended William Prescott. In Lowell's absence the impractical and somewhat vulgar Carter let the magazine slide. On his return, Lowell found the magazine bankrupt and facing court action for compensation. With the help of his family, Lowell personally assumed the major financial losses, and, after several years, doggedly paid off the debt completely.

Miscellaneous Poems, Lowell's second volume of verse, appeared in 1843, bearing the unmistakable marks of Maria's antislavery influence on the increasingly radical young Brahmin. Some found Lowell's poetic strictures against slavery didactic, but most shared Fanny Longfellow's appraisal of the poems' "pure and Christian spirit," and Lowell's identification of the Negro slave's battle for freedom with the greater human struggle against all forms of tyranny. The volume, of which 1,500 copies were printed, sold well and again resulted in new writing assignments for Lowell from prominent journals.

Lowell ventured beyond his study, if not as fanatically as Abolitionists like William Lloyd Garrison, to join Maria in reform movements, urging better conditions for northern factory workers, fighting capital punishment, and unfurling the flag of temperance "to the point," a biographer notes, "where an alarmed Longfellow feared Lowell was on the verge of asking him to destroy his wine cellar."

All the while the shadow of death stalked the once idyllic Lowell home, taking one of their children after another. Their first child, Blanche, born on December 31, 1845, lived only fifteen months. A bereft Lowell again gave voice to his grief in "She Came and Went" and in another poem, "The Changeling." The Lowells' hope was renewed in the birth of Mabel in 1847, the only child to survive them. But a third daughter, Rose, born in 1849, survived only a few months; and Lowell's only son, Walter, born in 1850, died in 1852. On October 27, 1853, not quite a year after Lowell's first trip to Europe, he faced the ultimate tragedy. Stricken with grief over the loss of her children, frail and exhausted by a cough that had plagued her for years, Maria died of tuberculosis. Lowell was almost delirious with grief, dreaming once that he saw the dead Walter on her knee and hearing Maria say with pride "See what a fine strong boy he has grown!" He felt within "an indefinable sense of having begun to die." Lonely at Elmwood in the presence of his deaf father and silent sister, he lay awake at night for hours, "thinking," he told a friend in confidence, "of my razors and my throat and that I am a fool and a coward not to end it all at once."

But Lowell's nature, as he said, was "naturally joyous." He knew he must rally, and he did, building anew on the literary reputation already firmly established by 1848, certainly his most productive year. In 1848 alone, a year of revolution throughout Europe, appeared Lowell's two most important works, *The Biglow Papers* and *A Fable for Critics*.

Phrased in the caustic, disarmingly ungrammatical Yankee dialect of one Hosea Biglow, the archetype of his no-nonsense rustic kin, *The Biglow Papers, First Series*, for all its humor, is a damning assault on the evils and pretensions of mid-nineteenth-century America: American aggression in Mexico, the moral evil of war itself, slavery, the smug myth of white racial superiority, the blatant imperialism Americans liked to call Manifest Destiny. For a while, in its pages, Lowell seems at last to have found his metier:

On the Mexican War, Lowell rebukes those who insist:

> . . . Thet our nation's bigger'n therin, an' so its rights
>   are bigger,
> An' thet it's all to make 'em free thet we air pullin'
>   the trigger. . . .

More devastating still was his comment on the broader moral issue:

> Ez fer war, I call it murder,—
>   There you hev it flat;
> I don't want to go no furder
>   Than my Testyment fer that;
> God hez sed so plump an' fairly,
>   It ez long ez it is broad
> An' you've gut to git up airly
>   Ef you want to take in God.

It was Lowell at his best, and of all his works remains ideologically at least the most relevant.

Lowell lost friends but gained new notoriety with the publication of *A Fable for Critics*, in which he takes splendidly funny, not to say devastating pokes at the leading literary arbiters of his day, notably at Emerson, Margaret Fuller, James Fenimore Cooper. Edgar Allan Poe, he announced, was "three-fifths genius . . . and two-fifths sheer fudge." Nor did he spare himself, cheerfully allowing that he would never amount to a single thing until he learned the difference " 'twixt singing and preaching." In three swift editions, the *Fable* alone sold three thousand copies.

In 1848, too, Lowell published *The Vision of Sir Launfal*, a highly derivative poem, inspired by Tennyson and the legend of the Holy Grail, Sir Galahad, and King Arthur's court. But Lowell's Launfal is scarcely credible, his story attenuated, and the poetry itself imitative and numbing.

The years 1854 and 1855 found Lowell sharing the literary limelight with Longfellow as a nationally respected poet sought out by magazines and lecture committees. It was during one lecture series on the English poets presented by the Lowell Institute in Boston in the 1854–55 season that Lowell, without seeking the post, was appointed to succeed Longfellow at Harvard as Smith Professor of Modern Languages. He was to serve at a salary of $1,200, which, added to his private income of $600 and his fees for articles and lectures, stood him in fair stead.

Before assuming his Harvard post, Lowell was granted a year abroad to strengthen his grasp of German and Spanish. Leaving Mabel at home in the care of a governess, Miss Frances Dunlap, a once wealthy woman and friend of Maria's in reduced circumstances, Lowell left for the Continent. Europe was good to him. He delighted in almost daily visits to the inexhaustible Louvre. He stood enraptured before the Gothic majesty of the cathedral at Chartres, inspired to write one of his better poems, "The Cathedral." In England he visited Stonehenge, chatted with Browning and Thackeray. In Dresden he maintained an exacting schedule of German studies, immersing himself in detail. But no change of environment could assuage his still lingering grief at Maria's loss. Homesick, still plagued by thoughts of suicide, Lowell decided against a visit to Spain, and after fleeing to Italy's sedative beauty and warmth, returned to America in the late summer of 1856.

Back in Cambridge, Lowell found Elmwood so depressing that he moved with Mabel and Miss Dunlap into the home of his sister-in-law, Mrs. Estes Howe. Accepting the advice of Dr. Oliver Wendell Holmes that he retire early to bed and abstain from coffee, Lowell rallied. A major factor in his recovery was his growing attachment to Frances Dunlap, whom he found "very agreeable," and "intelligent, sensible, with several accomplishments." To the surprise and chagrin of close friends, including Mrs. Longfellow, Lowell and Miss Dunlap were married in December, 1857. He had found in Frances, Lowell said, "remarkable strength & depth of character & of corresponding gentleness." Cambridge and Boston society might look askance at his marriage to this restrained, plain woman from Portland, Maine, but Lowell was undeterred: "My second marriage," he declared, "was the wisest act of my life, & as long as I am sure of it, I can afford to wait till my friends agree with me." It is clear that Lowell was most happy in the married state, and equally clear that he needed the company and counsel of a strong woman. Frances Lowell managed even his finances and provided more than wifely care. Apart from her, Lowell said, "I miss you every hour of the day, for you know that I always run and hide my face in your lap when I am troubled." And Frances's silent, patient manner finally won over Lowell's skeptical friends.

At Harvard, where he taught for almost twenty years, Lowell's function, like Longfellow's, was not to instruct students in the actual mechanics of language but to deliver general lectures on the thrust of national literatures. Lowell's favorite course was one on Dante, which he conducted not only in the classroom, but by the fireside of his library at Elmwood to which he had returned with Frances. Of the Dante course, one student recalled: "Mr. Lowell . . . never, from the beginning, bothered us with a particle of linguistic irrelevance. Here before us was [*The Divine Comedy*]—a lasting impression of what human life had meant to a human being, dead and gone these five centuries. . . . Let us read, as sympathetically as we could make ourselves read, the words of one who was as much a man as we, only vastly greater in his knowledge of wisdom and beauty." In one month, the student added, he "could read Dante better than I ever learned to read Greek, or Latin, or German."

As he poked about its streets, Lowell seemed less to be in than to *be* Cambridge to his students and friends. Returning to America after twenty years' absence, the novelist Henry James recalled Lowell in that college town as "the very genius of the spot, who had given it from so early the direct literary consecration, without which even the most charming seats of civilization go through life awkwardly and ruefully, after the manner of unchristened children."

Lowell by no means confined himself to the Harvard campus. From 1857 to 1861 he served as founding editor of the *Atlantic Monthly*, its very first issue graced by articles from Emerson, Holmes, and Longfellow, and Lowell himself was to be a major contributor to this immensely successful magazine. Lesser known writers did not fare so happily, given Lowell's somewhat casual methods as an administrator. On one occasion a number of rejected manuscripts met a watery end, when Lowell's hat, crammed with the offerings of would-be contributors, blew off into the

Charles River. Again, in 1863, Lowell returned to the magazine business, agreed to coedit the prestigious *North American Review* with Charles Eliot Norton, and again Lowell was a major contributor, his distinguished political articles reflecting a growing appreciation of Lincoln's moderate policies as maintaining the ship of state in "the main current" of American political life. Between 1862 and 1875, Lowell published several highly discursive volumes of criticism, travel essays, and general commentary, came out with the second series of *The Biglow Papers,* and contributed to the *Nation,* as well as to the *Atlantic Monthly* and the *North American Review.*

Alarmed by the venality of the Grant administration and the departure of the Republican Party from its initial idealism, Lowell actively entered Republican politics and was at least marginally instrumental in securing the nomination of Rutherford B. Hayes over boss-ridden James G. Blaine. A victorious Hayes rewarded Lowell with the post of Minister to Spain, in which he served capably from 1877 to 1880. The Court of Saint James next welcomed him as American minister, as did London society, which he beguiled as an after-dinner speaker. The British valued him as a realistic diplomat, aware, as in the controversy over Irish-American revolutionary activity against the Crown, that the practical political interests of both countries must be squarely faced if viable solutions were to be reached. Lowell did much to establish Anglo-American relations on the cordial and stable basis on which they have since largely rested. Oxford and Cambridge awarded him honorary doctorates in 1873 and 1874, and in 1885, when Lowell was recalled by President Cleveland, he received new evidence of British esteem: Oxford offered him no less than its University Professorship of English Language and Literature. To be sure, there were some who questioned the propriety of naming a foreigner to that distinguished post, but the very fact that this and other generous offers were made to Lowell attests to the high regard in which he was held in the land of his forbears. Queen Victoria herself averred that during her reign no ambassador had "created so much interest and won so much regard as Mr. Lowell."

For his part, despite his anger over British conduct during the Civil War, Lowell was deeply impressed by England, not to say charmed, and he never got over the love affair. The expatriate American novelist Henry James saw much of Lowell during his years in England and noted a "strange" duality in his character and conduct. "That is," James observed, "I don't know how English he was at home, but he was conspicuously American here." Once home, Lowell would adopt the top hat of the British court, and, as long as his health held out, would return to England every summer for visits to town and country.

At home, Lowell once again moved cheerfully in the company of friends, the great scientist Agassiz, who shared his opposition to Darwin, and, always, his good neighbor Henry Longfellow. If Henry Thoreau could dismiss the Parker House—and the Saturday Club—as "all [cigar] smoke, and no salt," and mock its patrons "deposited," he said, "in chairs over the marble floor, as thick as legs of bacon in a smoke house," Lowell relished the sprightly talk and genteel camaraderie of that august group, even there at no loss for words. Not all of his social peers, to be sure, ranked him high. In his often patronizing *Journal*, his old chum Ned Dana observed: "Jimmy is very clever, entertaining & good humored, & thoroughly independent, but he is rather a trifler, after all. His feelings cannot be deep." And in 1869, Emerson had a judgment of his own to pronounce about poetry. While acknowledging Lowell's technical skill, the Sage concluded that Lowell's poetry in general "rather expresses his wish, his ambition, than the uncontrollable interior impulse which is the authentic mark of a new poem . . . and which is felt in the pervading tone, rather than in brilliant parts or lines. . . ."

Two modern critics support Emerson's view. In his classic critical work, *American Poets from the Puritans to the Present*, Hyatt Waggoner concludes that "reading Lowell straight through is next to impossible. Most of the poems . . . are simply failures, and a large number of the long ones are quite unreadable—long-winded, repetitious, and imitative . . . of English Romantics and Victorians." In *The Flowering of New England* Van Wyck Brooks adds: "That [Lowell's poetry] added much to other sums, local, moral, political, hardly affected the question. . . . The fact remained that one forgot his poems. One read them five times over and still forgot them, as if this excellent verse had been written in water."

There is evidence that Lowell, in his most candid moments, would have agreed with both critics. Again, he knew his limits. He conceded, with no obvious pain, that he was better at "thoughts" than at "thought," that he preferred the *hors d'œuvre* of literature to its full-course dinners. Besides, he was equally honest, if perilously incorrect, in his condemnation of the art of others. Declaring Swinburne's sensuous love poetry to be fit more for the "cellar" than for "those fair upper chambers which look toward the sunrise" of Easter, he laid down the law: "Let no man write a line that he would not have his daughter read." The great

domes of Rome, he announced, were "the goiter of architecture." And again he lashed out at Poe: "He probably
cannot conceive of anybody's writing for anything but a
newspaper reputation."

It is true that Lowell opposed the Fugitive Slave Act
and that while Maria was alive joined ranks with antislavery
moderates. It is also true that Lowell saw through the de-
ception of *laissez-faire* economics as a barrier to social
progress. In a deft image he rejected the idea that the
Constitution was a "sacred parasol" designed to prevent the
Goddess of Liberty from getting a tan. But on balance,
Lowell was an unreconstructed Tory. In biographer Ernest
Samuels' words, he had nothing but "amused contempt
[for] the perspiring crusaders who proclaimed the New
Jerusalem in strident treble voices." He felt "blue," he said,
about "our penny-paper universal education and our work-
ingmen's parties, with their tremendous lever of suffrage,
decrying brains." Of labor movement radicals sentenced to
death despite lack of criminal evidence in Chicago's Hay-
market Riot of 1886, Lowell could say only that he "thought
those Chicago ruffians well-hanged." Lowell was more casual in religious matters. The Universe, he believed, must be
"fire-proof," otherwise God "would not let us get at the
match-box so carelessly." The theory of evolution, despite
Mr. Darwin's stature as "almost the only perfectly disin-
terested lover of truth [Lowell had] ever encountered," was
"mush . . . a poor substitute for the Rock of Ages. . . ."

Lowell was smitten, too, with an ethnic and religious bias
bewildering in a man intellectually so urbane. Negroes, he
pronounced, were "incapable of civilization from their own
resources." He looked nostalgically back to a happier day
"before our individuality had been trampled out of us by

the Irish mob." Jews, he conceded, were admirable for their love of learning, but were possessed of "the most intense, restless, aspiring and unscrupulous blood of all." Lowell, in short, shared the central prejudices of an ingrown Brahmin caste aware of its declining hegemony in the wake of massive immigration and social upheaval. On his own class, however, he could pronounce judgments equally harsh. "The Americans I remember fifty years ago," he wrote, "had a consciousness of standing firmer on their feet and in their own shoes than those of the newer generation. We are vulgar now precisely because we are afraid of being so." The Athens of America had become a babble of merchants and mill-owners, cheap politicians and half-educated parasites, and he would have none of it. While insisting that he was reconciled to his age of transition, that signs of change had ceased to alarm him, he remained, in fact, unreconciled, even to the microscope, which, he said, "had made us heirs / To large estates of doubts and snares." Lowell, again in Hyatt Waggoner's words, was "suspended between a world he loved but could not quite believe and a world he understood but could not love." So, for lack of an alternative he stood his Brahmin Yankee ground: "I would not give up a thing that had roots to it," he declared, "though it might suck up its food from graveyards." If the sun were, in fact, setting on the long Brahmin reign, he preferred its light, however dim, to the darkness he saw in the changed world about him.

By 1890, Lowell's health had so declined that he had to abandon his cherished walks for his carriage. He was alone again. Frances Lowell had died five years before, succumbing at last to a mental and nervous derangement from which she had only intermittently recovered since her collapse into utter madness during Lowell's term of service in Madrid. In July, 1891, struck down by cancer of the stomach, Lowell sank into delirium at Elmwood, convinced, under opium, that he was entertaining royalty, and begging to be taken to the home in which he lay. Following services in the Harvard chapel, he was buried at Mount Auburn Cemetery.

"Give my love to Longfellow," Lowell had written from England in 1855, "and tell him that to know him is to be somebody over here." Lowell had miscalculated Longfellow's importance, as, at first, he had his own. History would be kind to neither of them as poets. It would revere both as gentlemen.

OLIVER
WENDELL
HOLMES

HE SAW NEW ENGLAND'S SUNSET

The doctor, over eighty now, was lonely. "I feel like my own survivor," he told a friend. Emerson was gone, and Longfellow, Lowell, Hawthorne. And Oliver Wendell Holmes of 296 Beacon Street, Boston, who had presided unchallenged over their Saturday Club sessions of wit and philosophy, was feeling his age. "We were on deck together as we began the voyage of life," he wrote the poet Whittier. "Then the craft which held us began going to pieces." Now, he said, he was clinging to a "solitary spar, which is all that still remains afloat of the sunken vessel." At twenty-one he had laughed at Melville's grandfather as the old major made his rounds in his colonial three-cornered hat, knee breeches, and silver-buckled shoes. But even then he knew that age would claim him, too, and in "The Last Leaf," a poem that Lincoln would commit to memory, young Oliver begged a future indulgence:

> . . . If I should live to be
> The last leaf upon the tree
>   In the spring,
> Let them smile as I do now,
> At the old forsaken bough
>   Where I cling.

Now, indeed, the Sage of Boston—physician, medical reformer, essayist, poet, and conversationalist supreme—*was* the last leaf on New England's once flowering tree of literature. "The prologue of life," he had said at sixty, "is finished here at twenty: then come five acts of a decade each, and the play is over, with now and then a pleasant or a tedious afterpiece. . . ." Dr. Holmes could take comfort in his son Oliver, who, with his wife Fanny, had moved into the Beacon Street home when death claimed his wife and daughter in quick succession; Oliver was already well on his way to fame as a United States Supreme Court justice. And from his study window, the doctor commanded a view "over all creation," he had said: Bunker Hill, the spires of Harvard, Boston itself. But his city's hour of splendor, the hour in which one of Holmes's characters could pronounce Boston's State House "the hub of the solar system," the hour in which a city father could solemnly concede that there were not twenty men in Boston who could have written the plays of Shakespeare, was clearly over. Holmes himself had declared his city "the thinking centre of the continent, and therefore of the planet," the nonpareil of "free thought and free speech and free deeds." But the golden age of his "Yankee Athens" was ending, just as certainly as the age of Calvinism, epitomized by his father, the Reverend Abiel Holmes, had ended years before.

The "Gambrel-Roofed House"—just outside Harvard Yard—in which Oliver was born on August 29, 1809, rang with the echoes of the Revolution. It was said that the Battle of Bunker Hill had been planned there, that the very dents on the floor of this former military headquarters had been made by the muskets of patriots. Oliver's grandfather, Captain David Holmes, had fought the redcoats, and in the French and Indian Wars before them. But the home in which Wendell—the fourth of five children—was reared, was considerably more sedate. The Reverend Abiel Holmes was the prototype of gown-and-bib Calvinism, before that gloomy theology of human depravity and preordained damnation gave way to the more amiable dogmas of Unitarianism. Minister of Cambridge's First Church, a graduate of Yale, and possessed of a proper Federalist fear of

Jeffersonian democracy, Abiel Holmes had all of the determination of his son and grandson, with little of their open-
mindedness to fact. To be sure, his *Annals of America* was
"the first attempt to record events on this side of the Atlantic as *American* rather than Colonial," and had led to his
admission to the American Academy of Arts and Sciences
and the American Philosophical Society. But Abiel's primary concern was the salvation of his partially doomed
flock, and the gate that he opened to heaven was narrow
indeed. The stern language of his public excommunication
of an erring woman parishioner for "contumacious behavior" is reminiscent of the trial and condemnation of
Hawthorne's Hester Prynne. Abiel's library might boast two
thousand volumes, but it consisted chiefly of arid volumes
of latter-day theology, the inevitable *Pilgrim's Progress*,
Latin books on alchemy, the Westminster Catechism. The
good doctor of divinity considered it his paternal duty to
tear out certain pages of Dryden's "All for Love," lest they
excite young libidos, noting archly in Latin in the mutilated
book: "The omission is by no means to be mourned." There
was no compromising revealed truth. Faced with a revolt
by his more liberal parishioners against his even then dis-
credited orthodoxy and finally dismissed from his pulpit,
Abiel Holmes remained adamant: "If I seem to disregard
the wishes or the taste of my hearers," he declared from
his pulpit, "it is because I am more desirous to *save* than
to *please* them."

The morbid atmosphere of the minister's house—not
even study was permitted on Sunday—was somewhat relieved by the bright presence of Holmes's mother Sarah,
daughter of the Boston merchant Oliver Wendell, and
descended from early Dutch settlers in Albany and from

the Boston Quincys and Jacksons. Sally Holmes would gather her children around the piano every now and again to sing the gay Irish melodies of Thomas Moore, and if she catechized them she did so less ominously than her husband. Besides, to an enterprising prankster like Wendell, Cambridge, then "a village . . . of open fields where raspberries grew wild," offered many a challenge: sneaking up to the old Craigie House, knocking on its windows to alarm its owner and fleeing in laughing panic; smoking behind the minister's barn; taking his brother John to see the last public hanging in Cambridge on Gallows Hill. And Oliver thrilled to the Boston Navy Yard guns of "Mr. Madison's War" as Longfellow did in Portland, and he delighted in the romantic poetry of Byron and Goldsmith.

Young Oliver's life was blighted, however, by the obsessive piety and petty moralisms of his father, whose lifelong negative influence on Holmes cannot be exaggerated. Even a bookworm that had bored its way clean through a volume of ecclesiastical history was held up to the young boy as a paragon of industry. In that mordant atmosphere, Holmes came to think of the clergyman—as a type—as a "moral bully," a "lean phantom, whose extended hand points to the text of universal love," and whose "acrid words / Turn the sweet milk of kindness into curds, / Or with grim logic prove, beyond debate, / That all we love is worthiest of our hate. . . ." Of a particularly morbid clerical visitor to his father's house, he declared that he "did more in that one day to make me a heathen than he had ever done in a month to make a Christian out of an infant Hottentot." Nor did he spare his father: "I might have been a minister myself for aught I know," he said, "if [a certain] clergyman had not looked and talked so like an undertaker."

After sending Oliver to the customary private schools, including the "Port School" in nearby Cambridgeport, where Ned Dana and Margaret Fuller were among his classmates, Reverend Holmes packed his son off at fifteen to Andover Theological Seminary, a safe twenty miles away and a center of orthodoxy. Andover's instructors ruled with the canons of Calvin in one hand and the ferrule in the other and Wendell seems to have gotten his full share of both; on one occasion he was struck on the hand so hard that it turned black, his tormentor apologizing for the barbarism some twenty years later. At Andover, too, only five feet three in his boots, Holmes was made more conscious still of his elfin height and weight. A boorish desk-mate exulted in kicking him regularly under the desk. "You are a bully," young Oliver informed him, prophesying correctly: "When you are a man you will be a murderer."

Far from restricting Holmes, as his father had hoped, to the straight path of Calvinism, Andover only confirmed him in his biases. Oliver was delighted in September, 1825, to exchange the seminary's "doctrinal boiler" for the "rational ice-chest" of Harvard. To be sure, Harvard was scarcely permissive in his undergraduate days. A Committee on Dress laid down the law on the number and kind of buttons one wore on one's black suit, even regulated student parties and departures from Cambridge. Holmes escaped much of this regimen by living until his senior year at home, and while he looked in vain, he said, for "a girl in the neighborhood whose blood ever rose above the freezing point," or "who ever dreamed of such a thing as opening her lips without her whole family in attendance" he sought refuge from the "vinegar-faced old maids" of Cambridge by rowing on the Charles or downing a furtive beer

at the Porter House. He joined the "Puff" club, dedicated
to cigar-smoking fellowship, was elected to Hasty Pudding,
and joined "The Medical Faculty," a club consecrated to
solemn parodies of Harvard's starchy examination of can-
didates and its pedantic catalogue.

Academically, Holmes applauded Ticknor's introduction
of modern languages, taking French and Italian. He signed
a class petition to substitute science for additional courses
in Greek and warmed to chemistry and mineralogy. Holmes
was privileged, as Thoreau and Emerson had been, to polish
his writing style under the brilliant eye of Edward Tyrrel
Channing, who moved him to versified praise:

> Channing, with his bland, superior look,
> Cold as a moonbeam on a frozen brook,
> While the pale student, shivering in his shoes,
> Sees from his theme the turgid rhetoric ooze.

Already established as a versifier *d'occasion*, Oliver was
named class poet, but even upon graduation in 1829—he
was seventeenth in a class of fifty-nine and elected to Phi
Beta Kappa—he remained uncertain about his professional
future. "I wear my gills correct," he wrote an old Andover
chum, "and do not talk sentiment. I court my hair a little
more carefully, and button my coat a little tighter; my
treble has broken down into a bass, but still I have very
little of the look of manhood." All this, Holmes sighed,
despite his smoking "most devoutly." In addition, he was
"totally undecided what to study," wavering between "law
or physick," for, he told his friend, "I cannot say that I
think the trade of authorship quite adapted to this merid-
ian."

Still in his father's house, Holmes plunged wearily into

the study of law, poring through Blackstone. By January,
1830, he had already despaired of the legal calling. "I am
sick at heart," he said, "of this place and almost everything
connected with it. I know not what the temple of the law
may be to those who have entered it, but to me it seems
very cold and cheerless about the threshold." September
found him in better spirits, however, with the publication
of his still beloved "Old Ironsides," which brought him
instant national fame. Learning that the Revolutionary
War frigate *Constitution*, docked in Boston, had been ear-
marked for destruction, an indignant Holmes—standing on
one foot, legend has it, in Abiel's attic—dashed off his still
ringing lines on a piece of scrap paper:

> Ay, tear her tattered ensign down!
>   Long has it waved on high,
> And many an eye has danced to see
>   That banner in the sky . . .
> Oh, better that her shattered bulk
>   Should sink beneath the wave;
>
> Her thunders shook the mighty deep,
>   And there should be her grave;
> Nail to the mast her holy flag,
>   Set every threadbare sail,
> And give her to the god of storms,
>   The lightning and the gale!

Printed in the *Boston Daily Advertiser*, and hawked
through the streets of Washington, D.C., and the nation,
Holmes's poem won high public favor. It clearly saved the
ship through the pressure of public opinion on the Navy
Department and continued to as late as 1944. With the

publication of "The Last Leaf," the poem inspired, as we have seen, by Melville's grandfather and the pathos of old age, Holmes won new acclaim. The often irascible Poe thought it "an excellently well conceived and well managed specimen of versification."

The success of these poems did not, however, propel Holmes into a full-time career as a professional writer; nor did the publication in the *New England Magazine* of November, 1831, and February, 1832, of the first articles bearing the title of the greater series that would ensure Holmes's literary fame: *The Autocrat of the Breakfast-Table.* His success did, however, buttress him in his decision to abandon study of the law and adopt medicine as a career. Now he left his father's house for a boarding house room in Boston where he studied at the Massachusetts Medical College (later Harvard Medical School). An eager student, Holmes attended lectures, followed the doctors on their rounds and studied their movements in the dissecting room, where he pronounced himself guilty of "slicing and slivering the carcasses of better men and women than I ever was myself or am like to be. It is a sin for a puny little fellow like me to mutilate one of your six-foot men as if he was a sheep,—but *vive la science!*"

Holmes entered the world of medicine in its less eminent era, an era in which the theory of contagion was unknown or mocked, an era of crude, unsterilized surgical instruments when operating rooms rang with the screams of patients, before anesthesia replaced whiskey as a release from pain. Within the limits of the medicine then known, however, Holmes did well, earning the praise of Dr. James Jackson, uncle of his wife-to-be. "Holmes knows more about my courses this winter than anyone," Jackson wrote to his son in Paris, where Holmes was about to continue his studies. "Do not mind his apparent frivolity and you will soon find that he is intelligent and well-informed. He has the true zeal."

In Paris, then one of the world's most advanced medical centers, Holmes followed a Spartan regimen arising early to follow the noted pathologist Pierre Louis and other physicians on their rounds. He learned a clinical detachment that served him well through life in all matters: "not," he said, "to take authority when I can have facts; not to guess when I can know. . . ." But Holmes was not immune to the pleasures of the Continent. He relished table talk with Jackson's son and others at the cafe where Voltaire had held forth. He defied his father, frequented the theater, and told the old minister not to waste his time scolding him. He toured Heidelberg, took in the derby at Epsom Downs, England, and drew a memorable word portrait of William IV: "The King blew his nose twice, and wiped the royal perspiration repeatedly from a face which is probably the largest uncivilized spot in England."

Holmes was awarded his M.D. from Harvard in 1836 and, announcing that small fevers would be gratefully received, hung out his shingle in Boston. He did not build a large practice, first because he was less than zealous in seeking out clients and second because his reputation as a poet and wit did not strike Bostonians as an ideal qualification in a physician. Nor was his standing among his colleagues enhanced by such remarks as his announcement that if the entire lot of medicines then prescribed for the ailing body were tossed into the sea "it would be all the better for mankind—and all the worse for the fishes." And his boyish appearance still plagued him. A leading physician who took Holmes along to visit an invalid old lady was asked by the patient to Holmes's mortification: "Why do you bring that little boy in here? Take him away!"

Holmes made his medical mark as a reform writer, exposing such medical quackery as phrenology and homeopathy, and what he called "other methods of getting a living out of the weakness and credulity of mankind." His major papers were generally well received, ultimately even his at first controversial paper "The Contagiousness of Puerperal Fever," which he delivered in 1843 before the Boston Society for Medical Improvement. In this epochal work, hailed one hundred years later as "the most important contribution made in America to the advancement of medicine" until its time, Holmes cited chapter and verse to prove that this childbed fever, which killed an astonishingly high percentage of otherwise healthy mothers, was in fact caused by a uterine infection carried from patient to patient by doctors and attendants. For years Dr. Holmes was bitterly attacked by outraged colleagues, but he stood his ground; he was right. And in 1855 he reprinted his work. "I had rather rescue one mother from being poisoned by her attendants," he declared, "than claim to have saved forty out of fifty patients to whom I had carried the disease." And he added: "I am too much in earnest for either humility or vanity, but I do entreat those who hold the keys of life and death to listen to me also for this once. I ask no personal favor; but I beg to be heard in behalf of the women whose lives are at stake, until some stronger voice shall plead for them." Holmes also had the distinction of being the man to give a name to the sulphuric ether first used in 1846 at the Massachusetts General Hospital. The name "letheon" had been advanced. But Holmes didn't like it. "I would have a name pretty soon," he advised a colleague, "and consult some accomplished scholar . . . before fixing upon the terms, which," he underlined, "*will be repeated by the tongues of every civilized race of mankind.*" He recommended the term "anaesthesia."

Holmes excelled, too, as a professor of anatomy, first at Dartmouth and later at Harvard, where for a time he also served as Dean of the Medical School. To Harvard men he was "Uncle Oliver." Even his 1:00 P.M. class was popular among students wearied from a whole morning of classes and yet to have lunch. His lectures were, in fact, more like stage appearances, with students vying to get front row seats. "He enters," an assistant recalled, "and is greeted by a mighty shout and stamp of applause. Then silence, and there begins a charming hour of description, analysis, simile, anecdote, harmless pun, which clothes the dry bones with poetic imagery, enlivens a hard and fatiguing day with humor, and brightens to the tired listener the details for difficult though interesting study." Once pointing to the soft underside of a cadaver, Holmes announced: "These, gentlemen, are the tuberosities of the ischia, on which man was designed to sit and survey the works of Creation." Holmes could be less blasé on other occasions. If, for example, a rabbit had to be chloroformed, he would dash from the lecture room, "beseeching his assistant not to let it squeak."

Professor Holmes had not abandoned poetry. He rarely declined an invitation to deliver occasional verse—on the birthdays of notables, at a temperance dinner, and, always, at reunions of his beloved Class of 1829. He shared the platform with Emerson when the Sage of Concord delivered his address "The American Scholar," which Holmes called America's "intellectual Declaration of Independence." He lectured for the Lowell Institute on English poets, and was sufficiently *au courant* with the literary world to picnic in the Berkshires with Hawthorne and Melville. But Holmes's poetic output in these early academic years was distinctly amateurish. Besides, he had three children to bring up. He had married Amelia Jackson, daughter of Justice Charles Jackson of the Massachusetts Supreme Court, in June, 1840. And Amelia, in biographer Catherine Drinker Bowen's words, "Amelia of the warm heart, the quick tongue and bright brown eye," bore him Oliver Wendell Holmes, Jr., destined to be a great liberal United States Supreme Court Justice; a daughter, Amelia, who would comfort the doctor in lonely old age; and Edward, a Boston attorney. At once practical and indulgent, Mrs. Holmes proved a good listener to the loquacious doctor, who liked to dominate family table talk, but she knew how to silence him, too, and how to moderate his frequent clashes with young Wendell, who found Holmes's constant flow of speculative chatter as abrasive as Holmes had found his father's pieties. In general, though, the Holmes household was a pleasant and creative one, as the doctor added to the joys of the hearth and of Harvard those of a good row on the Charles, a ride in a fast horse and chaise, or planting trees at his country home in Pittsfield and sitting by the sea at his cottage at Beverly Farms on the Massachusetts shore.

But Holmes was not to escape literary distinction, after all. His friend Lowell had agreed to edit the *Atlantic Monthly*—which Holmes had named—on the condition that the doctor contribute to it. And contribute Holmes did, publishing in 1857 the first in a series of scintillating articles entitled *The Autocrat of the Breakfast-Table.* Published in book form in 1858, *The Autocrat* is a discursive volume of philosophic gems ranging from the virtues of much money to the colloquies of Erasmus and is studded with witticisms and observations on the human character. *The Autocrat* was to prove Holmes's most enduring work, not least because it contained his best poems: "The Chambered Nautilus" and "The Deacon's Masterpiece, or the Wonderful 'One-Hoss-Shay.'"

"The Chambered Nautilus," best remembered, perhaps, for its exquisite line "Build thee more stately Mansions, O my soul . . ." draws a weighty moral lesson from the pearly nautilus which secretes a new, larger shell around itself each year, "growing physically," in one critic's words, "as we must mentally and spiritually until at last, in death, the walls that shut it from heaven, that kept it from attaining the absolute in life, were at least less restrictive than formerly. . . ."

"The Deacon's Masterpiece, or the Wonderful 'One-Hoss-Shay,'" for all of its Yankee humor, comparable in a sense to Lowell's Hosea Biglow's, was angrily received by Holmes's clerical contemporaries, who took it for what it was: a gentle, but no less devastating celebration of the collapse of Calvinism. The deacon's shay, like the theology of Calvinism, is perfectly constructed at every point, impervious to decay, in no need of repair. When it does fall apart it does so all at once, even as Calvinism falls apart when, in the light of new knowledge, its premises become not only untenable but irrelevant. Faced with the evangelical clergy's frenetic reaction to his delightful verse, Holmes permitted himself some bitterness: To the historian John Motley he wrote: "There must be a great deal of weakness and rottenness when such extreme bitterness is called out by such a good-natured person as I can claim to be in print." But Holmes's self-defense misses the mark. Derision is the *one* reality which the intellectually insecure cannot endure.

Of the rest of Holmes's verse, as the critic Hyatt Waggoner suggests, "very little . . . survives the occasions that produced it"—a Boston dinner for President Rutherford B. Hayes, a memorial to Francis Parkman, or "My Hunt After the Captain," in which Holmes, to his son's chagrin, sentimentally related his search for young Oliver wounded in the Civil War. Holmes was lionized as an after-dinner speaker of the first rank and he reveled in notoriety. "I was always patient," he quipped, "with those who thought well of me." Little of this praise outlived him, however, and it is difficult to reject the judgment that he was, after all, a literary amateur, that he was a dilettante, that, as one critic puts it, "life was too agreeable for him to take the trouble to become an artist." But, like Lowell, Holmes had a redeeming knowledge of his limits. He knew, he said, that he wrote "not verses so much as the stuff verses are made of." Holmes has suffered, too, by comparison with Emerson, Thoreau, Hawthorne and Melville, whose importance and influence on American thought and letters are so great as to resist definition.

The Autocrat was followed by *The Professor at the Breakfast-Table* in 1860, *The Poet at the Breakfast-Table* in 1872, and *Over the Teacups* in 1891, all unsuccessfully imitative of *The Autocrat*. Holmes's novels, *Elsie Venner* (1861), *The Guardian Angel* (1867), and *A Mortal Antipathy*—all of which have to do with the effects of inherited physiological or psychological abnormalities—while they still command clinical study, are literary failures. Time has supported the reaction of a critic of the *Nation* to the publication of *The Guardian Angel:* "When he had written the *Autocrat of the Breakfast-Table,*" the critic observed, "Dr. Holmes would have done well, as it has since appeared, had he ceased from satire. . . . He has never stopped hammering at the same nail which he hit on the head when he first struck."

Despite the passing of old friends, Holmes's mature years were good to him. He took pleasure in microscopy and photography, improved the stethoscope, invented the very popular hand stereoscope, a device that gave three-dimensional depth to regular photographs. He indulged his fondness for naming things by discovering the Boston Brahmin caste. He took up the fiddle—disastrously—at fifty, was a founder of the American Medical Association and a patron of the Boston Symphony. Despite chronic asthma, which limited his travel, he set out, at seventy-four, for England, where he met with Tennyson and Browning and received honorary doctorates from Cambridge, from Edinburgh, and from Oxford, where cheering students shouted their question: Had Dr. Holmes come in his "one-hoss-shay"?

Throughout life, Holmes remained actively opposed to supernatural theology. Independent of Revelation, he argued, Nature itself is a continuing miracle, in the formation of a crystal, in the fall of a stone. True religion, he believed, consisted not of credal affirmations but in the evidences of a "righteous life." Nor was religion a matter of mere appearances; he had seen "plenty of praying rogues and swearing saints." He rejoiced in the theory of evolution, because, he said, it had replaced despair in the human species with hope. And he urged the study of anthropology as a more reliable key to the nature of man than theology. Still, he worshiped regularly at King's Chapel in Boston, explaining that there was "a little plant called *Reverence* in the corner of my Soul's garden which I like to have watered about once a week." And as late as 1871 he confessed to Harriet Beecher Stowe that "even to that day [he] didn't read novels on Sunday, at least not until 'after sundown'. . . ."

In matters of politics and economics, Holmes was candidly conservative, committed to the mythology of his caste. He derided the "mesmeric pamphlets" of Utopian reformers of the ultra-Transcendentalist stamp; they were, he thought, as naively optimistic as their Calvinist forbears had been pathologically pessimistic. And he believed that an economic elite was as ineluctable as rain. "You can't keep a dead level long," he was convinced, "if you burn everything down flat to make it. Why, bless your soul, if all the cities of the world were reduced to ashes, you'd have a new set of millionaires in a couple of years or so, out of the trade in potash." Still he bridled at the label "conservative," and in the argot of the clinic he declared: "If to be a conservative is to let all the drains of thought choke up and keep the soul's windows down—to shut out the sun from the east and the wind from the west—to let the rats run free in the cellar, and the moths feed their fill in the chambers, and the spiders weave their lace before the mirrors, till the soul's typhus is bred out of our neglect, and we begin to snore in its coma or rave in its delirium—I, Sir, am a *bonnet-rouge*, a redcap of the barricades, my friends, rather than a conservative." And in fact he refused to share the pretense of a Beacon Hill that loved its Madeira no less heartily than the Irish railroad worker fancied his beer. Of the temperance movement, he observed acidly, "Yet better even excess than lying and hypocrisy; and if wine is upon all our tables, let us praise it for its color and fragrance and social tendency, so far as it deserves, and not hug a bottle in the closet and pretend not to know the use of a wine-glass at a public dinner!" Indeed, the doctor considered wine no less than "the grand specific against dull dinners."

With young Oliver in the field of battle, Holmes took a passionate personal interest in the Civil War. He was angered by the suggestion that the North was fighting for industrial hegemony and denying the South its inherent right of self-government. But he took a less than zealous interest in the abolition movement, to which Lowell had been converted, replying to Lowell's scolding about his silence: "Let me try to improve and please my fellowmen after my own fashion at present." But it is clear, as Vernon Parrington notes, that while Holmes might share a sentimental concern for the slave in the abstract, "he shared the Beacon Street dislike of agitation—it was not well bred and it might bring down more things than he cared to have brought down."

For all his superb open-mindedness, Holmes remained until his death a favored son of the status quo: of his Beacon Street which he had called "the sunny street that holds the sifted few;" of his Saturday Club, "the crown," he had declared, "of a literary metropolis," hated and envied by "foolish people" because it was "lofty, serene, impregnable, and, by the necessity of the case, exclusive." He might concede that the seedling tulip of Brahmin culture was breaking down into "high-caste colours," but it reigned in his mind as the world's finest flower.

The end came for Dr. Holmes and, in a sense, his era, quietly, on Sunday afternoon, October 7, 1894, as the sunset cast its gray-rosy glow across the Charles. Judge Oliver and Fanny were sitting with him in his study when his head sank as if he were going to sleep, and, with no time for farewells, the effervescent little man, whom the elder Henry James had declared "intellectually the most alive man I ever knew," was dead. A memorial tablet in King's Chapel recorded his achievements in the order he had requested: "Teacher of Anatomy, Essayist and Poet." The inscription concludes with a citation from Horace's *Ars Poetica: Miscuit Utile Dulci:* "He mingled the useful with the pleasant."

BIBLIOGRAPHY

GENERAL

Brooks, Van Wyck. *The Flowering of New England*. New York: E. P. Dutton, 1952.

Higginson, Thomas Wentworth. *Old Cambridge*. New York: Macmillan, 1900.

Levin, Harry. *The Power of Blackness: Hawthorne, Poe, Melville*. New York: Alfred A. Knopf, 1958.

Parrington, Vernon L. *Main Currents in American Thought*. Vol. II, *The Romantic Revolution in America, 1800–1860*. New York: Harcourt, Brace and World (A Harvest Book), paperback, 1954.

Quinn, Arthur Hobson. *The Literature of the American People*. New York: Appleton Century Crofts, 1951.

Van Doren, Carl. *The American Novel, 1789–1939*. New York: Macmillan, 1940.

Waggoner, Hyatt H. *American Poets from the Puritans to the Present*. Boston: Houghton Mifflin, 1968.

RALPH WALDO EMERSON

Aaron, Daniel. *Men of Good Hope: A Study of American Progressives*. New York: Oxford University Press, 1951.

Crothers, Samuel McChord. *Ralph Waldo Emerson: How to Know Him*. Indianapolis: Bobbs-Merrill, 1921.

Emerson, Ralph Waldo. *Basic Selections from Emerson. Essays, Poems and Apothegms*. Edited by Eduard C. Lindeman. New York: New American Library (A Mentor Book), paperback, 1954.

——. *The Conduct of Life*. New York: A. L. Burt, no date.

——. *Essays. First and Second Series*. Boston and New York: Houghton Mifflin, c. 1903.

——. *The Heart of Emerson's Journals*. Edited by Bliss Perry. New York: Dover Publications (paperback), 1958.

——. *Miscellanies*. Boston: Houghton Mifflin, 1900.

——. *Nature, Addresses, and Lectures.* Boston: Houghton Mifflin, 1883.

——. *The Poems of Ralph Waldo Emerson.* Selected and edited with a commentary by Louis Untermeyer. New York: Heritage Press, 1945.

——. *Representative Men.* Seven Lectures. Boston and New York: Houghton Mifflin, c. 1903.

——. *Selected Essays, Lectures and Poems of Ralph Waldo Emerson.* Edited by Robert E. Spiller. New York: Washington Square Press (paperback), 1965.

——. *The Works of Ralph Waldo Emerson.* Vol. III: *Nature, Addresses, and Lectures.* Philadelphia: John D. Morris and Co., 1906.

Hawthorne, Julian. *The Memoirs of Julian Hawthorne.* New York: Macmillan, 1938.

Hoeltje, Hubert H. *Sheltering Tree: A Story of the Friendship of Ralph Waldo Emerson and Amos Bronson Alcott.* Durham, North Carolina: Duke University Press, 1943.

Holmes, Oliver Wendell. *Ralph Waldo Emerson.* Boston: Houghton Mifflin, 1884.

Konvitz, Milton R. and Stephen E. Whicher. *Emerson: A Collection of Critical Essays.* Englewood Cliffs, New Jersey: Prentice-Hall (A Spectrum Book), 1962.

Perry, Bliss. *Emerson Today.* Princeton: Princeton University Press, 1931.

Schneider, Herbert W. *A History of American Philosophy.* New York: Columbia University Press, 1946.

Witham, W. Tasker. "Panorama of American Literature." Stephen Daye Press, 1947.

HENRY DAVID THOREAU

Canby, Henry Seidel. *Henry David Thoreau.* Boston: Houghton Mifflin, 1939.

Derleth, August. *Concord Rebel: A Life of Henry David Thoreau.* New York: Chilton Books, 1962.

Emerson, Ralph Waldo. "Biographical Sketch of Henry David Thoreau," published as the introduction to the Houghton Mifflin Sentry Edition of Thoreau's *A Week on the Concord and Merrimack Rivers* (paperback).

Harding, Walter. *The Days of Henry David Thoreau: A Biography.* New York: Alfred A. Knopf, 1965.

——. *The Variorum Civil Disobedience.* New York: Twayne, 1967.

Krutch, Joseph Wood. *Henry David Thoreau*. American Men of Letters Series. New York: Dell (A Delta Book), paperback, 1948.

Longstreth, T. Morris. *Henry Thoreau, American Rebel*. New York: Dodd, Mead, 1963.

Miller, Perry. *Nature's Nation*. Cambridge, Mass.: The Belknap Press of Harvard University Press, 1967.

Sanborn, F.B. *The Life of Henry David Thoreau*. Boston and New York: Houghton Mifflin, 1917. Republished in 1968 by Gale Research Co., Book Tower, Detroit.

Thoreau, Henry David. *Cape Cod*. New York: Bramhall House, copyright 1951 by W.W. Norton.

——. *The Heart of Thoreau's Journals*. Edited by Odell Shepard, Boston and New York: Houghton Mifflin, 1927.

——. *Journals*. In Walden Edition of *The Writings of Henry David Thoreau*. In twenty volumes, 1906, fourteen volumes of which contain all of extant *Journals*, excepting entries from April, 1843, to July, 1845.

——. *The Maine Woods*. New York: Bramhall House, copyright 1950 by Dudley C. Lunt.

——. *Men of Concord*. (Based on *Journals*.) Edited by Francis Allen. Boston: Houghton Mifflin, 1936.

——. *"On the Duty of Civil Disobedience"* in *Walden*. New American Library (A Mentor Book) paperback, 1956.

——. *Walden*, with an introduction by Basil Willey. New York: Bramhall House, copyright 1951 by W. W. Norton.

——. *A Week on the Concord and Merrimack Rivers*. Boston: Houghton Mifflin (The Riverside Press Sentry Edition), paperback, 1961.

NATHANIEL HAWTHORNE

Arvin, Newton. Introduction to *Hawthorne's Short Stories*. New York: Random House (A Vintage Book), paperback, 1946, pp. v–xvii.

Cohen, B. Bernard, editor. *The Recognition of Nathaniel Hawthorne*. Ann Arbor: University of Michigan Press, 1969.

Crews, Frederick C. Excerpts from Crews's *The Sins of the Fathers: Hawthorne's Psychological Themes*, reprinted, in Cohen volume cited directly above, pp. 290 ff.

Hawthorne, Julian. *The Memoirs of Julian Hawthorne*. Edited by his wife Edith Garrigues Hawthorne. New York: Macmillan, 1938.

———. *Nathaniel Hawthorne and His Wife.* 2 vols. Boston: Houghton Mifflin, 1893.

Hawthorne, Nathaniel. *The Complete Short Stories of Nathaniel Hawthorne.* Garden City, New York: Hanover House, Doubleday copyright, 1959.

———. *Hawthorne's Short Stories.* Edited and with an introduction by Newton Arvin. New York: Random House (A Vintage Book), paperback, 1946.

———. *The Scarlet Letter.* New York: Heritage Press, 1946.

Hoeltje, Hubert H. *Inward Sky: The Mind and Heart of Nathaniel Hawthorne.* Durham, North Carolina: Duke University Press, 1962.

Pearson, Norman Holmes. Introduction to Modern Library edition of *The Complete Novels and Selected Tales of Nathaniel Hawthorne.* New York: The Modern Library, 1937.

Stewart, Randall. *Nathaniel Hawthorne. A Biography.* New Haven: Yale University Press, 1948.

Turner, Arlin. *Nathaniel Hawthorne: An Introduction and Interpretation.* New York: Barnes and Noble, 1961.

Van Doren, Mark. *Nathaniel Hawthorne.* New York: The Viking Press (A Compass Book), paperback, 1966.

Wagenknecht, Edward. *Nathaniel Hawthorne: Man and Writer.* New York: Oxford University Press, 1961.

Waggoner, Hyatt H. *Hawthorne: A Critical Study.* Rev. ed. Cambridge, Mass: The Belknap Press of Harvard University Press, 1967.

RICHARD HENRY DANA, JR.

Adams, Charles Francis. *Life of Richard Henry Dana, Jr.* 2 vols., 1890. Reprinted by Gale Research Co., Detroit, Michigan, in 1970.

Bartlett, Irving H. *Wendell Phillips, Brahmin Radical.* Boston: Beacon Press, 1961.

Dana, Richard Henry, Jr. *The Journal of Richard Henry Dana, Jr.* Edited by Robert F. Lucid. 3 vols. Cambridge, Mass.: The Belknap Press of Harvard University Press, 1968.

———. *Two Years Before the Mast.* New York: The Heritage Press, 1947.

Hart, James D. Foreword to Modern Library edition of *Two Years Before the Mast.* New York, 1936.

McFee, William. Introduction to *Two Years Before the Mast.* New York: Heritage Press, 1947.

HERMAN MELVILLE

Finkelstein, Dorothea Metlitsky. *Melville's Orienda.* New Haven and London: Yale University Press, 1961.

Howard, Leon. Chapter on Melville, pp. 82–117, in *Six American Novelists of the Nineteenth Century,* edited by Richard Foster. Minneapolis: University of Minnesota Press, 1960.

Matthiessen, F. O. *American Renaissance: Art and Expression in the Age of Emerson and Whitman.* New York, London, and Toronto: Oxford University Press, 1941.

Melville, Herman. *The Battle-Pieces of Herman Melville.* New York: Thomas Yoseloff, 1963.

——. *Billy Budd and Other Tales,* with an afterword by Willard Thorp. New York: New American Library (A Signet Classic), paperback, 1961.

——. *Journal of a Visit to London and the Continent.* Cambridge, Mass.: Harvard University Press, 1948.

——. *Moby Dick.* New York: Macmillan, 1962.

——. *Typee, A Peep at Polynesian Life During a Four Months' Residence in a Valley of the Marquesas.* Special limited edition, copyrighted by the West Virginia Pulp and Paper Company, 1962.

Miller, Perry. *The Raven and the Whale.* New York: Harcourt, Brace and World, 1956.

Sealts, Merton M., Jr. *Melville as Lecturer.* Cambridge, Mass.: Harvard University Press, 1957.

FRANCIS PARKMAN

Doughty, Howard. *Francis Parkman.* New York: Macmillan, 1962.

Farnham, Charles Haight. *A Life of Francis Parkman.* Boston: Little, Brown, 1901.

Parkman, Francis. *Count Frontenac and New France Under Louis XIV.* Boston: Beacon Press (paperback), 1966.

——. *The Discovery of the Great West: La Salle.* New York: Holt, Rinehart and Winston (paperback), 1965.

——. *The Journals of Francis Parkman.* Edited by Mason Wade. 2 vols. New York: Harper, 1947.

——. *The Letters of Francis Parkman.* Edited by Wilbur Jacobs. 2 vols. Norman: University of Oklahoma Press, 1960.

——. *The Oregon Trail.* New York: New American Library (paperback), 1959.

Wade, Mason. *Francis Parkman: Heroic Historian.* New York: Viking, 1942.

WILLIAM HICKLING PRESCOTT

Angus-Butterworth, L. M. *Ten Master Historians.* Aberdeen, Scotland: The University Press, 1961.

Bassett, John Spencer. *The Middle Group of American Historians.* New York: Macmillan, 1917.

Gardiner, C. Harvey. *Prescott and His Publishers.* Carbondale: Southern Illinois University Press, 1959.

Ogden, Rollo. *William Hickling Prescott.* Boston and New York: Houghton Mifflin, 1904.

Prescott, William Hickling. *The Conquest of Mexico.* 2 vols. New York: E. P. Dutton, 1921, 1922.

——. *History of the Conquest of Peru.* New York: A. L. Burt, no date.

——. *History of the Reign of Ferdinand and Isabella.* Edited by C. Harvey Gardiner. With the author's preface. New York: Heritage Press, 1967.

——. *The Papers of William Hickling Prescott.* Selected and edited by C. Harvey Gardiner. Urbana: University of Illinois Press, 1964.

——. *Prescott's Histories: The Rise and Decline of the Spanish Empire.* Selected and edited and with a biographical introduction by Irwin Blacker. New York: Viking Press, 1963.

Ticknor, George. *Life of William Hickling Prescott.* Philadelphia, J. B. Lippincott, 1875.

——. *Life, Letters and Journals of George Ticknor.* 12th ed., 2 vols. Boston: Houghton Mifflin, 1876.

Williams, Stanley T. *The Spanish Background of American Literature.* 2 vols. New Haven: Yale University Press, 1955.

HENRY WADSWORTH LONGFELLOW

Arvin, Newton. *Longfellow—His Life and Work.* Boston and Toronto: Little, Brown (An Atlantic Monthly Press Book), 1962, 1963.

Gorman, Herbert S. *A Victorian American: Henry Wadsworth Longfellow.* New York: George H. Doran Co., 1926.

Hirsh, Edward L. *Henry Wadsworth Longfellow.* University of Minnesota Pamphlets on American Writers. Minneapolis: University of Minnesota Press, 1964.

Long, Orie William. *Literary Pioneers: Early American Explorers of European Culture.* New York: Russell and Russell, 1963.

Longfellow, Henry Wadsworth. *The Complete Poetical Works of*

Longfellow. Boston: Houghton Mifflin (The Cambridge Edition), no date.

Macy, John, ed. *American Writers 'on American Literature*. New York: Horace Liveright, 1931. Cf. Chapter ix on Longfellow by Howard Mumford Jones.

Nemerov, Howard. *Poetry and Fiction: Essays*. New Brunswick, New Jersey: Rutgers University Press, 1963.

Shepard, Odell. *Henry Wadsworth Longfellow—Representative Selections, with Introduction, Bibliography, and Notes*. New York: American Book Co., 1934.

Thompson, Lawrance. *Young Longfellow, 1807–1843*. New York: Macmillan, 1938.

Wagenknecht, Edward. *Longfellow: A Full-Length Portrait*. New York, London, Toronto: Longmans, Green, 1955.

JAMES RUSSELL LOWELL

Duberman, Martin. *James Russell Lowell*. Boston: Beacon Press (paperback), 1966.

Greenslet, Ferris. *The Lowells and Their Seven Worlds*. Boston: Houghton Mifflin, 1946.

Hale, Edward Everett. *James Russell Lowell and His Friends*. Boston and New York: Houghton Mifflin, 1899.

Howard, Leon. *Victorian Knight-Errant—A Study of the Early Literary Career of James Russell Lowell*. Berkeley and Los Angeles: University of California Press, 1952.

James, Alice. *The Diary of Alice James*. Edited by Leon Edel. New York: Dodd, Mead, 1964.

James, Henry. *The American Scene*. Bloomington and London: Indiana University Press, 1968.

Lowell, James Russell. *The Biglow Papers*. Boston and New York: Houghton Mifflin, 1891.

——. *The Complete Poetical Works of James Russell Lowell*. Boston and New York: Houghton Mifflin, 1899.

——. *Letters of James Russell Lowell*. Edited by Charles Eliot Norton. 2 vols. New York: Harper and Bros., 1893.

McGlinchee, Claire. *James Russell Lowell*. Twayne's United States Authors Series. New York: Twayne, 1967.

Samuels, Ernest. *The Young Henry Adams*. Cambridge, Mass.: Harvard University Press, 1948.

Sutton, Walter. *Modern American Criticism*. Englewood Cliffs, New Jersey: Prentice-Hall, Inc., 1963.

Wagenknecht, Edward. *Longfellow: A Full-Length Portrait*. New York, London, Toronto: Longmans, Green Co., 1955.

OLIVER WENDELL HOLMES

Bowen, Catherine Drinker. *Yankee from Olympus, Justice Holmes and His Family*. New York, Toronto, London: Bantam Books (paperback), 1968.

Holmes, Oliver Wendell. *The Autocrat of the Breakfast Table*. New York: New American Library (A Signet Classic), paperback, 1961.

———. *The Complete Poetical Works of Oliver Wendell Holmes*. Boston: Houghton Mifflin (The Cambridge Edition), no date.

———. *Over the Teacups*. Boston and New York: Houghton Mifflin, 1891.

———. *The Poet at the Breakfast-Table*. Boston and New York: Houghton Mifflin, 1894.

———. *The Professor at the Breakfast Table; With the Story of Iris*. Boston: Ticknor and Fields, 1866.

———. *The Wit and Wisdom of Oliver Wendell Holmes: Father and Son*. Edited with an introductory essay by Lester E. Dannon. Boston: The Beacon Press, 1953.

Macy, John, ed. *American Writers on American Literature*. New York: Horace Liveright, 1931. Cf. Chapter XII on Holmes by Harold deWolf Fuller.

Morse, J. T., Jr., ed. *Life and Letters of Oliver Wendell Holmes*. 2 vols. London: Sampson Low, Marston, 1896.

Oberndorf, Clarence P. *The Psychiatric Novels of Oliver Wendell Holmes*. New York: Columbia University Press, 1946.

Small, Miriam Rossiter. *Oliver Wendell Holmes*. Twayne's United States Authors Series. New York: Twayne, 1962.

Tilton, Eleanor M. *Amiable Autocrat: A Biography of Dr. Oliver Wendell Holmes*. New York: Henry Schuman, 1947.

INDEX